DATE DUE

AUG 1 6 1996 Thompson—Nicole due May 5/01	

BRODART, INC.   Cat. No. 23-221

The Stroessner Era

The Stroessner Era

Authoritarian Rule in Paraguay

Carlos R. Miranda

Westview Press
Boulder, San Francisco, & Oxford

Copyright © 1990 by Westview Press, Inc.

Published in 1990 in the United States of America by Westview Press, Inc., 5500 Central Avenue, Boulder, Colorado 80301, and in the United Kingdom by Westview Press, Inc., 36 Lonsdale Road, Summertown, Oxford OX2 7EW

Library of Congress Cataloging-in-Publication Data
Miranda, Carlos R., 1954–
   The Stroessner era: authoritarian rule in Paraguay/Carlos R.
Miranda.
      p.   cm.
   Includes bibliographical references.
   ISBN 0-8133-0995-6
   1. Paraguay—Politics and government—1954–1989.   2. Stroessner,
Alfredo, 1912–   3. Authoritarianism—Paraguay—History—20th
century.   I. Title.
F2689.M54   1990
989.207′3′092—dc20   90-30613
                                                                    CIP

Printed and bound in the United States of America

The paper used in this publication meets the requirements
of the American National Standard for Permanence of Paper
for Printed Library Materials Z39.48-1984.

10   9   8   7   6   5   4   3   2   1

To the memory of my father

Contents

Preface

I was a sixth-grader when an authoritarian regime came to power in my native Argentina. With the exception of a three-year interlude between 1973 and 1976, I lived under military governments until I left Argentina in 1981. During all those years, I experienced life under autocratic rule in a variety of roles and circumstances: as a high school student active in church organizations, as a university student, as a sociology professor, and in a variety of other jobs I held.

The literature on Latin American authoritarian regimes attracted my interest in trying to understand more deeply the ways in which authoritarian governments work. My contact with the writings of Juan Linz, Guillermo O'Donnell, Alfred Stepan, Fernando H. Cardoso, and others prompted my commitment to study further the implications of authoritarian rule for the political development of Latin America.

I conducted the research for this study during three trips to Paraguay and Argentina. I talked extensively with people in the streets, in the buses, and all around Asunción. I met with several opposition leaders in Buenos Aires. Throughout this entire effort, I became indebted to many people. At the University of Connecticut, I would like to thank Professors Frederick C. Turner, Cyrus Zirakzadeh, Francisco Scarano, and Ilpyong Kim. In Paraguay, I was encouraged and helped most prominently by Dr. Adriano Irala Burgos of the Universidad Católica Nuestra Señora de la Asunción. He suggested ideas, materials, contacts, and logistic help each time that we met. Members of his staff were just as kind. In Buenos Aires, Dr. Luis A. Bogado Poissón was invaluable in lining up interview subjects and devising questions. Our common experiences within Catholic church organizations helped to establish a very interesting dialogue.

Staff members of the Homer Babbidge Library at the University of Connecticut provided inestimable help. I would like to mention especially that of Robert Vrecenak, Mohini Mundkur, and Pamela Skinner. Kenneth Trayes of the Roper Center for Public Opinion Research assisted in obtaining some of the survey data. Betty Seaver had the monumental task of editing the manuscript. Carmelita Shepelwich and Marilyn Eudaly, at Texas Christian University, provided welcome secretarial skills.

Throughout preparation of the manuscript, many people offered suggestions and encouragement. At the University of Connecticut, I appreciated the aid of Professor Larry Bowman, Chair, Department of Political Science, and also of Professor J. Garry Clifford. At the University of Tampa, I would like to thank Professors Richard Piper and Robert Kerstein. At Texas Christian University, I was encouraged by all my colleagues in the Department of Political Science, most particularly by J. Michael Dodson and Donald Jackson. I drew much of my energy to carry on from my undergraduate students, who were a source of inspiration on a daily basis. I would like to mention especially members of my class in authoritarian regimes at TCU, who shared my interest in the subject and learned along with me.

I am grateful for generous financial support from the Research Foundation of the University of Connecticut, the University of Connecticut Center for Latin American and Caribbean Studies, and the Department of Political Science.

I would like to thank three anonymous reviewers for their insightful comments and criticisms. Special gratitude goes to Professor Paul H. Lewis, whose suggestions at several stages in the preparation of the manuscript were crucial.

I have been honored to work with Barbara Ellington at Westview Press. She believed in the potential of this book when I was almost ready to give up.

I would like to thank my "two" families for having always backed my endeavors with loving patience. And at last, I want to thank my wife, Heidi Josephine Golicz. She has been involved with this book in so many ways that I can hardly imagine having completed it without her help. Her patience and support maintained me when I no longer had energy to spare.

Any errors remain my own.

Carlos R. Miranda
Clinton, Connecticut

PARAGUAY

International boundary
National capital
Railroad
Road
International airport

0   50   100 Kilometers
0   50   100 Miles

Introduction

Alfredo Stroessner ruled Paraguay from 1954 to 1989—the longest-lasting dictator in the country's history—yet he went largely unremarked by the outside world because of the deliberately low profile of his regime. He was an atypical ruler, not the flamboyant caudillo-style dictator characteristic of other Latin American nations. Stroessner masterfully reorganized Paraguayan politics to fit his own script. His ability to maintain personal control was matched by his skill at manipulating constituencies. He stirred deep emotions: detractors vehemently condemned his style and his substance, but many supporters lavished praise upon his every act. Stroessner unquestionably left an indelible mark on the culture, politics, and society of Paraguay.[1]

Much about Stroessner and his regime challenges some of the stereotypical assumptions about dictatorships in Latin America and the Third World.[2] Was he successful in controlling, inspiring, and mobilizing the masses or did he preside over a military regime akin to the bureaucratic experience of neighboring Argentina and Brazil? Actually, neither. One might suppose that because of his long tenure, he was gifted with popular appeal, but he was not. Although he assiduously courted the masses, Stroessner was not possessed of charisma. In fact, he had no gift for rhetoric and had an unappealing public presence; his was the air of a military functionary—concerned, hard working, and committed. What, then, does account for his durability? The reasons must be looked for in the fabric of Paraguayan society, and in the way he tailored his role to that society.

Stroessner presided over a country geographically isolated, economically deprived, and undergoing a political-identity crisis due to years of political infighting between groups. Landlocked, Paraguay throughout its history played its relationships with Argentina and Brazil to its own advantage by drawing closer to either one if economic or political gains could be materialized. Because it lacked resources and because of a devastating war over boundaries in the 1930s, Paraguay was a backward nation when Stroessner came to power in 1954. It had been unable to develop strong institutions that could mitigate its tendency toward instability, chaos, and strongman governance.

Part of the reason for the absence of institutional development is that Paraguayan politicians have had a disposition to gather around individual men rather than institutions or ideas, a proclivity that carried great costs as the country moved between democratic and authoritarian governments. Acting as if democracy were not in the Paraguayan nature, Stroessner gained ascendancy by surmounting partisan differences and by becoming a catalyst of unity. Still, to last longer than every other dictator in the world, Stroessner obviously did more than reconcile groups at odds with one another.

Stroessner effectively altered the nature of Paraguayan politics by taking over the Colorado party, by delimiting the opposition, and by catering to the armed forces. In a nation not lacking in towering historical figures, Stroessner became a symbol of Paraguay itself: cities, streets, buildings, currency, stamps—everything carried his name. Achievements of all kinds were ascribed to him. Prosperity during the 1970s was deemed to be his doing. When organized groups sought to gain a toehold on power, he choked off their ambitions by controlling or co-opting their leaders. He declared that he was not a dictator, yet he had laws tailored to conduct systematic harassment of the opposition, earning one of the worst human rights violation records in Latin America.

Stroessner banked on the loyalty of some, the skills of others, and the support of many. By the end of the 1970s, his position was rock-solid and he seemed poised for a fourth triumphal decade. Yet, the dismantling of his regime that began early in the 1980s proved once again that invincibility is not a permanent condition. Elected for the eighth time only a year before his downfall, Stroessner was ousted because he could no longer make his political machine work. The duplicitousness, cunning, and repression that marked his reign were no longer enough to keep things going. And finally, the corruption that had built the fiefdom brought it down.

The process of modernization that encouraged the nation to consume during the 1970s had aroused expectations among the populace. Unmet in the 1980s, those expectations created strong divisions throughout Paraguayan society, including the Colorado party. Stroessner lost the unified support he had once enjoyed, and a sizable faction in the party considered him and his system of governance detrimental. Further, it became increasingly troublesome to keep the opposition in line because a process of social mobilization had now validated the necessity for the opposition to function. Facing potential unrest, the armed forces forsook Stroessner. Stroessner's exile brought to an end a period of Paraguay's history that warrants our attention if only to probe for its lessons.

In contrast to the extensive attention given to other authoritarian regimes throughout Latin America, that of Stroessner long remained virtually unknown outside the Southern Cone.[3] The regime has been defined as traditional, in contrast to the populist and bureaucratic types. To many, it seemed Stroessner survived because of cultural elements that made possible his unprecedented longevity—and that would almost preclude the possibility of future change. But it was the keen political skills of Stroessner himself that rendered the regime unique, at least within the context of Latin American dictatorships.

Successful dictatorships in Paraguay did not begin with the Stroessner regime. Certain historical events have predisposed Paraguayans to accept authoritarian forms of government. The country's colonial experience was far different from that of the other countries in the region. Paraguay had few natural resources, and its conquest had much to do with the appealing Río de la Plata territory. There was little to foster creation of powerful elites because business was confined to a small number of artisans, and there were no ports to speak of that could allow commerce to flourish.

In some senses, Stroessner's Paraguay recalled the colonial period and the influence of the Jesuit order with its *reducciones,* places where the natives were introduced to the cultural forms of the "civilized" world. The population of Paraguay remained quiet and accepting, a condition reflective of a fatalistic and apathetic view. Another authoritarian institution of the colonial period, the *encomienda,* was abolished much later in Paraguay than in the rest of Latin America. The encomienda system, whereby the Indians exchanged labor for protection, may have conveyed the notion of authority as not clearly defined but highly centralized. The character of the tribes and the high degree of racial protectionism may have further accentuated the Paraguayan tendency to search for and support strong centralized government in order to assert cultural identity.

Paraguayans have also accepted strong forms of authoritarian rule since the achievement of national independence. The leader José Gaspar Rodríguez de Francia (1814–1840) initiated a period of almost total isolation from the outside world. Carlos Antonio López (1840–1862) and Francisco Solano López (1862–1870) reinforced authoritarian structures by means of their styles of ruling as they envisioned a larger role for the nation on the world stage. The three dictators made Paraguay a self-sufficient nation during the nineteenth century, perhaps creating the notion that such governance promoted stability and progress.

The personalism and centralism of nineteenth-century Paraguay proved disastrous. In 1864, a major confrontation with three neighboring nations devastated its human and economic potential. The War of the Triple Alliance slowed economic growth and threw roadblocks in the way of institutional and political development. The early part of the twentieth century proved inauspicious as well. Plagued by short-lived dictatorships, instability, and poverty, Paraguay found itself battling Bolivia over boundaries in 1932. A vigorous figure in the victorious Chaco War, Marshal José Félix Estigarribia, became president in 1939. His death in a plane crash the following year opened the office to General Higinio Morínigo, the fourth strongman. Five governments followed him between 1949 and 1954. Then, after having taken part in several military coup attempts, Stroessner took center stage in Asunción.

Stroessner did not go unchallenged, but he survived by setting in motion the consolidation of a distinct brand of authoritarianism. He delineated his goals of modernization: eradicating domestic chaos and providing the people with some degree of political participation. To increase the internal security of the system, the administration prohibited any questioning of, and attacks upon, its legitimacy as well as challenges to its policy orientations and ideological positions. The rupture between the social system and the political system grew evident. The regime was attending to the needs and expectations of a smaller and smaller number of citizens. Repressive measures preserved the institutional arrangements.

The administration also co-opted potential dissidents. At a very high level, it allowed military officers to participate in the profitable smuggling activities for which Paraguay is famous. A number of goods that can enter into Brazil and Argentina only after paying high duties are brought into Paraguay duty-free and then smuggled into the neighboring countries for large profits. Military and police officers received posts that provided them with economic benefits. At the middle level, a thoroughly bureaucratized structure created government jobs in an effort to portray the regime as a paternalistic provider of opportunities for all. At the lowest level, a large informal or "underground" economy was permitted to operate in the capital with the benign semisanction of the authorities. A very relaxed migration policy also encouraged those who did not do well at home to search for jobs in neighboring countries.

Perceiving that politics was not an arena for everyday citizens, Paraguayans thereafter turned to the economic performance of the system. Sensitive to this circumstance, the regime pressed high growth to guarantee its own welfare. Expansion thrived on the strength of the agricultural sector and of the hydroelectric and construction industries, and a very favorable exchange policy that kept the currency overvalued and made imports cheaper—all of which helped raise the standard of living. Paraguayans enjoyed levels of consumption and spending that were high by historical standards.

The regime's fulfillment of Paraguayans' expectations earned it widespread "consensual" support, even though the greatest benefits accrued to the elite that monopolized politics. After the boom of the 1970s, though, growth and plentiful investment opportunities did not produce structural changes. Thus, Paraguayans' expectations prompted social mobilization in the 1980s. Stroessner's underlying source of legitimacy—coercion—would no longer suffice.

The political system that developed under Stroessner is an interesting case of authoritarianism for several reasons: first, because socioeconomic changes produced alterations in political demands and in the amount of mobilization and popular participation only when the regime entered its final stages and unavoidable crisis; second, because the consensual support enjoyed by the Stroessner regime shows how an authoritarian regime becomes consolidated by resorting to coercive measures; third, because minimal political participation made challenges to the regime difficult even for organized interest groups; and fourth, because corruption allowed the regime to operate successfully as long as there were enough resources to be distributed among different groups.

Even so, the character and the spirit of the Stroessner years are difficult to define. The regime has been described as personalistic, as an authoritarian political culture, and as institutionalized authoritarianism. However, it cannot be simplistically categorized. Whether any or all of those labels fit is uncertain. Under Stroessner, organizational efforts were so intertwined with repressive policies that the resultant political culture established conditions especially propitious for the emergence and continuation of authoritarianism.

Furthermore, the Stroessner regime produced a series of experiments that should enlarge our perception of authoritarianism in the Latin American context. Paraguay can no longer be considered a country based on a largely agricultural economy, just as its leadership did not present a typical case of *caudillismo.* Unquestionably, economic development has taken place, albeit within a slower process of modernization. To refer to Paraguay as an unimportant, traditional, agrarian nation is far from accurate.

Paraguay also developed under Stroessner a remarkable brand of politics, one that no single concept can accurately describe. Discussions of Paraguay among scholars and policymakers tend to extremes. Some define it as dictatorial, others as the natural outcome of the country's history and culture. The latter group tends to justify the regime as a precondition for a more stable, durable, and competitive democracy. In all likelihood, the authoritarian experience of the Stroessner era can provide us with useful information about the process of authoritarian consolidation. The regime ruled the country for thirty-five years, and its control was complete. Despite its critics and its excesses, the ways in which it solved problems are evidence of its ability to constrain challengers from within and from without and to gather popular support.

Election results are another important indicator of the high degree of consolidation achieved by the regime. Stroessner won elections in 1954, 1958, 1963, 1968, 1973, 1978, 1983, and 1988. After 1963 he allowed some opposition parties to participate in the electoral process, but he never received less than 80 percent of the vote, and surpassed the 90 percent mark in two of the last three elections. Although the context of election politics in Paraguay was quite special, receiving more than 90 percent of the vote in a presidential election is rare. Further, most Paraguayans in the opposition believed that even in a "clean" election Stroessner would have been victorious, although not by such very large margins. The conclusive support given to the regime can be understood in several ways: first, the amount of control exercised by the regime affected the election results; many feared to vote for another party. On the other hand, citizens could have been comfortable with the election results and the political system under which they lived. Many of them actually believed that in the aggregate the country had never before enjoyed so much "peace, work and well-being"—as the slogan of Stroessner and the Colorados kept assuring them.[4]

The Organization of This Study

The creation of a multifactor approach to the issue of stability in an authoritarian context requires discussion of the cultural elements that define the political system. Chapter 2 traces those elements, noting that Paraguay has presented an idiosyncratic situation since colonial times. The exchange between the native population and the Spanish conquerors created a milieu that defined the contemporary political culture under Stroessner. This fact is more evident at the grass-roots level and in the political attitudes of the Paraguayan people.

Because of an environment that sanctioned authoritarian politics, authoritarianism flourished in Paraguay after independence. The third chapter introduces a survey of the historical conditions that brought authoritarianism to the fore and the forces that have contributed to its consolidation. Institutional instability, external political pressure, and political conflict within the Paraguayan elite certainly influenced the developments that ultimately led in 1954 to the Stroessner presidency.

The fourth chapter argues that the regime was consolidated because of its efforts to encourage a ideological uniformity within the ranks of the Colorado party. The constitution allows the creation of an authoritarian regime by providing extensive latitude to the executive; the result is a power structure that rests on the triad composed of the military, the president, and the single party. The elimination of competing ideological leaders within the party structure long reinforced the position of the Stroessner administration. Stroessner's "new" doctrine focused on a number of interrelated issues, such as a vehemently anticommunist position, a strong popular appeal, an obvious nationalism, and a thirst for economic development, in creating its distinctive orientation.

The fifth chapter discusses issues concerning the policies of control exercised by the regime. The focal points are the limitations on the party structure and interest groups. The human rights record and mechanisms of control over other government institutions, such as the judiciary and the bureaucracy, are also examined. The single party as an instrument of control must also be seen as contributing to the atmosphere of fear fostered by the regime. The fear was heightened by the persecution of certain groups and individuals, those who dared challenge the decisions made by the regime.

The sixth chapter introduces issues of co-optation that result from the economic development strategies the administration followed during its second and third decades. The analysis concentrates on the role of the external sector, balance-of-payments difficulties, and regional and international economic ties that helped the country achieve a high rate of economic growth. The role of smuggling in the economy and the proposed industrialization projects stand out as examples of the relationship between economic development and the politics of consolidating the authoritarian regime.

The seventh chapter focuses on the factors that brought about the departure of the regime. The lengthy process of deterioration began in 1983, accelerating just before the 1988 elections. With an economic crisis affecting key sectors of Paraguayan society, and confrontations within the Colorado party over transition to a more democratic future, the regime faced its own demise. When the Stroessner inner circle failed to unite the party, to keep the benefits of corruption flowing, and to control the opposition, the regime collapsed in a matter of months.

The concluding chapter summarizes the findings and considers the implications of the Paraguayan case in light of recent literature concerning the transition to democracy in Latin America.[5] The complicated nature of the transition process makes Paraguay all the more relevant, due to the difficulty of breaking the tradition of autocratic rule so prevalent for many years. Moreover, the consolidation of the Stroessner regime and its impact on the political development of Paraguay are important in view of the new regime elected in May of 1989. The question posed concerns not only the political process under way during the administration of General Andrés Rodríguez but the creation of an eventual alternative to Paraguay's authoritarianism.

Notes

1. Latin America has a long tradition of authoritarian rule. During the nineteenth century, strong caudillos monopolized power in rural areas by creating peasant armies. In the early part of the twentieth century, *dictadores* ruled by virtue of their military experience and personal control of economic and political power. More recent authoritarian regimes have brought more sophisticated kinds of autocratic rule in which the military as an institution usually plays the dominant role.

2. Some of the most relevant works include David Collier, ed., *The New Authoritarianism in Latin America* (Princeton: Princeton University Press, 1979); Juan J. Linz, "An Authoritarian Regime: Spain," in *Mass Politics: Studies in Political Sociology*, ed. Erik Allardt and Stein Rokkan (New York: Free Press, 1970); Juan J. Linz, "Totalitarian and Authoritarian Regimes," in *Macro-Political Theory*, ed. Fred I. Greenstein and Nelson W. Polsby (Reading, Mass.: Addison-Wesley, 1975); Juan J. Linz and Alfred Stepan, *The Breakdown of Democratic Regimes: Latin America* (Baltimore: Johns Hopkins University Press, 1981); James Malloy, ed. *Corporatism and Authoritarianism in Latin America* (Pittsburgh: University of Pittsburgh Press, 1977); Guillermo O'Donnell, *Bureaucratic-Authoritarianism: Argentina, 1966–1973, in Comparative Perspective* (Berkeley: University of California Press, 1988); Guillermo O'Donnell, *Modernization and Bureaucratic-Authoritarianism: Studies in South American Politics* (Berkeley: Institute of International Studies, University of California, 1973); Alfred Stepan, *The State and Society: Peru in Comparative Perspective* (Princeton: Princeton University Press, 1978); Alfred Stepan, *Authoritarian Brazil: Origins, Policies and Future* (New Haven: Yale University Press, 1973).

3. The scarcity of works on contemporary Paraguayan politics is sad, almost shocking. See Paul H. Lewis, *Paraguay under Stroessner* (Chapel Hill: University of North Carolina Press, 1980); Paul H. Lewis, *Socialism, Liberalism and Dictatorship in Paraguay* (New York: Praeger, 1982); Russell H. Fitzgibbon and Julio A. Fernández, *Latin America: Political Culture and Development* (Englewood Cliffs, N.J.: Prentice-Hall, 1981); and Riordan Roett, "Authoritarian Paraguay: The Personalist Tradition," in *Latin American Politics and Development*, ed. Howard Wiarda and Harvey Kline (Boston: Houghton Mifflin, 1979).

4. A neon sign above the National Development Bank in downtown Asunción reminded the population of the three major accomplishments of the Stroessner regime.

5. The issues involved in the transition to democracy in Latin America are discussed in Guillermo O'Donnell, Philippe C. Schmitter, and Laurence Whitehead, eds., *Transitions from Authoritarian Rule: Latin America* (Baltimore: Johns Hopkins University Press, 1986).

The Political Culture
of Paraguay

2 The stability achieved by the Stroessner regime of Paraguay can be traced to a combination of historical and cultural elements that allowed the leadership to manipulate and play up the authoritarian tradition of the nation. Yet, per capita income and other indices of modernization improved greatly after 1954, raising the question as to whether such changes make a democratic political culture more likely or whether, in fact, this was impossible due to the Stroessner administration's policies.

Evaluating the Paraguayan cultural context more thoroughly even necessitates some rethinking of the concept of political culture itself, especially as it relates to entrenched authoritarian regimes. The policies of the Stroessner regime certainly undermined tendencies toward democracy, but the underlying values of the Paraguayan people—their political culture, which antedated Stroessner and which survived him—may be an even more fundamental force affecting the transition to democracy in the Paraguayan case. At the very least, then, we need to assess Paraguayan values, to relate them to broader issues of political culture and the policies of the Stroessner government, and to question how they may affect the norms and institutions of the country's future.

Paraguay developed its social and cultural values in wake of the contact between the native Indian culture and the Spanish culture of the conquerors. The Indian population mixed with the Spanish, accepted the teachings of the proselytizing religious orders, and emerged with a new set of values that formed the core of contemporary Paraguayan values. External influences altered the original value system of the inhabitants of the region, but the encounter of the two cultures also reinforced some of the traits peculiar to the Guaraní culture. The cultural mix affected the pattern of social organization and also left an important mark on the perceptions, ideas, and values of the native population.

9

Even to this day, intellectuals and visitors witness the cultural traits described during the times of the conquest.

The social and political institutions that emerged after independence, therefore, reflected a culture wherein a simplistic institutional organizational pattern coexisted with very particularized interpersonal relationships. In this sense, the political culture prevailing in Paraguay prior to the emergence of the Stroessner regime reflected a tendency toward authoritarian values, ingrained submission to authority, and a unique perception of power relationships. For the majority of the population, a sense of normalcy prevented development of forceful feelings of antagonism between social classes and political groups. The only sphere where power relationships manifested themselves openly was at the personal level. The upshot was a polity that tolerated politics more on an individual than group basis. Intermediaries between the population and key institutions of government became, then, the safeguards of the system. To this extent, certain members of society became spokesmen for entire sectors of the population, who by the very nature of their cultural orientation could not themselves express their demands openly and freely.

The Guaraní Culture

The traditional character and culture of the indigenous Paraguayans were quite idiosyncratic. Most other tribal groups within Latin America used their talents for war, but the Guaraní wandered extensively without seeming to consider any land as their own. They covered long distances, cultivated maize intensively, and practiced ritual cannibalism. The Guaraní were in contact with other South American Indian cultures due to their settlement pattern and geographical distribution. Of good physical build and relatively short, they shared the general anthropometric characteristics of other Meridional American Indians. They were quiet, subdued, and spoke generally in a very low tone of voice, never establishing eye contact while engaging in conversation. The attitude they presented was cold and reserved.[1]

The Guaraní also possessed striking qualities not found in other Indian cultures of the Americas. For example, they were peaceable, not having adopted the warlike deportment of their original Indian competitors or their later Spanish conquerors. This was a major reason for the success of the Jesuits in establishing a close and personal relationship with them. The order had attempted to civilize other Indian groups—such as the Lulis, Tobas, and the Lenguas Mocobíes, all Indians who inhabited the Chaco region[2]—but had met stubborn opposition. Many of the priests had been killed, and the order had continued to look for a friendlier group more amenable to the message of civilization.

Although there were groups of Guaraní scattered over a large geographical area, they spoke a common language. Most groups shared a linguistic heritage, even if they had achieved different levels of cultural development. In matters such as political organization, social conditions, economic resources, and daily life, the Guaraní resembled a unified group with distinctive features, something usually found only in the superior Indian civilizations.[3]

The original pattern of settlement was defined in terms of a *guára*, meaning a particular region easily recognizable because of being bounded by rivers. Different guáras constituted the original societal environment of the Guaraní. To them, the concept of guára meant a region where they found their own "space." The Guaraní were deeply attached to their individual guáras. They never rejected the notion of the guára, the idea that their own lives were confined to a particular area, and they strongly believed in their right to possess the resources of their region.[4]

The Guaraní also developed their own worldview, in a sense, their own ideological distinctiveness. They felt close to the land and created more detailed and philosophical interpretations of life and the objects around them. In an illustrative work, Juan Natalicio González shows how, among other characteristics, the Guaraní imputed spiritual meaning to material objects. They also tended to define things quite precisely and clearly. They were not fatalists because they believed that they could conquer the universe around them, because they had developed a notion of the soul, and because they maintained a strong sense of the truth.[5]

The Guaraní thus had developed a culture immersed in their natural environment. They enriched their lives with concepts captured etymologically in their concern with language and communication. In all, their civilization's foundations went beyond the mere practice of war rituals or the hunger for material conquest. There was a constant effort at establishing a relationship with the environment that was proof of the Guaraní's peaceful concept of life, and the positive, useful, and beautiful sense with which they conveyed it.[6]

The Impact of the Religious Orders

The religious orders that were brought by the conquerors had a significant impact on the existing Guaraní culture.[7] The orders' mission was twofold: to introduce the Indian population to civilized forms of life, and to initiate the Indian population into the Catholic faith through the education of youth. The most important of these orders were the Franciscans, the Jesuits, the Mercederians, and the Dominicans. All except the Mercederians established institutions that proved vital to the new order of Paraguay. The overall impact of the orders upset the nature of the Guaraní culture and produced a new cultural environment, laying the political foundations of modern Paraguay.

A great religious and cultural impact on the native population was achieved over time by the Jesuit order.[8] The Jesuits' creation of different missions was the most important and far-reaching effort at influencing the cultural and political evolution of the region. Although the Jesuits arrived with the same goals as the other orders, they attempted to introduce the Indians to the faith by supporting a different pattern of social, economic, and political organization. Their efforts subverted the nature of the Guaraní culture, and due to the quite special character of the Jesuits, they were able to establish a social experiment whose goal was to bring the "Kingdom of God to earth." Charles A. Washburn, resident commissioner of the United States in Asunción during the 1860s, wrote of the Jesuits:

> They sought not earthly possessions for themselves but said to the trusting Indians, "Come and live with us; we will teach you to live in greater ease and comfort; we will instruct you in the ways of peace, security and bliss; and we will show you how, when this brief life is past, you may live with us in Paradise. . . ."[9]

The attitude of the Indians toward the Jesuits was different from their attitudes toward the Spanish and Portuguese conquerors. They assumed the missions to be places not only where material well-being could be achieved but also where spiritual rewards were at stake. At the same time the Guaraní leaders who had had previous contacts with the *colonizadores* knew that the *reducciones* would alter significantly the social and political structure of the Guaraní community.[10] The organization of the reducciones followed a general model. Members of the order kept the higher positions for themselves, maintained the Indian chieftains in their positions, and nurtured a small *cabildo.* The cabildo was an institution of town government consisting of Indians who did not have much effective power but who were able to collaborate with the priests. Physically, the reducciones were of an urban nature, even if the population ran its economic activities in the fields. Activities were strictly managed. The members of the order instilled in the Indians notions of discipline, work, and communal values, and protected them from exploitation and disease. The natives' labors were split between supporting the church and sustaining themselves. The reducciones became small centers of economic prosperity, independent of the other institutions of colonial Paraguay.[11]

Although much has been said and written about the impact of the reducciones, it is important to note that even though the reducciones restricted the Indians' movement and forced them to accept a lifestyle foreign to their own, the priests concurrently managed to teach crafts and skills to a large number of Indians. At the end of the experiment, the trained Indians were able to live in urban settings and could earn their livelihoods by a variety of activities. In essence, the relationship between the Guaraní and the Jesuits was a positive one because the work of the latter helped the former to become politically organized within a cohesive community.[12]

The contact between the Guaraní culture and the new norms and practices introduced by the religious orders created a cultural environment distinctively different from that of the rest of the region. The tendency of the Guaraní indians to avoid conflict, together with the imposition of a hierarchical social order, prompted them to submit unquestioningly to strong forms of authority. Although the impact of Catholic organizations also encouraged authoritarian rule in other parts of Latin America, the notable influence of the Jesuit order may have conditioned Paraguay to a certain proneness to extreme forms of authoritarian leadership.

Remarkably, the traits of both the Guaraní culture and the religious orders provided the cultural hallmark of contemporary Paraguayan values. It is not surprising, then, to find that little cultural change has taken place since independence and that the country has been unable to maintain nonauthoritarian forms of government. To the extent that old values have remained the same, contemporary Paraguayan politics reflects a relationship between the people and their leaders based on the early experience of the native culture with the dominant Spanish-Catholic values. Those practices are ingrained in the character of the people and are most evident in the manner that they affect politics at the grass-roots level.

Political Culture at the Grass-Roots Level

Sociological and anthropological studies allow us to understand the cultural context in which politics takes place in Paraguay, especially because it is at the grass-roots level where the true manifestations of the citizenship can be observed. For the purpose of our discussion here, it is important to identify the elements that define the political orientation of the population first, and then see whether the orientation correlates with the findings of recent survey research studies. If there is a close relationship between the two, the analyses would allow us to reach two conclusions: (1) that the Stroessner regime correctly tailored its political style and rhetoric to the cultural orientation of the citizenry, and (2) that the authoritarian political culture of Paraguay was reinforced by the style and the politics of the regime.

One of the first landmark studies of Paraguayan culture was conducted by Elman and Helen Service and reported upon in 1954. The Services were interested in probing the extent of Indian cultural practices within a single rural town, Tobatí. They concluded that only the language had outlasted the colonial period. A few elements, such as culinary practices and native foods, could be traced to the original Guaraní, but the Services pointed out that similar elements had also survived in other Indian cultures throughout the world. Some important Indian institutions, like *compadrazgo*,[13] the Services indicated were European in origin. Even the complete census of the town's families revealed few surnames of Indian origin.[14]

The social and political structure of a small rural town is a good description of the cultural context in which politics takes place in Paraguay. The Services suggested that the most peculiar trait of contemporary Paraguay is the fact that "early colonial cultural patterns have been preserved into modern times . . . unusual acculturation situation in the early period of adjustment between the Spanish settlers and the Guaraní Indians."[15] One of these colonial traits is the structure of authority they found in Tobatí. The Services tell us that the most powerful political figure in Tobatí was the *comisario,* who together with a small group of young officers was in charge of the town's security. Another prominent figure was the town priest, although the Services attributed his status to the personality of the priest himself and did not look upon the role of the priest as crucial in institutional affairs.

The political attitudes of the population in a small town are reflective of the tendency of the national population to accede to a style of political participation not conducive to the establishment of a democratic system. At the grass-roots level, in the opinion of the Services, politics was considered purely a channel for personal economic and social mobility. In this context, they defined political parties in this small town as

> not compact and disciplined with the pretension of an ideology related to policy: they are, rather, loose aggregations of small bodies of factions of would be office-holders, professing personal allegiance to their leaders but continually jockeying for greater power by forming new alliances and destroying old ones.[16]

The alliances follow in some cases a pattern of interpersonal relations related to the role of the ranchers and landowners. Although in the rural areas ownership of land is not legally established but, rather, determined by simple occupation, the landowning elite around Tobatí maintained a relationship with tenants on the basis of an exchange of benefits. The formation of patron-client relationships has its origin in the compadrazgo, which, according to the Services, proceeded more from the traditions imposed by Roman Catholicism than from the native Guaraní themselves.[17]

Another scholar who looked at the grass-roots political culture in Paraguay was Frederick Hicks, who wrote about how interpersonal relationships encouraged the expansion of caudillismo.[18] Hicks argued that a system of "dyadic contracts" defined such relationships in the political culture. They affected most notably the role of the political parties, and fostered the emergence of strongmen with personal followings. The relationships achieved "the effect of politicizing the peasantry (and the urban lower masses), yet directing their political energies to the support of conservative groups which do not usually act in their interest."[19]

In practical terms, interpersonal relationships of this kind operated at several levels. Patron-clientelism allowed for the formation of different kinds of interpersonal exchange, depending on the context of the relationships themselves. One of the most culturally accepted practices of clientelism in Paraguay is the institution of compadrazgo. Although in most of Latin America co-parenting as a ritual is practiced, in Paraguay the relationships provide an opportunity for giving mutual aid, sometimes between individuals and sometimes between individuals and children who are given a "godfather" for the same purpose. These ties foster networks of dependency, and as a general rule, people tend to depend more on individuals than institutionalized channels, wherever they may exist.

Hicks described a second level of interpersonal relationships that affect the evolving Paraguayan culture, namely, paternalism. In this type of relationship the performing of certain personal favors creates a tie that normally goes beyond those formally defined by the relationship itself. Hicks points out that this is normally found in economic relationships between employers and employees, for employers are expected to furnish benefits to workers beyond regular salaries. What ties the two parties together are the benefits, which create a two-way obligation.

Dyadic relationships do not involve only individuals of different socioeconomic status. When people belong to the same social stratum, notably the upper class, collegial relationships develop. One grants friends and relatives whatever benefits are associated with one's position within the political or economic system. The favors are then returned, encouraging a system of exchange. Most practically, the relationships thus occurring are used to bypass the bureaucracy, to gain positions without having to compete for them, or simply to increase one's sense of personal prestige and power.

Grass-Roots Political Culture
and Institutional Politics

A culture based on strong interpersonal loyalties may be the reason that institutional politics has not developed in Paraguay. Indeed, political parties have been struggling to survive and gain ground in the now-modernizing political system, but they are up against the cultural context and old values. What seems so ironic in the case of Paraguay is that the sources of support for political change—obviously those who are deprived economically, socially, or politically—do not play a more prominent role in institutional politics. The tendency to limit the scope and role of institutional politics may largely be explained by the fact that the lower strata do not know what gains can be realized by changing loyalties. Hence, ingrained interpersonal dependency continues to define the nature of politics. Even in light of some economic modernization and progress, as long as the members of the elite can maintain their ability to dispense favors to their personal constituencies, the system is likely to remain unchanged.

Beyond the problem of attracting the allegiance of individuals accustomed to receiving favors from persons rather than from institutions, there is also the problem of resource distribution. Hicks argued that the tendency of Paraguayans to divide themselves between two major political groups or parties (Colorado or Liberal; *oficialista* or *oposición*) reinforces a form of clientelism practiced by the parties. Because the parties are utilized at the local level as channels for distribution of political benefits, memberships must be kept at manageable levels. If party memberships suddenly were to skyrocket, benefits would be insufficient. Unmet expectations would give rise to instability. Hicks's analysis perfectly describes the situation that others have indicated exists within the party structure of Paraguay: strong allegiance on the basis of class, status, or family background and potential personal economic gains.

The impact of the cultural context on the role of political institutions is such that almost no institution escapes the paternal and patronal role. This is most evident in the role of political parties at the local level. The possibility of not belonging to a political party is understood as a tacit rejection of the premises under which the system itself operates. Party affiliation is a matter of personal importance. Switching from one party to another is frowned upon because it is interpreted as evidence of infirm commitment. Allegiance to party for reward's sake means that the parties *raison d'être* is not ideological competition but patronage distribution to those who lend their support.

Hicks posited that the institutional problems created by this kind of cultural orientation affect the prospect for achieving positive results in community development objectives. He argued that the Catholic priests fill the void created by this system of intense loyalties on the basis of personal gain. Because community interests never outrank partisan loyalties, the priests become the settlers of disputes over local policies. The need for people without allegiance to parties allows them to operate at a nonpolitical level. They normally achieve a great deal of success in the activities they undertake, thereby reinforcing their ascendancy.[20]

All these patterns suggest that one of the reasons that the political culture of Paraguay remains authoritarian may be the network of interpersonal relationships that are at its base and to the extension of those relationships to institutions that are key to more competitive politics. To circumvent social practices that are all-pervasive in the population is well-nigh impossible, and for the most part Paraguayans accept the status quo as normal. They do not become impatient at the slow pace of modernization, the accumulation of personal wealth by patrons, or the advantages that inhere in political office. In fact, these very cultural values were promoted by the Stroessner administration through the provision of government jobs, through the expansion of the role of the committees at the local level, and defending the official position of the Colorados as the most patriotic—all in a deliberate effort to maintain the system in place.

The Paraguayan poor were surprisingly supportive of the Stroessner regime, and demonstrated their support openly when the government faced serious organized opposition efforts throughout the country. To this extent, the Paraguayan peasants, poverty stricken and without hope, found at least that they had been given a political role in a political system that worked against their own best interests. But, their lack of preparation prevents them from understanding the situation, and as long as authorities showered praise upon the role of Paraguayan citizens, their support for the regime was insured.

The Political Culture Under Stroessner

The Paraguayan political culture reflects many of the cultural traits found at the grass-roots level. Originally, the colonial period conditioned postindependence institutional development. Efforts to adopt a liberal government proved a great source of conflict, partially because the culture was countervailing. After the advent of the Stroessner regime, the country was involved in a process of modernization of enough magnitude to create the frictions that are common in this kind of social process. Yet, the political culture showed little tendency to change, and remained a cornerstone of the effort toward consolidation made by the Stroessner regime.

Amidst the moves to modernize, certain patterns of social and institutional relationships remained the same. The rather rigid social stratification born during the colonial period operated against forging a more profound sense of national identity. The liberal views of the Enlightenment dominated the behavior and expectations of only the elite segment of the population; the large majority was intellectually unprepared to understand political issues, lacked formal education, and was therefore relegated to a condition of marginality. The result of this compartmentalism was a pattern of interclass relationships that permeated every aspect of Paraguayan social life: relationships based on a calculation of economic and personal benefits to be derived therefrom.

Paraguayan political culture served well to strengthen the political power of the Stroessner regime. The elite that ruled for more than three decades did not change. Most cabinet officers were recirculated within the administration, and in some cases lifetimes were spent in one post. By appearing to be concerned about the fate of the masses, members of the elite achieved a degree of respect that had very little to do with their formal roles. Because the same kinds of interpersonal relationships obtained at all levels of society, the dependent ties between the peasantry and the elite also existed between leaders of the regime itself. Coups and double-crosses were limited only by the fact that every member of the system gained by supporting the regime in place.

The Paraguayan elite played up to the submissiveness of the peasantry. In other Latin American countries like Bolivia or even Argentina, a social and political experience such as Paraguayans underwent would have eventuated in a much more politicized and popular activism. The distinctive submissiveness was reinforced by policies of repression, but it would not be entirely correct to say that the repression brought the submissiveness into being. Repression was also used to restrain potential adversaries who could put the entire system in jeopardy. The usual Paraguayan citizen understood the governance that existed in Paraguay, related to it, and benefited from it to the extent possible. Although it is possible that the economic gains achieved during the past few decades might have changed attitudes toward politics, the gains were normally evaluated in a purely economic context.

The Authoritarian Tradition Reinstated

In a cultural context prone to authoritarian rule, Stroessner's politics were widely accepted because Stroessner himself came to personalize the authoritarian tradition of the country. His ability to manipulate historical events, figures, and records convinced Paraguayans that he possessed visionary powers in policy-making. He managed so to present his administration that any democratic development, however insignificant, was taken as an affront to the established order. The few who requested a more competitive political system were seen as moving against the best interests of the nation. Most Paraguayans understood the punishment meted out to regime opponents in cultural terms: people should accept things as they are. Just as most Paraguayans go along with accepting benefits from patrons, they took for granted the patronage politics of the political elite. The message that Stroessner was good for the country echoed the idea that as benefits continued to be distributed by the political elite and the political parties, little was about to change. By becoming the symbol of what the regime had achieved for the nation and its citizens, Stroessner received dedicated support from the population.

The regime also played up certain other symbols of Paraguayan politics that accentuated the need for the kind of politics that Stroessner sanctioned.[21] Paraguay has always made extensive use of the fact that because of geographic location and environmental limitations, the country is at the mercy of its enemies. During the nineteenth century, the enemy was defined in regional terms: Argentina and Brazil could not be trusted, and therefore, fabrications about their intentions vis-à-vis Paraguay were ever present in policy-making.

Concerned over the country's inability to resist foreign aggression and intervention, Paraguayan leaders constantly praised the heroic nature of the Paraguayan people. The two major confrontations the country has experienced—the Triple Alliance War and the Chaco War—are solid proof of the reality of the foreign aggression and of the glorious character of the Paraguayan people. These wars enlisted the active participation of the population at large, and regardless of the result of each confrontation itself, therefore, Paraguayan leaders promoted this sense of national identity. The people feel, then, intensely proud of their resistance capability and enshrine it as one of their most salient collective traits. In a sense, the symbolic value of having stood against the enemy from the outside provided the Stroessner regime a legitimizing element for fighting those who opposed the system from the inside.

The effort to reinforce authoritarian politics forced Stroessner to play up all possible symbols that were associated with the successful policies of the past. Therefore, even though the leaders of Paraguay during the nineteenth century—José Gaspar Rodríguez de Francia, Carlos Antonio López, and Francisco Solano López—were true tyrants, they are seen by Paraguayans as archetypes of nationhood. In fact, Francia was one of the nation's founding fathers, and the man who molded its politics. Francisco Solano López is portrayed as a leader who succumbed to a much more powerful external force. That Solano López lost the confrontation and plunged Paraguay into long-term sacrifice for reconstruction are not significant elements when compared with what he means to the Paraguayan psyche. Solano López has symbolic value for what his life tells about the Paraguayan people. It is a message that everyone can clearly understand and relate to; it validates the values that made the Paraguayan people truly distinct in the eyes of the regime.

Political Orientations in Paraguay

There are few systematic studies of Paraguayan political culture, although some survey research conducted in recent decades can give us some relevant insights. It would be advantageous to learn how attitudes toward the political system change after long exposure to authoritarianism, but the limitations of the data make such analysis problematical. In a country where most personal activities were subject to institutionalized harassment, it was not easy to assess political orientations. There are, however, several benchmark studies that help us to understand the distinctive culture of Paraguay. In particular, it is important to ask how far and in what direction Paraguayan political culture departs from the general orientations of Latin America. Such tendencies should further illuminate the relationship between authoritarian politics and political culture.

The Lipset Study

One of the first systematic studies of Paraguayan public opinion was the 1966 Lipset survey of university students in several disciplines that measured their outlook on life, importance of family ties, concern for academic issues, and perception of national and international issues in politics. The sample comprised 482 students, most eighteen years of age or older, who attended universities in Asunción. Principally middle class, the students saw education as an important element in upward mobility. Although Lipset did not measure overall orientations toward politics, his findings still bear on the political culture of Paraguay.[22]

The survey revealed a low level of interest in politics. When students were asked if they thought it desirable that their professors be politically active, almost six out of ten indicated that it was "undesirable" or "very undesirable." National politics did not rank high among subjects students talked about among themselves. From a list of choices, they indicated that they discussed "professional and career problems" on a daily basis, followed by "personal problems." Thirteen percent discussed national politics daily; 20 percent did so every two or three days; 25 percent, once a week; some 20 percent, once a month; and another 20 percent did not respond.

Students held a very negative image of politics and politicians. When asked to choose between becoming a professor/researcher or a politician, such as a deputy or a senator, 73 percent of the sample overwhelmingly settled on the former. Opinion on whether the student government should be concerned with national or international politics split almost evenly: half the sample said yes, half said that student and academic activities should be topmost. Seven out of ten students also held that student leaders should not have any affiliation with national political parties or ideologies.

Levels of participation demonstrated that university students believed in involving themselves more in campus politics than in national politics: almost six out of ten did not belong to a national party, but more than six in ten belonged to a student party. When asked how much interest they had in student politics, 40 percent answered "a lot," but the interest figure was 33 percent in regard to national politics. Almost 12 percent had no interest whatsoever in student politics, but the no-interest figure increased to almost 21 percent in relation to the national scene. The country's needs were very clear in the minds of most students. When asked which was most important for Paraguay, economic development, political democracy, or social and economic equality, students ranked them in that same order. However, by a margin of ten to one, they were in favor of agrarian reform.[23]

The students' attitudes were also revealing of the cultural and political traditions of the nation. More than three out of five students declared a preference for hiring a relative instead of a stranger to fill a job opening, clearly demonstrating the affinity of kinship and personal trust. By a margin of two to one, students agreed that there were two kinds of people in the world: weak and strong. They declared, too, that the most important thing a child should learn is to obey his or her parents. Questions about the way the Paraguayan government operated were also revelatory. More than half the students disagreed with the statement that "political corruption has decreased in recent years," and almost seven out of ten disagreed with "the majority of the politicians are still honest." Half the sample said that a rapid increase in economic development would require a stronger national government.

The attitudes of the students showed a lack of identification with problems of a national character. For the most part, they were more concerned with their own future and status than with the promotion of political goals.[24] Although they appeared to be interested in participating in politics within their own environment, they were in fact detached from the political realities of their wider surroundings. Their decision to disassociate themselves from the political process at the national level indicates their realistic understanding of the limitations imposed by the system itself.

The Nichols Studies

Byron Nichols of Union College conducted two studies in Paraguay. Although the data are unfortunately not available for reanalysis, the responses still can serve to illustrate the political attitudes of Paraguayan citizens. In the first study, Nichols, believing that parties had both a political and a social function, interviewed three hundred Paraguayans, with reference to four parties. He assumed that partisan loyalties would vary according to age because each cohort had grown up under different political circumstances, and political preferences change as level of education rises.[25]

Among the more revealing findings of this survey was the tendency of Paraguayans to see ideology as the way for a party to increase its membership. By "developing an ideology that involved all aspects of the social life of the country," respondents said, a party could appeal to a larger number of constituents.[26] Partisans differed sharply in choosing the goals that their parties should pursue. Members of the Colorado party indicated that "peace" was of foremost importance; members of the Liberal Radical party opted for "honest government." Members of both parties strongly supported the idea that achievements in "development" determined their rating of the capabilities and performance of the government.

Respondents also recognized that opposition parties lacked the ability to influence government decisions, that parties were excellent recruitment tools, and that the party programs affect what each party can actually do in government. The most informative part of the study, however, measured the function of the community roles of the parties. Respondents identified a party as one of the most important organizations in their lives, together with the Catholic church and the extended family. Members of the traditional parties indicated that they belonged because of family custom, but members of the modern parties were more pragmatic.[27]

Nichols undertook a more comprehensive study of Paraguayan political culture in 1970 along the lines of the categories developed by Almond and Verba in *The Civic Culture*. He utilized a sample provided by the Centro Paraguayo de Estudios Sociológicos and interviewed 269 household members, using closed-ended questions. Costs prohibited inclusion of a rural sample, but the results are accurate for urban Paraguayans.[28]

Nichols's first set of questions measured knowledge of politics. Some 98.9 percent of the respondents could name the president, from which Nichols concluded that there were no parochials in urban Paraguay. And although the leader of the Partido Liberal Radical (PLR) had been in his post for only four years, 33 percent identified his name correctly; 75 percent correctly identified the leader of the Asociación Nacional Republicana (ANR).

Other questions measured recognition of the political institutions. One question asked about "who" makes laws according to the Constitution and who puts laws into practice. More than half the sample could not identify the functions of the president or the Senate. These data reveal an implicit understanding of the personalism of Paraguayan politics. The respondents all knew of President Stroessner, but they were far less informed about the formal structures through which his policies were implemented. Another question asked whether certain products were provided by the private or public sector. Here almost three out of four respondents managed to recognize the kinds of services furnished by the government, suggesting a subjective political culture. It can be inferred, then, that the main political orientation of Paraguayan citizens is toward the outputs of the political system.[29]

The survey also asked about political perceptions. Almost 30 percent indicated that the government never makes mistakes; 14 percent said that mistakes were made "rarely"; and about 31 percent responded "sometimes." This form of political cynicism was much more evident among the less educated and the older respondents. But, overwhelmingly, the greatest influence was party identification. Forty percent of the sample were members of the Colorado party, and they said that the government "never" made a mistake.[30] Similarly, almost half of all respondents indicated that they thought that the government would come to their aid, but more significantly, most of these people also said that they were members of the Colorado party.

Nichols also sought opinions concerning the realities of Paraguayan politics. Of the 53 percent who said that there would be differences in government according to which party ruled, about half were unable to give reasons for such differences. Most respondents named personal prestige and personal gain as the reasons that most politicians enter government service. When asked about criteria by which to judge a particular political system, the respondents named peace and order, followed by honesty and by development. The answers did not correlate with party identification, so the criteria by which most Paraguayans evaluate government seem to be tranquillity, honesty, and economic well-being.

When the respondents were asked to indicate how satisfied they were with their government, most said they were happy with the way things were. The answers correlated strongly with party identification and with level of education; those who were outside the sphere of power and who had more education tended to be less happy about the way politics were run.

An excellent way to understand how politics is ingrained in Paraguayan society is through citizen expression of political beliefs. Nichols found that Paraguayans speak little about politics in their youth, and that most do not feel comfortable talking politics outside the family. People clearly understand that a wider discussion of politics can lead to social and even legal sanctions. Knowledge of politics is acquired from the press, the church, and the media. Few people give credence to the speeches of politicians, perhaps believing that there is not much objectivity to be found in what they say. Concerning socialization practices, Nichols found that the family remains the focal institution providing political socialization.

The last issue looked into by Nichols was political participation. Some 79 percent of his sample had participated in the national election of 1968, and more than 90 percent of the sample had received assistance from the state. It is natural for Paraguayans to view government as a source of largesse because so many of them have benefited thereby. On the other hand, more than half the sample had never attended political rallies or party activities, 30 to 35 percent did so only "rarely." Some 70 percent said that they never presented complaints or requests to government officers or party leaders—something that must in fact be done with great caution in Paraguay. Overall, then, it was quite natural for Nichols to conclude that in Almond and Verba's terms Paraguayans manifest a subjective political culture.

The Silvero Studies

Professor Ilde Silvero of the Catholic University of Asunción conducted an investigation of the attitudes of Paraguayans toward their political system. The sample was 242 respondents in Asunción, eighteen years or older, mainly from three classes: workers and employees, independent professionals, and entrepreneurs. The interviews took place in September 1982, and the results were published in 1983.[31]

The Silvero study allows some useful comparisons. Most of the questions were similar to those in the Nichols survey on political culture, even though Silvero sought only to measure attitudes about "political life in Paraguay" and asked questions that were not part of the theoretical propositions in *The Civic Culture*. The questions pertained especially to political participation. Three-quarters of the respondents indicated that they had never attended a course, seminar, or meeting in which they had received political training. When asked about party ideology, only half the sample knew about the ideology of the Colorado party,

30 percent knew about that of the Liberals, and 20 percent were familiar with that of the Febreristas.

Other questions also showed low levels of political knowledge and participation. More than half the respondents could not name the leaders of all three major parties, and 35 percent could not name the leaders of the Colorado party, even though the leaders have remained the same for more than four decades. Only three out of five correctly identified the Acuerdo Nacional as an organization of political parties that opposed the administration of President Stroessner. Almost half were not enrolled in a political party. Half of those interviewed had not participated in the latest municipal elections, even though voting is mandatory for all citizens over eighteen. Even more revealing, perhaps, is that eight out of ten had not participated in a party-organized activity in the previous six months.

Like Nichols a decade earlier, Silvero found little interest in political activities. About half said the political situation of the country was "favorable," and half said it was "unfavorable." Almost 40 percent indicated no interest whatsoever in the presidential election of 1983, and only 6 percent were very interested. People between eighteen and twenty-five years of age were less interested in politics, voted the least, and seldom participated in party activities.

The most interesting of Silvero's findings also indicates subject orientations. The group that earned the least tended to have a better opinion of the political situation. The most affluent saw the situation as only partially favorable or as totally unfavorable. The lower classes, which remain outside the mainstream of politics, thus appear to measure performance on terms different from the terms used by those who expect more personal benefits.

Silvero and José Morínigo in 1986 conducted a more comprehensive study sponsored by the Friedrich Naumann Foundation and the Catholic University of Asunción. The sample comprised 1,803 respondents from Asunción and its surrounding areas, 331 from medium-sized cities, and 264 from small cities. The purpose of the survey was to enlarge the findings of the previous study.[32] The researchers reported a strong fear of participating in the survey on the part of many citizens, manifested by the high percentage of individuals who answered no questions. The survey found political parties to be in institutional crisis because they were not typically deemed the most credible institutions; respondents placed more trust in members of the clergy, the press, and even the military. Asked whether "political parties serve only to distribute personal services to their memberships," 75.9 percent of the sample replied that a party that would not provide services to its membership was not fulfilling its reason for being.

A strong willingness for change throughout the country was revealed. Of the total sample, 31.8 percent thought that "some" things must change, 36.9 percent, that "many" things must change, and 18.0 percent, that there must be a "total change."[33] The difficulty was to find ways to bring change about. When asked about possible options, most respondents could not think of an alternative to the power structure currently in place. Almost half of the sample could not identify the Acuerdo Nacional, and more than half of the sample could not name another political party that could do well if in office. Low voter turnout and an opposition force that is not fully active within the political system mean that the possibility of change is indeed quite limited.

Paraguay: An Authoritarian Variant

Although the relative scarcity of data concerning the political culture of Paraguay points to an area that deserves further exploration, the evidence gathered so far comports with the foregoing analysis of Paraguayan politics in general. For a century and a half, Paraguayan politics has been little more than a series of confrontations between parties or party factions. By now, people's lack of satisfaction with party politics has long encouraged acceptance of a government that maintains order and peace, one that promotes sound economic policy above partisan preferences. The apathy so evident in survey responses thus reaffirms the criteria by which authoritarian politics became and remained dominant within Paraguay.

The focus of the population on the benefits received from the government regardless of party affiliation affects the views that Paraguayans have about their individual role in politics. Citizens have come to see political parties as no more than institutions wherein a few politically involved individuals "weather" their differences. People are more interested in the results of politics than in the political process, hence the parties have not found an effective area of competition. Partisans view the parties as institutions that will bring them personal economic benefit, and ironically, when Paraguayans 'refer to the parties' programs, their primary if unspoken concern is with the goods they will gain or lose by bringing a particular group to power.

The most striking dimension of Paraguayan political culture in the 1980s was the general lack of interest in politics, in the population at large and especially in the younger generation. In light of the internecine quarrels affecting the major parties, youth is further convinced of the wisdom of remaining outside the political domain. When an entire population concludes that politics is an arena that one enters only in pursuit of personal benefits, the prospects for developing a participatory political culture are dim. And when the entire system is securely controlled by a small group, the task of delivering the system from its authoritarian mode may be impossible.

Notes

1. For the way in which the Tupí-Guaraní are related to other South American and to North American Indians, see Paul Radin, *Indians of South America* (Garden City, N.Y.: Doubleday, Doran, 1942), pp. 75ff.

2. *Chaco* is a Quechua word that means hunting or hunting ground.

3. On the character of the Guaraní culture, see Gaspar N. Cabrera, *Carácter peculiar de la cultura Guaraní* (Asunción: Imprenta Zamphirópolos, 1965).

4. Fourteen "guáras" were found at the beginning of the conquest, and they were populated by different Guaraní groups: the *Carios*, the *Tobatines*, the *Guarambarenses*, the *Itatines*, the *Mbarakayúenses*, the *Mondayenses*, the *Paranáes*, the *Ygañáenses*, the *Yguazúenses*, the *Uruguayenses*, the *Tapes*, the *Mbiazás*, the *Guairáes*, and the *Chandules*. On the role played by each and their characteristics, see Branislava Susnik, *El rol de los Indígenas en la formación y en la vivencia del Paraguay*, vol. 1 (Asunción: Instituto Paraguayo de Estudios Nacionales, 1982).

5. On the traits of Guaraní ideology, see Juan Natalicio González, *Ideología Guaraní*, Ediciones Especiales, No. 37 (Mexico: Instituto Indigenista Interamericano, 1958), chap. 10.

6. For a strong argument on the cultural accomplishments of the Guaraní, see Juan Natalicio González, *Proceso y formación de la cultura Paraguaya* (Asunción: Editorial Guarania, 1948).

7. On the different religious orders operating in Paraguay, see Rafael E. Velázquez, *Breve historia de la cultura en el Paraguay*, 10th ed. (Asunción: El Gráfico, 1985).

8. An excellent account of the activities of the Jesuit order in Paraguay can be found in R. B. Cunninghame Graham, *A Vanished Arcadia* (New York: Haskell House, 1968).

9. Charles A. Washburn, *The History of Paraguay*, vol. 1 (Boston: Lee & Shepard Publishers, 1871), p. 76.

10. See Bartomeu Meliá, S.J., "Las reducciones jesuíticas del Paraguay: Un espacio para una utopía colonial," *Estudios Paraguayos* 6 (September 1978): 159.

11. For a detailed analysis of the economic, social, and cultural environment of the reducciones, see Ramón Gutiérrez, "Estructura socio-política, sistema productivo y resultante espacial en las misiones jesuíticas del Paraguay durante el siglo XVIII," *Estudios Paraguayos* 2 (December 1974): 83–140.

12. A short description of the relationship between the Indians and the religious can be found in Bartolomé Meliá, S.J., *Guaraníes y Jesuitas* (Asunción: Ediciones Loyola, 1969).

13. *Compadrazgo* is an institution widespread in Latin America. It involves a special type of interpersonal relationship normally established as a result of a

religious ritual—typically baptism, confirmation, or marriage—for the purpose of showing spiritual affinity.

14. See Elman R. Service and Helen S. Service, *Tobatí: Paraguayan Town* (Chicago: University of Chicago Press, 1954), pp. 284–85.

15. Ibid., p. 26.

16. Ibid., p. 129.

17. The Services point out that the mode of the compadrazgo in Paraguay resembles that of southern Brazil, where the influence of the Roman Catholic church was strong. In other Indian cultures of Latin America, notably Peru, Guatemala, and Mexico, the institution of compadrazgo was the result of aboriginal culture. Ibid., p. 284.

18. Frederick Hicks, "Interpersonal Relationships and Caudillismo in Paraguay," *Journal of Interamerican Studies and World Affairs* 13 (January 1971): 89–111.

19. Ibid., p. 90.

20. Frederick Hicks, "Politics, Power and the Role of the Village Priest," *Journal of Inter-American Studies* 9 (April 1967): 273–82.

21. The symbolic character of Paraguay's political culture was suggested to me by Paul H. Lewis. Although he sees this symbolic content as a comprehensive explanation for political culture in Paraguay, I believe it is manipulated by the authorities simply to reinforce the authoritarian tradition.

22. The data correspond to the survey conducted by Lipset as part of his study "Values, Vocations and Political Orientations." The data are available from the Inter-University Consortium for Political and Social Research at the University of Michigan.

23. This point demands an explanation. Although most Paraguayans accept the class-oriented nature of their society, they can also see the benefits of a program like agrarian reform. The empirical evidence from which students gathered their notion was probably the program instituted in 1963 by the Institute for Rural Welfare. The program was a colonization effort, and it did not achieve the impact that agrarian reform could have had.

24. This tendency to overvalue the role of the university in providing status, income, or knowledge is what Rivarola has called the "mediatization" of the university. See Domingo Rivarola, "Universidad y estudiantes en una sociedad tradicional," *Aportes* 12 (April 1969): 47–84.

25. See Byron Nichols, "Las expectativas de los partidos políticos en Paraguay," *Revista Paraguaya de Sociología* 5 (December 1968): 22–61. Nichols used the Asociación Nacional Republicana and the Partido Liberal Radical as examples of the traditional parties, and the Partido Demócrata Cristiano and the Partido Revolucionario Febrerista as examples of the modern parties.

26. The response of the sample is interesting in that Paraguayans conceive their political parties to stand for different ideologies insofar as they portray different elements of the social history of Paraguay. The Colorados stress the role of Francia and the Lópezes in building the nation against the aggression of foreigners; the Liberal party portrays the brutality of the dictatorial past.

27. Nichols explains that although respondents defined the difference between parties as differences between the programs pursued by each, in reality the

programs are quite similar and tend to remain unchanged. Most respondents also indicated that they "belong" or "are" of a particular party affiliation, which is suggestive of the notion that programs do not make much difference. See Nichols, "Las expectativas de los partidos políticos," p. 45.

28. See Byron Nichols, "La cultura política del Paraguay," *Revista Paraguaya de Sociología* 8 (January-April 1971): 133-60.

29. Ibid., p. 141.

30. Nichols concluded that there were different perceptions within the Paraguayan population about politics. Perceptions were strongly influenced by party allegiance, but education, age, and sex had little bearing on them. See ibid., p. 147.

31. See Ilde Silvero, "Opinión, interés y participación en la vida política Paraguaya," *Estudios Paraguayos* 11 (June 1983): 215-44.

32. José N. Morínigo and Ilde Silvero, *Opiniones y actitudes políticas en el Paraguay* (Asunción: Editorial Histórica, 1986).

33. Ibid., p. 200.

The History of
Authoritarianism
in Paraguay

3 Some observers speculate today that Paraguay remained highly authoritarian because of the indigenous character of its people or the long Jesuit tutelage of the Indians in the *reducciones* of the colonial period. Others look to nineteenth-century authoritarianism as the key to the authoritarianism of the twentieth. At the very least, then, the analysis of Paraguayan authoritarianism presupposes an inquiry into the special historical experience of the nation. We must try to gauge its relevance for present-day Paraguay.

The Colonial Period

The incorporation of the Spanish into Guaraní society produced a different social order. Several classes emerged, each with its own characteristics, especially in Asunción and nearby areas. The highest class comprised the Spanish, a small minority that enjoyed privileges like those of the original conquerors. The next class comprised the *criollos*, people of solely European blood but born in the New World, who enjoyed some benefits but did not achieve preeminence due to their small numbers. The third and largest group comprised *mestizos*, the offspring of miscegenation between the Spanish and the Indians. The Indians, together with the Negroes and mulattos, were brought to a condition of virtual slavery, forming the lowest class, as a result of the economic need for agricultural labor.

The method used to secure agricultural labor was the *encomienda*, a privilege granted by the crown. In return for the Indians' work, the *encomendero* provided the necessities of life. Conquistadores were awarded portions of land that they would then exploit through the administration of an encomendero. Ultimately, the Indians were not subject to the encomendero but indirectly to the Crown. Initially, an encomienda was given for the duration of two lives, that of the beneficiary and his heir; the rule was altered in 1718.[1] The encomienda was different from the *repartimiento.* The former was the allocation of land with its Indian families; the latter consisted of the distribution of Indians for agriculture, mining, or other pursuits. At first Indians who were part of encomiendas were not included in repartimientos, but when labor became scarce, both institutions could apply for the same Indians.[2] There were two kinds of repartimientos: *mitas,* groups of Indians who would provide their services for specific periods of time, rotating in their assignments, and *yanaconas,* Indians at the personal disposal of the conquistadores who were considered members of the family and expected to give almost unlimited service.

Two early events show that the Spanish conquest not only had altered the peaceful culture of the Guaraní but also had introduced competition between groups. The insurgency of the *comuneros* in 1717 and the expulsion of the Jesuit order in 1767 reveal that tensions were mounting. The comuneros were the catalyst of a strong popular sentiment that spread throughout the province; they promoted the idea of independence from the crown long before other countries in the region conceived a similar notion. Two main causes prompted the comunero revolt: first, the social composition of the Cabildo of Asunción had changed by the end of the seventeenth century; and second, sentiments toward the crown had grown hostile because of the perceived notion that it had little concern for Paraguayans. The imperious and persecutory actions of Governor Diego de Reyes Valmaseda, in charge since 1717, stirred an organized challenge, in consequence of which in 1721 the Audiencia de Charcas sent José de Antequera y Castro to investigate. Antequera found Reyes guilty, whereupon Reyes fled and Antequera assumed power. The viceroy then appointed a former governor, General Baltasar García Ros, to confront the usurper. Antequera, in agreement with the Cabildo and militia of Asunción defeated Ros and the royal army in 1724. On his way to present his case to the Audiencia, Antequera was apprehended and imprisoned. Concerned over the apparent success of the comunero movement, the viceroy ordered a new expedition against the comuneros, under the governor of the Río de la Plata, Bruno Mauricio de Zabala. The retaking of the government was unimpeded.

In 1730, Ignacio de Soroeta, who had close ties with the Jesuit order, was appointed governor of the province of Paraguay. The comuneros did not recognize him, electing instead revolutionary leaders who remained in charge. In 1733 the comuneros marched against a second crown appointee, Colonel Manuel Calderón de Ruyloba, who was killed in the confrontation. An expeditionary force led by Zabala smashed the comunero movement in 1735. A smaller effort in 1747 to confront the governor was made public and its leaders were executed.[3]

The comunero movement was also against the increasing economic power and dominance of the Jesuit order. The Jesuits had gained a virtual monopoly over labor resources and also enjoyed taxation benefits from the crown. By 1730 they controlled thirty reducciones, with a total labor pool of about 150,000. But, such extraordinary assets inevitably brought enemies. The comuneros had expelled the Jesuits of the Colegio de la Compañía de Jesús in Asunción during the Antequera administration because of suspicion that they would collaborate with the royal forces.

The Jesuits suffered another crisis as a result of the treaty between Portugal and Spain signed in 1750. The treaty provided Spain with the jurisdiction over Colonia in exchange for land located east of the Uruguay River. In 1754, the Indians of seven Jesuit missions revolted against the decision to relocate them to Brazilian jurisdiction. The disruption was indicative that the Jesuits' position was making them troublesome to the Spanish empire, which itself was being pressed by domestic unrest and European problems. At one and the same time the Jesuits were finding themselves at odds with the crown, the native population, and the Catholic authorities. The climate was propitious for a royal move against the order, and it was expelled from Paraguay in 1767.

The Postindependence Era

The events that led to the independence of Paraguay were to a remarkable degree foreign to the nature of domestic affairs. The relationship with Buenos Aires was an easy one throughout the colonial period. On July 24, 1810, the Cabildo of Asunción declared Paraguay's allegiance to the Spanish Regency Council, opposing subordination to the leaders of the Argentine revolution. Buenos Aires responded by sending troops under the command of General Manuel Belgrano, but their defeat in Paraguarí in January·and Tacuarí in March of 1811, meant the end of Buenos Aires supremacy over the province.

The leadership of this insurrection was shared by Pedro Juan Caballero, Fulgencio Yegros, and Blás José de Rojas Aranda, who led the young officers in Asunción, Ytapúa and Candelaria, and in Corrientes, respectively. During June 1811, the General Congress declared that the first national government of Paraguay would be headed by a five-man junta: Fulgencio Yegros, Pedro Juan Caballero, Francisco Javier Bogarín, José Gaspar Rodríguez de Francia, and Fernando de la Mora. Francia resigned on several occasions from the junta, but returned in November of 1812 when pressure from Buenos Aires demanded a man of his qualities at the helm. The General Congress in 1813 announced the Republic of

Paraguay, adopted thirteen principles of governance, and declared the state was to be ruled by a two-man council composed of Yegros and Francia. In spite of admirable efforts to remain democratically organized, the General Congress on October 3 and 4, 1814, created the position of Dictador Supremo de la República, with power over the cabildo and over its armed forces for a period of three years, and elected Francia to the position. The General Congress of 1816 gave him life tenure.[4]

Authoritarianism I: The Franciata, 1814–1840

The role given to Francia indicated the renunciation by popular groups of aspirations to gain participatory positions within the power structure.[5] On the same day that Francia was elected, several resolutions assured him total control. The republic would have a general congress only when the dictator called for one, and the congress that elected him would be dissolved. The clergy were instructed on how to refer to him in front of the people. In short, Francia enjoyed undisputed power and limitless authority.

The character of the Franciata was clear a few years later.[6] Most of Francia's support was based on his decisions to increase expenditures on defense, to provide an expanded role to the military and police forces, and to keep a close watch on the membership of the cabildo. Although he would later dispose of this institution, at first he handpicked its members.

Opposition to Francia soon arose. He responded firmly to his challengers and was quick to limit their activities. Even with Fulgencio Yegros, he did not compromise. Discovering that Yegros held meetings in his *estancia* with possible dissidents, Francia ordered him to establish residence in Asunción, where he could be watched more closely. The accumulation of such repressive measures brought about the elimination of the national elite as potential challengers to state power.[7]

A source of discontent that presented problems for Francia was the Catholic church. He attempted to gain control over ecclesiastical institutions by reducing the influence of the respective orders. Most of the priests were well educated and had foreign contacts, a condition that rendered them even more the objects of Francia's strategies. In 1819 he demanded that a church council study the relations between church and state, and in 1823 he closed down the seminary and the monasteries. Priests who were involved with these institutions were sent to parishes in the interior. With the secularization of once-independent church institutions, such as the seminary and monasteries, Francia's grip over the Catholic clergy was almost complete.[8]

The reining in of the Catholic church and the repression of the domestic elite gave Francia domination over the politics of the nation. He solidified his power when he abolished the cabildos of Asunción and Villa Rica in 1824. By indicating that *alcaldes* would continue to mind administrative matters, he cleared the way for his own personalized control over those two administrative posts as well.

Francia's policies created an institutional arrangement whereby no organized countermovement could materialize. Paradoxically, however, Francia also helped to create an institutional army, which proved to be unwise from his standpoint. By drawing men mostly from the interior, he at first assured himself of loyalty within the ranks. The professionalization of the army gave him a seal of approval from the population. Many citizens appear to have seen it as a demonstration of Francia's concern for protecting Paraguayans from foreign threats.[9]

The Franciata, then, was organized along authoritarian lines and was welcomed by most of the population. Paraguayans accepted the leadership style of El Supremo with the same quiet attitudes that had characterized the relationship of the Guaraní Indians with the Jesuit order. Once the old institutions had been subverted, Francia governed personalistically. His policies were clear, decisive, and popular. The hallmark of his tenure was the isolation of Paraguay from international and regional developments, so that the consolidation of his power would suffer no unexpected surprises. The dictator was not so much preoccupied by the possible arrival of foreign forces upon Paraguayan soil—although this might have happened—as he was concerned about the penetration of ideas that would cause his countrymen to understand the true nature of his reign. Nevertheless, he permitted some commercial relations, especially through the ports of Candelaria and Ytapúa. He wanted a low profile of Paraguay abroad and to curtail the role of foreigners within Paraguay.[10]

A political system of extreme personalism, the Franciata reserved all decisions concerning the institutional life of the nation to El Supremo. The abolition of the old elite and the absence of a significant bureaucracy concentrated power in him. One of the few limitations was regional: Francia's grip was weak in the interior. He was far less popular there; post commanders received much of the local glory.

The economic policy of the Franciata was in line with the general orientation of the government. Francia strove for self-sufficiency and for a nineteenth-century form of state socialism. Agriculture and livestock growing increased substantially during his years, as did basic manufacturing, especially in clothing. Still, the most revealing dimension of his tenure was the heightened role of the state in the economy. He created an economic sector based on ranches owned by the state, to which he added the ranches of foreigners who had died, and those that belonged to the conspirators of the 1820s. What the ranches produced was usually sold in state stores. El Supremo monopolized the export trade, revenues, and the sale of stamped paper for official business. His budget surpluses attested the success of his policies.[11]

The Franciata came to an end in 1840 with the death of Francia. By then he had achieved a remarkable development record; Paraguay's situation was unparalleled in the region. Francia left a lasting mark on Paraguayan political culture. He reinforced the people's tendency to depend on personalism yet dismantled the domestic elite. He managed to maintain the country in peace when neighboring countries were riven by domestic chaos. More darkly, the underlying assumption that as a leader he was indispensable and that Paraguayans were unfit to participate in politics formed a legacy that continues to haunt Paraguayan politics today.

Authoritarianism II: The Lópezes, 1840–1870

The demise of El Supremo did not initially occasion many emotional or political consequences. The expectation that his death would cause profound instability was forgotten when domestic politics swiftly changed direction. Concerned with the fate of the republic, army officers gained control and summoned a congress to reorganize the country. With three contenders for the highest position, the congress arranged for a two-man junta to lead Paraguay for the next three years. Soon thereafter the officer nominated to be one of the pair returned to the barracks, convinced he had little contribution to make. Carlos Antonio López found himself the sole leader, a post that he had dared to try for only after Francia's death.

López was a lawyer with a good reputation. An imposing figure, he had a relaxed way of handling the business of government. Whether or not he would conduct politics different than Francia did at first seemed questionable. In fact, López attempted his own brand of leadership, but it turned out to be not much different from Francia's.[12] Fearful of the internal struggles plaguing Paraguay's neighbors, López worked to reinforce the Asunción army and to prepare the country for self-defense. Much of the infrastructure built during this period and the creation of naval forces were for the purpose of preparedness.

If López was more externally minded than Francia, his internal politics resembled Francia's to an extraordinary degree. He controlled the press, supported education (except for higher education), and although he released most of Francia's political prisoners, managed to collect a few of his own. The results of his administration were reassuring to Paraguayans; here was a man who clearly understood the destiny toward which Francia had labored, and López attempted to bring to fruition the visionary ideas of his predecessor.

The ideological nature of López's orientation was evident in the first constitutional document produced in Paraguay. In his Law That Establishes the Political Administration of the Republic of Paraguay, López condemned dictatorial power and introduced a simple yet original scheme of government organization that seemed tailored to the Paraguayan reality. He intended to promote stability in Paraguay in order to avoid the disarray characterizing its neighbors.[13] López started to open Paraguay to international trade, and suspicious Paraguayans erratically embarked upon wider commercial relations. At the same time, the López family increased its control over the economy, acquiring more land for the state. The gradual increase in contacts with foreign governments meant modernization and a range of external pressures.[14]

López was very fond of his children, especially of his eldest, Francisco Solano. He spent considerable time with him, had him tutored, and saw to it that he had an excellent education. After some military training, Francisco was sent to Europe in 1852 to build his diplomatic skills and to foster his country's international contacts. And contacts he did establish. Within two years, he brought about commercial agreements with Great Britain, France, and Spain, but he failed to obtain papal confirmation of his uncle as bishop of Paraguay. Francisco returned to Asunción with a red-haired Irish mistress, who caused a stir in traditional Paraguayan society.[15] Francisco seemed to be destined for great things.

On his deathbed in 1862, Carlos Antonio López named Francisco vice-president, counseling him to be careful in his relations with the neighbors, especially Brazil. When the younger López called a congress to decide upon the future of the country, he provided a first indication of what was to come. Disaffection even then suggested that his strong rule would not endure forever. Francisco jailed opposing Asunceños to obtain majority support, and the climate grew more combative. He increased his repressive activities, and an atmosphere of intimidation permeated the streets of Asunción after his inauguration as president. The population sensed that trouble was on the way.[16]

Francisco's youth and lack of experience shaped his actions. His contacts in Europe had provided opportunities to meet many notables, and Napoleon had become his special hero. As a result, he rethought the role of Paraguay in the region on the basis of what proved to be two very costly misunderstandings: first, that his neighbors were militarily weak, and second, that his own military was strong. In November of 1864 Francisco ordered the seizure of the Brazilian ship *Marqués de Olinda,* after the ship had spent a few days in Asunción on its way to the Matto Grosso with the Brazilian governor on board. The bold action sealed the fate of authoritarian Paraguay. The anticipated military confrontation became a reality, one that ended Francisco's meteoric career and tore apart what three generations of Paraguayans had wrought.[17]

The Triple Alliance War, 1864–1870

Solano López's motives for going to war appear to have been quite complex. There were several territorial disputes and claims, the question of navigation on the rivers of the Paraná-Paraguay system, and most important, the independence of Uruguay—crucial to regional stability in the opinion of Francisco. He feared an agreement between Brazil and Argentina that would relegate Uruguay and Paraguay to a secondary role in the region. Just in case, Francisco readied the military and increased arms imports from Europe.[18]

He warned the Brazilians to abstain from military intervention in Uruguay. But, rather than concentrating on supporting the independence efforts of Uruguayan rebels, he attacked Brazilian positions in the Matto Grosso. Achieving success at first because of the unexpectedness of his move, Francisco then sought approval from Buenos Aires to reach the region of Rio Grande do Sul in southern Brazil by crossing over Argentine territory. When his request was denied, he seized the Argentine port of Corrientes in April of 1865. The following month, Solano López found himself fighting an allied force composed of Brazilian, Argentine, and Uruguayan armies.[19]

Francisco attacked energetically but was defeated in the battles of Riachuelo, Yataí, and Uruguayana during 1865. When he ordered a retreat to the north bank of the Paraná River, the allied forces reorganized. The allied army crossed the Paraná River in April of 1866 under the leadership of General Bartolomé Mitre of Argentina. Heavy fighting took a devastating toll on the Paraguayan army in the battles of Estero Bellaco, Tuyutí, Yatayty Corá, Boquerón, and Curuzú between May and September; it was victorious only at Curupaití. The allies' disagreement over whether to end the confrontation or to wait for additional forces considerably slowed their advance. After Mitre left his command to Brazilian General Luis Alves de Lima e Silva, Lima ordered the troops to attempt a peaceful crossing in front of the Humaitá fortress and then to sail upriver, heading for Asunción.

The expectation of Paraguayan citizens that foreign troops would liberate the city from López's terror were not fulfilled until January of 1869. The expectation was shared by the foreign community, much of which had found refuge in the U.S. consulate. Panic in the city and the insistence of Colonel Venancio López, brother of Francisco Solano, led Vice-president Domingo Sánchez to call a council of war. The Paraguayan army's lack of resistance at Humaitá and the efforts of the council to protect Asunción from what seemed an inevitable attack led Solano López to regroup in San Fernando. There he tortured and murdered those he thought were challenging his power.[20]

López continued his retreat, reorganizing at Villeta. General Bernardino Caballero led the Paraguayan forces, but the Brazilians were able to overpower them. With few soldiers to defend the Paraguayan positions, Solano López lost several small battles. He was forced to establish quarters at Cerro León, so the allied forces found no practical impediment in reaching Asunción.

With the decision to occupy Asunción rather than pursue López, the allied forces gave the dictator valuable time to mount what turned out to be an ineffective defense. The foreign forces entered Asunción, looting wealth and documents, destroying everything they found in their path. While the allied forces made the best out of the occupation, López remained busy rallying support in the countryside. After a few skirmishes, the Brazilians attacked him at Cerro Corá and the dictator tried to flee on foot. He did not yield to an invitation to surrender and faced death shouting, "I die with my country!" It was the end of the most controversial leadership in Paraguayan history.[21]

The Aftermath of Defeat

The defeat sealed the fate of the nation for the immediate future. Paraguay was physically devastated. Reconstruction would soon bring clashes among groups, ideals, and political factions. If the elimination of vast economic and human resources profoundly affected the character of the nation, it also doomed Paraguay to an uncharted route in the search for its own identity. The chronic instability of the postwar years reflected the magnitude of the impact of the defeat.

During the postwar period, Paraguay welcomed back many exiles who had been living in Argentina and Brazil. Argentina and Brazil sought to recover by diplomacy lands that the Lópezes had annexed. The allies formed a provisional interim government that was to stay until a democratically elected government replaced it. In fact, neither the allies nor the Paraguayans were prepared to control the government.[22]

It was in the aftermath of the war that the division that led to Paraguay's major political parties developed. Political clubs served as the foundation for the Asociación Nacional Republicana—the Colorado party—and the Partido Liberal. Both parties were officially formed in 1887, although the Liberal party adopted this name only in 1893. The former party attempted to save the memory of Francisco Solano López; the latter party had been formed in exile during the Solano López administration and had fought against him during the war in the Paraguayan Legion. Although the ideological differences between the parties were not great, the Liberals tended to support democratic government and a laissez-faire position on most economic matters.

The Constitutional Assembly was convened in 1870. It drafted the Constitution of 1870 in the manner of the Argentine Constitution of 1853, the U.S. Constitution of 1787, and the French Constitution of 1789. The document represented neither the history nor the spirit of Paraguayan politics. Harris G. Warren writes:

> The Paraguayan experience had been with ruthless dictatorship for more than five decades and with a colonial authoritarianism that, while not without democratic aspect, could not be called rule by the people. Authoritarianism was as deeply ingrained among the people as the use of the Guaraní language, and any effort to deviate from it entailed serious dangers that could be overcome only by an ideological revolution in which Paraguayans would agree to observe democratic political principles. Paraguay did not achieve democratic government under the Constitution of 1870.[23]

The character of the new constitution notwithstanding, the convention elected Cirilo Rivarola to the presidency. The election was a milestone in the reconstruction effort, but the choice of Rivarola also exposed the deep divisions between parties and loyalties. Rivarola was opposed by the *bareiristas*, who supported Cándido Bareiro for the presidency and also enlisted the support of the Liberals. If anything was evident at the time of Rivarola's election, it was that factionalism had developed as a result of many years of unconditional loyalty to dictators. Paraguayan society was fractured by the maneuvering of rival factions.

The tenure of President Rivarola proved difficult. He needed to compromise with a very hostile Congress; he had very little support among political groups; and he was used by the Brazilians in their effort to regain lands also claimed by Argentina. Much of the first presidential term, completed by Salvador Jovellanos in 1874 due to Rivarola's resignation in 1871, became a period of high diplomacy, in which rival sympathies with Argentina and Brazil dominated the domestic political scene. Conferences were held to establish the terms under which Paraguay would reinstate its sovereignty, but the interests of Brazil and Argentina confused the situation, thereby slowing and endangering the process itself.

Postwar efforts at reconstruction were geared to expansion of the railroads, attracting immigrants, and procuring loans from the British banking system. All were intricately connected because immigrants would boost agricultural production and an improved railroad network would mean that the products could be brought to market. The Paraguayan Central Railway never operated at a profit, but it proved to be an instrument by which private firms could negotiate with the British for investment capital.

With the plots to oust Jovellanos in 1874, a vigorous new personage emerged in Paraguayan politics. Bernardino Caballero not only was a general in the army but had been close to Francisco Solano López. His leadership style won him the support of the Bareiristas. He later helped to found the Colorado party, and despite internal struggles managed to dominate Paraguayan politics from 1878 until 1904. Caballero did not share the political vision of José S. Decoud or Cándido Bareiro, but he is often referred to as the father of *Coloradismo*. He clung to Decoud to save himself from being overwhelmed by Paraguayan politics.[24]

The First Colorado Republic, 1878–1904

Throughout the postwar decade a single name had been associated with the creation of the Colorado party: Cándido Bareiro. Therefore, it was no surprise that in 1878 he assumed the presidency. His inheritance was economic and political chaos compounded by the murder of former President Rivarola. (Rivarola had been attacked by six men while he was walking on Palma Street in full daylight, and died no more than a block from the presidential palace and the police station.) The incident mirrored the general turmoil of Paraguayan affairs.

Bareiro also confronted the opposition presented by Juan Silvano Godoi, who had been involved in the murder of former president Juan Bautista Gill in 1877, but who had managed to escape to Buenos Aires. Godoi plotted in Buenos Aires to disturb the administration and purchased a ship with which he sailed upriver toward Asunción. Bareiro declared a state of siege, and sent a ship and troops to meet the rebels. The intervention of the Argentine authorities ended the Godoi adventure, and the entire episode helped Bareiro to increase his power. But Bareiro's remarkable efforts would not last long, for he died in office after completing only two years of his presidential term.[25]

Vice-president Adolfo Saguier was jailed and asked to resign in order to allow Caballero to become president. On September 4, 1880, Caballero assumed the presidency in the most peaceful coup that Paraguay has ever known. He was concerned with the need for reconstruction and reorganization of the country; his dedication and values appear not only in his policy orientations but also in his determination to gain popular support for his regime. Caballero moved quickly to restore financial and economic stability to the nation. He reduced the public debt, promoted land sales, and gained support in Buenos Aires and Rio de Janeiro. Caught in the confrontation between Argentina and Brazil, Paraguay remained independent because its neighbors were unwilling to pay the high cost of absorption. But Caballero was not intimidated by the troubled situation of the country, and he prepared very carefully for the elections of 1882.

Caballero became the constitutional, elected president on September 25, 1882. At his inauguration two months later, he said that efforts at reconstruction would begin immediately. His administration achieved several agreements in foreign affairs, establishing commercial ties with Uruguay and Argentina. It declared neutrality in the conflict between Brazil and Argentina over the disputed territory of Misiones. On the domestic front, he pursued an aggressive policy to attract immigrants, created several educational institutions, and promoted peace and stability. By the time Caballero was ready to deliver the presidency to Patricio Escobar in 1886, his mark on the nation was already indelible.

Colorado supporters have certainly played up the role of Caballero, trying to promote an image that remains a centerpiece of politics in contemporary Paraguay. But his contributions to the restoration of the country were not all so successful. The state of the economy was troublesome but, for more than a century, the mythicizing of Caballero has tended to reinforce the personalism so evident in the Paraguayan political culture.[26]

During the first Colorado republic, seven other leaders of the party exercised power. The administration of Patricio Escobar continued most of Caballero's policies. In 1887 the party structure was formalized, with the *caballeristas,* or Colorados, founding the Asociación Nacional Republicana and the opposition being organized as the Partido Liberal. The economy continued to stagnate, however, and the intrusion of the two powerful neighbors increased tensions within Paraguay.[27]

When Juan G. González assumed the presidency in 1890 he appointed key figures from different political groups to his cabinet, but his efforts at dealing with factions created further problems. Liberals revolted during 1891 and 1892, arguing that the Colorado administration was oppressive and warning that they were willing to take up arms against it. In the midst of the turmoil created by the Liberals, the country prepared for the presidential election of 1894.

The intrusion of Brazil into the domestic affairs of Paraguay altered the electoral process. Brazil pressed to help elect a president supportive of its cause, which was easy, given the number of factions competing for power. The Colorados had three subgroups: one led by Caballero; one led by Juan G. González; and one led by Juan Egusquiza. The Brazilians organized and paid for a coup, for they feared González planned to help Decoud to the presidency, a candidate whom the Argentines would probably have supported. In a bloodless coup, González was forced to resign, and Brazil supported the election of General Juan Egusquiza, a man who was thought to be no threat to its interests.

Egusquiza was a conciliatory president weary of the efforts of the Colorado party to design a new course for Paraguayan politics. He sought to introduce a new generation of leaders, and let some Liberals gain leverage in the internal affairs of the nation. With some improvements in the economy, Egusquiza kept the opposition in check, and he reached the end of his term in 1898.

In the 1898 election, Paraguay finally found a civilian leader who was competent and prepared. Emilio Aceval had received a formal education, had traveled extensively throughout Europe and the United States, and had won respect in economic and business circles in Asunción. He was a moderate Colorado, following *egusquicismo* more than *caballerismo* or *gonzalismo*. He fought the ills that afflicted the nation, and produced remarkable changes in education and administration, but the economy continued to show signs of strain. A coup by the military in 1902 defied the Constitution, sent him to prison, and placed Héctor Carvallo in the presidency.

The temporary presidency of Carvallo was followed by the most incompetent of all Colorado presidencies of the First Colorado Era. Juan Antonio Escurra had little preparation for the job and was unable to understand the risks and the problems of Paraguayan politics. Supported by the Brazilians, he achieved some mild economic improvements amidst a major recession. But in and out of Paraguay the opposition was organizing to depose the Colorado leadership. With strong support from Liberals residing in Buenos Aires and with the sanction of the Argentine government, General Benigno Ferreira launched the Liberal Revolution of 1904. Although the Escurra administration attempted to quell the revolution, the Colorado old guard had already lost its grip. After minor confrontations, the Liberals engineered Escurra's resignation. Juan B. Gaona was elected to the presidency in 1904, and he ushered in the beginning of the Liberal years.

The Colorado-backed military coup of 1902 had signaled a change in the direction of Paraguayan politics. The most remarkable phenomenon was the lack of respect shown by Colorado politicians for the Constitution. Its denominated freedoms were merely rhetorical expressions to the Colorados, and the Liberals took full advantage of this irreversible mistake. Paraguay also slipped back into the orbit of the Argentine government, probably because of the large economic enterprises of Argentine origin that had become so crucial to the Paraguayan economy. The Brazilians, concerned with the possible annexation of Paraguay by Argentina, had intervened in domestic affairs to no avail. With the Colorados in disarray, the Liberals embarked upon a leadership role that carried through the first half of the twentieth century.

The Liberal Years, 1904–1947

The early twentieth century marked a change of course in Paraguayan politics. The Liberal party, armed with the Constitution and a desire to oust the Colorados from their position of dominance, promised to guide the nation toward prosperity, stability, and peace. But, just as it was evident that the Colorados had little regard for the Constitution, it was also evident that the Liberals were not effective at defending the liberties that it proclaimed. The long-term result was further instability and civil war.

The principal reason for the inability to master domestic politics rests within the realm of party activity. The Colorados wrestled with a highly factional constituency and the Liberals were divided along ideological lines. Even if each party managed to subdue its opponents, it would have been unable to subdue intraparty confrontation. The instability of the Liberal period manifested itself in a succession of presidents. After the 1904 revolution, no president was constitutionally elected until 1912. In that same time period, nine presidents were seated for less than half the normal presidential term. Between 1870 and 1938 thirty-four presidents averaged a tenure of two years apiece.

The unstable political environment was further complicated by the need to expand the economy. From 1912 to 1915 the government of Paraguay took out more loans. The agricultural sector was picking up in importance, and Paraguay benefited from agricultural exports during the first two decades of the century, partially because of the war in Europe. The balance of trade, however, showed a large surplus only from 1921 to 1923. After several foreign loans went unpaid, the government was hard pressed to restore its financial reputation around the world.

Among the many confrontations of this period, the civil war of 1922–1923 brought internal struggles to a head. A singular figure resulted from the civil war, one who would become prominent: Eligio Ayala. He assumed the presidency provisionally to placate the rebel military forces but resigned in 1924 to become a candidate for a constitutional term. His presidential tenure, from 1924 to 1928, was the only one since 1870 until the Stroessner era to undergo no organized challenge.

Ayala made fiscal responsibility the cornerstone of his administration. He was prone to methodical planning, and his government managed to bring about a lasting economic change. He promoted domestic stability and maintained fiscal parity with the Argentine peso, which increased confidence in Paraguay. Trade flourished, and the balance of trade started to show steady surpluses. Argentina served as the major trading partner, providing 33 percent of Paraguay's total imports and receiving 77 percent of Paraguay's exports.

The visionary administration of Ayala also predicted the necessity to prepare for war. Regional clashes with Bolivian forces had taken place and the prospective economic importance of the Chaco suggested an urgent need to arm. Ayala decided against modernization of the capital city in order to concentrate all the nation's economic capability on preparing for a possible war. Asunción remained without running water, sewage systems, and other modern amenities present in other Latin American capitals. But the cautious nature of the leader prevailed, and his intuition paid off when hostilities broke out.[28]

With the Wall Street crisis of 1929, economic troubles placed additional pressures on preparations for war. The administration of José Guggiari carried military expenditures to very high levels, taking advantage of the predepression state of the economy. It was hard to maintain the past levels of international trade because demand for Paraguayan products was slipping considerably. Still, the mobilization of 1928 had signaled the decision of Paraguay to wage war against Bolivia. Neither country was ready, however, and hostilities waited until 1932, when Lieutenant Colonel José Félix Estigarribia headed the military units in the Chaco. Paraguay was once again at war with a neighbor.

The Chaco War and the Febrerista Revolution

The Chaco War found Paraguay much better equipped for war. Paraguay easily beat back the attack from the West. The Bolivian army was composed to a large extent of Indians who had left the mountain region to fight, and they were no match for the determined Paraguayan peasants. The war ended in 1935 and Paraguay recovered all the land to the west, defeating the Bolivian army.

The results of the Chaco War were positive for Paraguay, especially because of the participation of such a large portion of the population. It was a popular war, and favorable sentiments about the role of government grew. In contrast, officers of the army believed that they had not been adequately prepared and that the nation had spent too much energy on the petty controversies over political power that accompanied the war. A generalized discontent began to grow among the ranks. The high-level participants in the war were given rewards, and Marshal Estigarribia received a generous life pension. With its sometime contempt for the contributions of the population and its favoring of Liberal officers who had not been very active at the front, the Liberal government of Eusebio Ayala sealed its fate.

The ideas of the army revolutionaries took physical shape in February of 1936. Led by Colonel Rafael Franco, the Febreristas spoke vehemently against the record of the Liberals who had ruled Paraguay since 1904.

They brought back images of the Franciata and the Lópezes, advocating a government with fascist orientations. A heterogeneous coalition, the Febreristas included a nationalist faction led by Juan Stefanich; the Colorados represented by Bernardino Caballero; a group with socialist ideas led by Anselmo Jover Peralta; and military men who had fought in the Chaco. Within one year, the Febreristas outlawed the Constitution, suspended political parties, and put all interest groups under the Interior Ministry. These moves were geared toward creating a one-party state, with support from students, labor, workers, and war veterans.[29]

A year later, the Febreristas were in total disarray. Taking advantage of the situation, the Liberals named a presidential candidate and pushed for elections in 1939. Marshal Estigarribia ran for office without opposition in August 1939, and a year later he forced the Liberal Congress to dissolve. He organized his government along highly authoritarian lines, wrote a new constitution, and formed the Council of State, whose major political figures advised him directly. The only group without representation was organized labor.

Estigarribia died soon after in an airplane crash, and the forces of the revolution mobilized again to support their choice for provisional president: General Higinio Morínigo. The Liberals backed down and decided to negotiate the tenure of Morínigo once he was in power, but they were surprised by events. Morínigo became the new authoritarian man of Paraguay, following in the tradition of Francia and the Lópezes.

Authoritarianism III: Morínigo, 1940–1948

General Morínigo set out to become a nonpartisan dictator with firm support from the armed forces. Although apparently not a skillful politician, he soon showed great ability in outdoing his opponents. He masterfully courted the masses with his fluent Guaraní, proudly proclaiming that he was neither a Colorado nor a Liberal. Given the favorable economic climate during World War II, Morínigo was also popular because of the general improvement in the standard of living.[30]

Still and all, Morínigo was a typical dictator. He provided two alternatives for his opposition: exile or imprisonment. His profascist tendencies were well known. At the outbreak of World War II his fervent nationalism was accepted, but once the Axis was defeated, it became increasingly difficult for regimes of this type to remain popular. Morínigo understood the situation, and he managed to orchestrate a return to more moderate positions.[31] He eliminated the right-wing generals first, and then worked for a coalition government with the Liberals, Colorados, and Febreristas. The parties all showed signs of internal conflict, but the Colorados were preparing most carefully to succeed Morínigo. The *guionistas*, led by Juan Natalicio González, had the semisanction of the president, and they were therefore able to harass the opposition at their pleasure.

Morínigo had other plans. In January 1947 he dissolved the coalition government, abandoned all efforts at reopening the country to democracy, and set up a new government with backing from Colorados, military officers, and the guionistas. But expectations had already mounted, and in March the Febreristas attacked the police station in Asunción. A civil war broke out, and Morínigo had to call on the peasant supporters of the Colorado party for defense. He also received help from General Juan Perón of Argentina. After a few months of fierce fighting, the rebel forces led by Colonel Franco surrendered. Although Morínigo was close to being deposed several times, his tenure was secured by the guionistas and the support of the Argentine government. Authoritarianism was set to dominate Paraguayan politics again.[32]

Prelude to Stroessner:
The Return of Authoritarianism

The guionistas emerged in undisputed control of Paraguayan politics.[33] The Colorados imposed a reign of terror around Asunción, and groups of guionistas searched for dissidents in house-by-house checks. Many Paraguayans fled to Argentina in fear of their lives. Moreover, the civil war created even deeper divisions within the Colorado party, as González was elected president, in highly unorthodox circumstances in February 1948, a post he would take in August.[34] Some dissident guionistas rallied around Felipe Molas López, and fearing a coup that would continue Morínigo's tenure, they deposed Morínigo on June 3, 1948, naming Juan Manuel Frutos provisional president. When González was inaugurated in August, he attempted to prevent followers of Molas López from taking positions in the cabinet. The military vetoed his choices, and he found himself surrounded by a strong opposition. Not having enough power to appoint military officers, he also lost some control over the military. González was at the mercy of Molas López and his people.[35]

Revolt broke out on October 26, 1948, when González attempted to replace the police chief of Asunción. At the time one of the infantry divisions, led by General Alfredo Stroessner, marched into Asunción. By contacting the few forces loyal to him, González managed to abort the coup. Many conspirators were exiled, among them Stroessner, who found asylum in the Brazilian embassy.

Continued fighting within the Colorado party brought General Raimundo Rolón to the presidency in 1949 before Molas López could take his turn. But the other Colorado faction, the *democráticos*, were already gaining popular support and Osvaldo Chaves and Eulogio Estigarribia encouraged public discontent and called for elections in April 1949. Because military officers wished to have Rolón elected again, the democráticos started to organize the coup that would eventually lead them to power. Stroessner was a key figure again. In February of 1949, during funeral services for Monsignor Juan Bogarín, the rebel forces marched into Asunción and staged their coup.[36]

Molas López had achieved his goals, but in reality he had lost power to the democráticos, who controlled key cabinet posts as well as the police station. Not satisfied with the new arrangement, Molas López organized a new coup to rid himself of the democráticos. He enlisted prominent democráticos, such as Eulogio Estigarribia, who was at odds with Federico Chávez over the presidency of the party. But, when the organizers went to Stroessner for support, he made the plot public and all the implicated civilians were arrested. The Colorado party demanded the resignation of Molas López and his supporters, and Federico Chávez was sworn in as provisional president.

Chávez had no choice but to reimpose the state of siege because both González and Molas López, from exile in Argentina, were actively planning to overthrow him. Concurrently, he called for elections in July 1950. He prevented the Liberals from running, and he managed to be elected for the remainder of the presidential term. With a deteriorating economic situation, Chávez was elected for a second term in 1952. Economic problems caused unrest within the military, especially when, on the advice of his police chief, Chávez increased the size of the police battalion to be able to counterattack plots by the military. With discontent prevalent in military ranks, a plot to overthrow him was set in motion by General Stroessner, Epifanio Méndez Fleitas, and Tomás Romero Pereira, the former president of the Colorados who was occupying the post of interior minister.[37]

The overthrow of Chávez was to occur when Argentine President Juan Perón arrived on a state visit on May 8, 1954. But suddenly the date was moved up because of an unexpected event. President Chávez had learned about the plot and ordered Major Virgilio Candia arrested while the chief of the army, Colonel Néstor Ferreira, was on an inspection tour. Stroessner, who had assumed Ferreira's duties while Ferreira was away, declared the decision of Chávez an insult to military honor and entered Asunción with cavalry forces. On May 5, Tomás Romero Pereira became provisional president.

The new strongman was actually Stroessner. His credentials were impressive, and he had masterfully prepared his own opportunity. On June 14, 1954, the Colorado party chose him as its candidate in the presidential election of July 11, which he won handily, Paraguayan style.

At his inauguration on August 15, not even Méndez Fleitas, his closest collaborator, was able to envision the impact that the new leader would have in the life of the nation.

Paraguayan politics had returned to the old authoritarian tradition. Stroessner managed to survive an environment prone to coups and countercoups, failed loyalties and betrayed friendships. His masterminded game was a mixture of ideological elements by which he exceeded the limitations of the party ideologies themselves; a strict policy of control within and outside government, by which he continually searched for any potential threat to his administration; and the co-optation of large segments of the army, by which he sanctioned illegal activities with very lucrative benefits. With this arrangement of ideology, control, and co-optation in place, it became pragmatically impossible to undermine his tenure. Serious economic problems, deep divisions within the Colorado party, and a general state of mobilization throughout society brought his regime to an end after thirty-five years of uninterrupted leadership.

Notes

1. The excessive nature of the *encomienda* in Paraguay caused the Indians to rebel against the authorities in 1660. Many Indians were supposed to provide services of various natures, such as opening paths through the forest, and they were also subject to mistreatment when they refused to work. See Rafael E. Velázquez, "Rebelión de los Indios de Arecayá en 1660," *Revista Paraguaya de Sociología* 2 (January-April 1965): 34.

2. See Harris G. Warren, *Paraguay: An Informal History* (Norman: University of Oklahoma Press, 1949), p. 135.

3. On the revolution of the comuneros, see Osvaldo Chaves, *La formación del pueblo Paraguayo* (Buenos Aires: Ediciones Amerindia, 1976), chap. 10; Carlos R. Centurión, *Historia de la Cultura Paraguaya*, vol. 1 (Asunción: Biblioteca "Ortíz Guerrero," 1961), chap. 8; and Rafael Eladio Velázquez, *Breve Historia de la Cultura en el Paraguay*, 10th ed. (Asunción: El Gráfico, 1985), chap. 7.

4. Francia's ascent is described in detail in John Hoyt Williams, *The Rise and Fall of the Paraguayan Republic, 1800–1870* (Austin: Institute of Latin American Studies, University of Texas, 1979). The confrontation between the military and Francia took place while Buenos Aires was pressuring Paraguay to join the *porteño* revolution. Francia negotiated skillfully and managed to convince the governing junta that Paraguay was heading for difficulties with its neighbors unless the military was kept at bay.

5. A description of Paraguayan society and its effect on the process of independence can be found in Rafael E. Velázquez, "La sociedad Paraguaya en la época de la independencia," *Revista Paraguaya de Sociología* 13 (January-April 1976): 157–69.

6. On the qualities of Francia, see Ezequiel González Alsina, *El Dr. Francia del pueblo y ensayos varios* (Asunción: Instituto Colorado de Cultura, 1978), p. 9.

7. A conspiracy had developed in 1820 to kill Francia and provide for Yegros to assume power. When Francia learned of the plot, he jailed the conspirators and pressed them to provide accounts of who was involved. Most were prominent members of aristocratic families, many having been active during the struggle for independence. See John Hoyt Williams, "The Conspiracy of 1820 and the Destruction of the Paraguayan Aristocracy," *Revista de Historia de América* 75–76 (January-December 1973): 141–55.

8. An account of the relationship between Francia and the church is found in John Hoyt Williams, "Dictatorship and the Church: Doctor Francia in Paraguay," *Journal of Church and State* 15 (Autumn 1973): 419–36.

9. The impact of the policy decisions made by Francia concerning the military are described in John Hoyt Williams, "From the Barrel of a Gun: Some Notes on Dr. Francia and Paraguayan Militarism," *Proceedings of the American Philosophical Society* 119 (February 1975): 73–86.

10. The character of the diplomacy practiced by Francia is analyzed in John Hoyt Williams, "Paraguayan Isolation under Dr. Francia–A Reevaluation," *Hispanic American Historical Review* 52 (February 1972): 102–22.

11. The kind of self-reliant attitude postulated by the Francia administration has been analyzed as a typical example of early efforts at articulating what has now become a widespread development policy. See Christian Lalive D'Epinay and Louis Necker, "Paraguay (1811–1870): A Utopia of Self-Oriented Change," in *Self Reliance: A Strategy for Development,* ed. Johan Galtung, Peter O'Brien, and Roy Preiswerk (London: Bogle-L'Ouverture Publications, 1980), pp. 249–68. On the role the *estancias* played during the Francia administration, see John Hoyt Williams, "Paraguay's Nineteenth Century Estancias de la República," *Agricultural History* 47 (July 1973): 206–15.

12. A personal account of the way that López ran his government and his effect on Paraguayan life appears in Idelfonso A. Bermejo, *Vida Paraguaya en tiempos del viejo López* (Buenos Aires: EUDEBA, 1973). Bermejo, a Spaniard who had returned to Paraguay after living in France, describes the atmosphere in and around Asunción with astonishing clarity.

13. On the ideology of Carlos Antonio López, see Efraím Cardozo, *Apuntes de historia cultural del Paraguay* (Asunción: Biblioteca de Estudios Paraguayos, 1985), p. 263.

14. On the gradual opening to international trade during the López administration, see Juan Carlos Herken Krauer, "Proceso económico en el Paraguay de Carlos Antonio López: La visión del Consul. Británico Henderson (1851–1860)," *Revista Paraguaya de Sociología* 19 (May-August 1982): 83–116.

15. Eliza Alicia Lynch became a prominent figure in Paraguayan politics. She was Francisco Solano's mistress as well as the centerpiece of Paraguayan social life during his presidency. For a discussion of Lynch's influence in Paraguayan social circles, see Josefina Plá, "Elisa Alicia Lynch," *Estudios Paraguayos* 6 (December 1978): 28–32. Also, Héctor P. Blomberg, *La Dama del Paraguay*

(Buenos Aires: Editora Interamericana, 1942); Henry Lyon Young, *Eliza Lynch, Regent of Paraguay* (London: Anthony Blond, 1966); Alyn Brodsky, *Madame Lynch and Friend* (New York: Harper & Row, 1975); and William E. Barrett, *Woman on Horseback* (New York: Frederick A. Stokes, 1938).

16. An indication of the climate growing in Asunción is the decision of the English minister to Paraguay, Mr. Thornton, to leave after advising all of his countrymen to do the same. See Charles A. Washburn, *The History of Paraguay,* vol. 1 (Boston: Lee & Shepard, 1871), p. 544.

17. A discussion of the process that led eventually to the confrontation is included in Williams, *The Rise and Fall of the Paraguayan Republic,* pp. 195ff.

18. The conflicts in the Plata region during the nineteenth century are explained in León Pomer, *Conflictos en la cuenca del Plata en el siglo XIX* (Buenos Aires: Riesa Editores, 1984). Pomer argues that the internal needs of the Mitre administration affected the Triple Alliance War.

19. An account of the confrontation can be found in Carlos Pereyra, *Solano López y su drama* (Buenos Aires: Ediciones de la Patria Grande, 1962). Also Gilbert Phelps, *Tragedy of Paraguay* (New York: St. Martin's Press, 1975).

20. See Williams, *The Rise and Fall of the Paraguayan Republic,* p. 223.

21. A discussion by several writers on the implications of the Triple Alliance War may be found in León Pomer, *Proceso a la guerra del Paraguay* (Buenos Aires: Ediciones Caldén, 1968).

22. On the politics of the postwar period, see Harris G. Warren, *Paraguay and the Triple Alliance: The Postwar Decade, 1869–1878* (Austin: University of Texas Press, 1978).

23. Ibid., p. 77.

24. José S. Decoud had been a shrewd member of the Club del Pueblo and a supporter of the *bareiristas,* and had been opposed to Brazilian intervention. He was one of the early philosophers of the Colorado party, and a political partner to General Bernardino Caballero. Cándido Bareiro, who had been secretary-general to President Rivarola, was a prominent Colorado politician who favored Argentina. He became president in 1878 after the short presidencies of Juan B. Gill (1874 to 1877) and Higinio Ugarte (1877 to 1878).

25. Warren indicates that the Bareiro administration was the transitional period between the postwar reality and the Colorado era. Remarkably enough, the most important result of Bareiro's death, Warren suggests, was "the swift coup that stole the presidency from Adolfo Saguier, for it was this act that restored military dictatorship to Paraguay." See Harris G. Warren, *Rebirth of the Paraguayan Republic: The First Colorado Era, 1878–1904* (Pittsburgh: University of Pittsburgh Press, 1985), p. 50.

26. An example is a speech given by the minister of foreign affairs on February 26, 1976, the anniversary date of the death of Caballero. See Asociación Nacional Republicana, *Homenaje de la Junta de Gobierno del Partido Colorado a la memoria del fundador Gral. de Div. Bernardino Caballero* (Asunción: Departamento de Prensa de la Junta de Gobierno de la ANR, 1976).

27. On the evolution of the major political parties in Paraguay, see José Gaspar Gómez Fleytas, "Ubicación histórica de los partidos tradicionales en el

Paraguay," *Revista Paraguaya de Sociología* 7 (September-December 1970): 144–64.

28. For a detailed account of the economic policies of the Ayala administration and Ayala's efforts to prepare the country for a possible war, see Alfredo M. Seiferheld, *Economía y petróleo durante la guerra del Chaco* (Asunción: El Lector, 1983), chap. 1.

29. The philosophy that guided the developments prompted by *Febrerismo* is explained in Juan Stefanich, *Paraguay nuevo* (Buenos Aires: Editorial Claridad, 1943).

30. On the Morínigo administration, see Michael Grow, *The Good Neighbor Policy and Authoritarianism in Paraguay* (Lawrence: Regents' Press of Kansas, 1981); and Carlos Pastore, *El Paraguay y la tiranía de Morínigo* (Asunción: El Gráfico, 1988).

31. See Grow, *The Good Neighbor Policy,* p. 63.

32. On the revolution of 1947, see Enrique Volta Gaona, *La Revolución del 47* (Asunción: By the author, 1982).

33. The Guión Rojo was part of the Colorado party's more authoritarian faction. It had developed through the leadership of Juan Natalicio González, and included a number of ready-for-action activists used in harassing members of the opposition.

34. The election of February 1948 was carried out in a tense atmosphere. Paraguayan voters were obliged to vote, and when they arrived at the polls they were handed slips of paper on which González's name appeared; they could not even use blank ballots. See Paul Lewis, *Paraguay under Stroessner,* (Chapel Hill: University of North Carolina Press, 1980), p. 42.

35. Molas López was a member of the left wing of the Colorado party and a man with a history of participation in politics. He had been a member of the Franco administration, had been mayor of Asunción, and had been strongly influenced by Peronism during his long exile in Argentina. Typical of Paraguayan political leaders, Molas López was also in search of personal power, and he was a master at orchestrating conspiracies and double-crosses.

36. The funeral services of Monsignor Bogarín drew a large portion of Paraguay's upper class. Bogarín was the prototype of Paraguayan churchmen. He had served as archbishop of Asunción for nineteen years and commanded much respect. After the services at the National Cathedral, Molas López held a dinner in Bogarín's honor. While all the leaders of the government were there, General Stroessner rallied his men, and with the help of Colonel Díaz de Vivar, entered the city.

37. The plot that brought Stroessner to the presidency is explained in Lewis, *Paraguay under Stroessner,* chap. 4.

The Ideological Bases
of the Stroessner Era

4 The ideology of an authoritarian regime constitutes one of the most controversial issue areas regarding this type of political system. In his definition of authoritarianism, Juan Linz indicates that the difference between typical totalitarian regimes and authoritarian regimes is basically one of ideological orientation. Authoritarian regimes exhibit a kind of mentality as opposed to a more fully developed ideology.[1] The concept of mentality describes the emotional and nonrational elements present in the ideological foundations of authoritarian regimes. Nevertheless, Linz warns about the difficulty of more precisely defining these mentalities, and he uses examples taken from Egyptian, Spanish, and Brazilian regimes to show that the tendency has often been for analysts merely to talk of the philosophy or the psychology guiding these leaders.

Bolivar Lamounier, a former student of Linz's at Yale University, has criticized and extended this conceptualization.[2] Lamounier advocates a deeper analysis of the *content* of different thought processes, and he emphasizes the importance of the legitimation of authoritarian regimes.[3] The concept of legitimacy provides the connection between ideology and power because it involves, on the one hand, the orientation of citizens and groups, and on the other hand, the power relations that exist between groups.[4]

The thinking of Karl Mannheim is also useful here, both as it complements that of Linz and Lamounier and also as it may be extended to the cases of recent authoritarian regimes in Latin America. Mannheim contrasts ideology with utopia, an idea somewhat similar to that of mentality. Ideology for Mannheim is "a set of ideas which function in the promotion and defense of interests." Although the concept reflects Marx's view of false consciousness, Mannheim also distinguishes between proper ideologies and what he calls utopias. When the ideas defend interests that are crucial to the social order, they are ideologies, but when they merely define the expectations of underprivileged groups, they are then utopias.[5]

It is clear from these conceptualizations that we need carefully to analyze the ideational self-justifications of regimes that are not tightly totalitarian; to examine how they work to build legitimacy; and to investigate who benefits most from their elaboration and their acceptance. In the recent experience of military authoritarianism in Latin America, the self-justifications have been variants of *doctrinas* (doctrines), especially the so-called national security doctrine. Accepted by the military, the concept that internal political change was understood as a security threat managed to create considerable ideological content in the political processes of authoritarian regimes in Argentina, Brazil, Chile, Paraguay, and Uruguay.[6]

Investigating the guiding principles of the national security doctrine and the way those principles have prompted the creation of national security states can help us better understand the character of authoritarian regimes in Latin America and the roles that the *doctrina* has come to play in each political system. In Paraguay, the Stroessner administration accepted the national security doctrine as the foundation of new ideological principles that sustain the regime. The doctrine was redefined according to the cultural and political legacy of the past. By redefinition, the regime masterfully established the rules of the game and extended the domain of its authority.

Under the *doctrina* of the Stroessner system, each ideological position was actually a set of symbolic elements that mapped the relationship between the structure of power and the roles of citizens. The Constitution of the nation provided the clearest indication of the regime's ideology. Most of the *doctrina* comes out clearly in the Constitution, which defines the authoritarian principles that regulate the political order. Although one needs to investigate the *doctrina* from other sources as well, the Constitution represents, legally and also symbolically, the most important link between the regime and the people, the instrument that provides Paraguayan politics with its content and meaning.

The Constitutional Dimension

The constitutional tradition of Paraguay is rooted in its authoritarian past. The country exhibits strong tendencies to accept personal leadership as a largely autonomous, almost self-sufficient agent of political power. In this context, efforts of the various Paraguayan constitutional conventions have often been limited in scope and ineffective in the creation of new institutional structures. The conventions have ratified power relationships in the country rather than trying to alter them.

The first Constitution, or "proto-constitution" as John Hoyt Williams calls it, was written by José G. Rodríguez de Francia in 1813.[7] The document proclaimed the independence of Paraguay and declared Fulgencio Yegros and Francia to be the leaders of the new nation. They were supposed to alternate in power and also to divide access to military and economic resources. In essence, the document was little more than a reflection of the nationalistic mood prevailing at the time and an indication of Francia's ability to control personally the destiny of Paraguay.

When Congress met in 1844, Carlos Antonio López used the opportunity to increase his political and personal stature. López had been worried about gaining recognition from neighboring states so as to further his quest for access to the Plata River system. The three hundred delegates proclaimed López as president and asked him to make another attempt at establishing a constitutional order. López had drafted a new constitutional document entitled The Law That Establishes the Political Administration of the Republic of Paraguay, hoping that it would provide a sense of legality for his tenure. Its basic purpose was to endow him with unlimited powers, although it recognized three branches of government. The Congress ratified the document as a new constitution and declared López president for ten years.

Although there was some effort at establishing at least an appearance of democratic practices under the López government, his "constitution" in fact represented the first effort at centralizing power in the hands of a single individual. Paraguayans not only had become convinced of the indispensableness of Francia and López but also tolerated their leadership principles and the principles' conversion to a written document that was supposed to guide political practices. As long as the president guaranteed the maintenance of order, his ability to do as he saw fit was to be undisputed. Ever since this era, centralized personalism has produced a unique brand of political organization in the country.

Thus, the creation of political institutions has provided a seal of approval for the highly authoritarian structures of Paraguayan politics. Nothing in the decisions made by the Congresses of 1813 and 1844 allowed an opportunity to establish constitutional principles that would have encouraged later democratic developments. The isolationist and controlled politics of Francia had been so successful that the representatives were almost obliged to endorse the actual pattern of organization. The first effort at establishing a truly political document took place in 1870, after the Triple Alliance War, when liberal thought changed the course of Paraguayan politics.[8]

The Constitution of 1870

The nature of the Paraguayan Constitution written in 1870 clearly reflects the devastating defeat suffered by the Paraguayan forces in the

Triple Alliance War. Under the allied occupation, Argentina and Brazil competed for preeminence in the domestic political processes of Paraguay. The liberal thinking prevailing in these neighboring countries at the time, especially in Argentina with the advent of the generation of 1880, naturally infused Paraguayan politics with new ideas and a new direction.[9]

The Constitution was drafted following the concepts expressed in the Argentine document written in 1853, the French Constitution of 1789, and the United States Constitution of 1787. Most prominently, the ideas embodied in the Constitution meant a radical departure from the authoritarian politics of the past. In a sense, the framers defeated themselves by creating political guidelines that could not be realized, given the tendency of the nation to accept authoritarian and personalistic forms of leadership.

The constitutional convention was controlled by the Liberals, who advocated a charter that would encourage free elections and participation through open discussion of political issues. The Constitution's introduction is very similar to the Argentine Constitution's preamble, even though in this document in particular it was ironic to speak of fulfilling "the will of the people." The objectives of justice, tranquillity, welfare, and common defense became part of the text. Catholicism was made the official religion, and immigration was to be a main concern of the new government. A state of siege could be declared, but the president enjoyed no official dictatorial powers. Nominally, support for dictatorships was to be penalized by law. The Constitution outlawed slavery, provided for a bicameral legislature, and gave the president customary powers. In essence, it seemed to provide all the necessary elements for good government. Although it left some areas not entirely defined, such as labor, social issues, and the state's relationship with the church, the Constitution as drafted appeared to provide the basis for legitimate and democratic processes.[10]

Paraguayans soon recognized that creation of a constitutional framework could not in and of itself produce a democratic political system. Lacking a distinctive party structure, and in the midst of total economic devastation, the actors in the Paraguayan drama could not envision the limitations that the expectations of their own people placed upon the results of the convention. The major drawback of the effort of 1870 was that the social and political realities had no relationship to the charter that the convention drafted. During the next two decades, the Colorado party dominated the political life of Paraguay precisely by ignoring many elements of the new Constitution. And the Liberals themselves found, once in power in 1904, that the Constitution of 1870 was very unrealistic, given the expectations, the sophistication, and the needs of the Paraguayan people.

Even if the Constitution was not to serve Paraguayan politics *strictu sensu*, it remained in force for over forty years. It certainly was not in tune with the internal nature of Paraguayan society, which had been born during the oligarchical rule of colonial times and then nurtured the dictatorial processes of the nineteenth century. To be congruent with political realities, constitutional norms required a return to authoritarian politics, the kind of political organization that Paraguayans had managed to make their own. After confrontations and internal drifting for decades, a new document was drafted by the Constitutional Convention of 1940.[11]

The Constitution of 1940

The Constitution of 1870 having proved inoperable, General José F. Estigarribia, who was elected president on August 15, 1939, called an assembly to rewrite it or to draw up an entirely new constitution. Estigarribia had achieved high recognition because he had led the Paraguayan Army to victory during the Chaco War, and his actions as leader of a Liberal government that had been forced to dissolve Congress because of internal divisions within the party. He unilaterally granted himself absolute powers, and he showed strong commitment to social reform.

Estigarribia's call for a constitutional convention revealed his determination to introduce institutional changes. The Constitution of 1940 provided the executive with all-encompassing power because Estigarribia wanted to establish his absolute mandate on constitutional grounds. The government was given the right to intervene in the economy, to control the press, and to regulate activities in which citizens could engage. The Constitution curtailed the powers of Congress, which was now unicameral, and established the presidential term at five years, with reelection limited to one additional term.

Three provisions of the new Constitution had particular impact. First, it gave virtually dictatorial powers to the executive; the president could dissolve Congress, dictate laws, and command the armed forces. Second, the armed forces were to be called on to guarantee order and respect for the Constitution, thus entrenching the political power of the military. And third, after Mussolini's example, the Constitution created a corporatist body that acted as the only institution representing interest groups. The Council of State would be composed of nine ministers and representatives from other sectors of society.[12]

Estigarribia subsequently commented on the need for the new Constitution, indicating that the limitations of the 1870 Constitution were actually "its slowness in the solution of problems, its lack of preparation to judge critical situations and efficiency to defend all the civilization of the country."[13] He encouraged the belief that the new Constitution was more nationalistic than the previous one, and that the extension of executive power was meant to reinforce the democratic character of the nation. The elimination of the Senate would perfect the unitary concept of power, and the Council of State as a consultant body to the president would be a communication channel between the Chamber of Representatives and the executive.

Although Estigarribia as well as the members of Congress who drafted the Constitution were convinced of its capacity to improve democratic aspects of governance, in effect the document provided the legal background for a return to the centralization of power that the nation had known during the nineteenth century. The framers also meant to provide in it an aura of legalism in which to preserve a political elite, one in charge of defending the values of civilization and of supporting a strong presidential system. Significant at this stage was the emphasis on nationalism, a trait then assumed to be especially useful for Paraguay. With concentration of power in a single individual, internal control exercised over Congress and the judiciary, and the expanded role provided to the armed forces, Paraguay had again embraced its authoritarian tradition. In fact, it had created more legally rooted dimensions for its authoritarianism, turning them into the distinctive landmark of its political organization.

It is not surprising, then, that the Constitution of 1940 launched a period of two strong dictatorships. After Estigarribia's sudden death in 1940, General Higinio Morínigo used his old network in the Liberal party to propel himself into power and to create a government strongly influenced by the military. Saying that he had no party allegiance, Morínigo set up his regime by playing masterfully on the loyalties of the Febreristas, the Liberales, and the Colorados. Colonel Alfredo Stroessner, head of the 1st Cavalry Division, was involved in the organization of the coup that ousted Morínigo from power. In 1954, he began his reign as Paraguay's longest-lasting dictator in a bloodless military takeover. Enjoying all the powers provided by the Constitution of 1940, his government called for a new constitutional assembly in 1967, mainly to introduce a constitutional amendment that would allow him to be reelected for more than the then-allowed two presidential terms.

The Constitution of 1967

Although the Constitution of 1940 provided enough support for an authoritarian government, the Stroessner administration moved to overturn its limited reelection articles by calling the special constitutional convention of 1967. The changes introduced were of a formal nature; most of the character of the old document was left intact, for it already served well the needs of a dictatorial regime. Nevertheless, a few changes strengthened the existing pattern of coercion, enhancing the capacity for domination that characterized the Stroessner regime.

The constitutional convention brought back the bicameral legislature by creating the Senate. The new body performed the same function as the House of Representatives, in that geographical representation in a country the size of Paraguay is almost a meaningless concept. Moreover, the government had in mind the creation of several additional, high-ranking posts to be used as instruments of internal control. The Senate thus became an institution of recruitment, one in which the official party could prepare its protégés, and show them how to maneuver politically.

Another constitutional convention meeting in 1977 allowed the president to be reelected regardless of the number of terms he had been in office.[14] As a result of making the law conform to actual practice, most Paraguayan officials recognized that the entire operation of the government has a solid foundation in the Constitution. Showing deep respect for institutional tradition, and equating constitutionalism with democracy, many members of the Stroessner government convinced themselves that the system was in fact democratic, for it rested on these pseudolegitimizing conditions provided by the constitutional framework.

Nonetheless, the constitutional tradition of Paraguay gave a legal spirit to an otherwise fraudulent political system. The machinery of politics made claims of representation, but its underlying ideological uniformity required explanation. However difficult it may be to define more precisely the ideology that the administration followed, the participants in Paraguayan politics under Stroessner nevertheless had to accept the strong ideological loyalties that he had professed in order to walk the thin line between participation and ostracism in his political system.

Authoritarian Ideology and Power Structure

The authoritarian thinking and institutions that are part of the constitutional tradition of Paraguay provided the foundations for an authoritarian power structure during the Stroessner regime. Constitutional principles gave wide latitude, under which the regime operated without major limitations. Although the government was formally organized along the lines of a representative and federal system, the administration managed to merge the roles and the jurisdictions of the executive, legislative, and judicial powers in a way that required careful explanation. The three branches did function in the political system; they simply did not operate separately and independently. Although they furnished a facade of organizational purity, their relationship was the underpinning of authoritarianism under Stroessner, the operational structure under which it became consolidated.

An important dimension of this problem was the distance among branches as opposed to the relationship among them. Distance among them means the relative autonomy that each enjoyed in the pursuit of its specific role. Although the formal specificity of each branch's independent role was beyond question, actual autonomy to elaborate policies was sharply limited, providing the informal structures of Paraguayan authoritarianism in the Stroessner era. In reality, the dividing line between power on paper and the actual exercise of authority lay in the autonomy enjoyed by each of the three branches of government.[15]

The relationship among the executive, legislative, and judicial branches took a back seat to the ties among the executive and two other powerful institutions: the dominant party and the military. These ties created a pattern of politics far more complex than the simplistic stereotypes of Paraguayan authoritarianism that abound outside the country. For example, the military was excluded from carrying out repressive activities. Most of the daily operations concerning political intelligence were the responsibility of the Asunción police. The military remained in the background, guaranteeing peace and order. By allocating such a visible and critical role to the police, Stroessner managed to protect the military from controversy.

A prominent political scholar in Paraguay argues that the relationship among the three institutions created an "immanent triangle" supported by the ideology of the regime, one that he labeled a "the Second Reconstruction." He stated that

> whether we accept it or not, the Second Reconstruction is an ideology because it fits perfectly in what every ideological process demands: to become a coherent structure of images, signs and symbols, values and ideas, that relate the theory with the praxis, with the evident purpose—like every other ideology—of shaping men and societies.[16]

A leader of the opposition Christian Democratic party suggested that this concept of the power triangle should also involve the judiciary and the legislature because they are extensions of the executive. He asserted that in Stroessner's Paraguay there was no notion of a separate role for the legislature and no tradition of independent courts. In my conversations with him, he mentioned that several prominent judges in Asunción called the head of the investigative section of the Asunción police to consult with him about decisions concerning their cases.[17]

The relationship among the three branches of government centered on the figure of the president, who was also the commander in chief of the armed forces and leader of the Colorado party. Because of the constitutional authority accorded the executive, the president could dissolve the legislature at any time that he deemed necessary. The judiciary could not be defined as an independent branch because its members were chosen by the executive in agreement with the Senate. The Constitution provides no mechanism by which the the executive could be sanctioned or judged.

The power structure embodied in the authoritarian ideology of the Paraguayan Constitution is also highlighted by the personal interpretation of President Stroessner. Stroessner understood early in the life of the regime that to consolidate his power, he needed to challenge the existence of potential rivals for leadership. In eliminating contenders who could unseat him, he also narrowed the range of ideological choices open to political factions. Stroessner not only decided to be the system but also to define the system in his own terms and according to his personal style. In two instances particularly, personal clashes with men who had been closely associated with him showed his ability to anticipate political trouble. The men had quite different orientations, but both were leaders who could have attempted to end the Stroessner reign had they remained unchecked. To appreciate how Stroessner dealt with Edgar Ynsfrán and Epifanio Méndez Fleitas, however, one first needs to appreciate more specifically the nature of the doctrine that he created.

Ideological Confrontations

If anything changed in Paraguay after Stroessner came to power, it was the extent to which the ideological orientation of the major political factions influenced politics. Transformations of the party system follow the changing pattern of the political ideas that the factions represent. However, although important factions emerged in each party after the Chaco War, the most prominent shift portrayed by Paraguayan politics has been to allow the creation of *stronismo* as a new political doctrine.[18]

Defining the roots and orientations of the *stronista* doctrine is prerequisite to understanding contemporary Paraguayan politics. Superficially, it seemed that the Colorado party and the president formed a strong political unit. The relationship between the party and the executive were not at all symmetrical, however, and the presidential power surpassed and penetrated the power and the structure of the party. In time, the doctrine of stronismo came to be far more than loyal identification with the Colorado party.[19]

Although the stronista doctrine achieved preeminence over traditional Colorado ideas, its origin undoubtedly comes from the party itself. The Colorado party emerged after the Triple Alliance War partly to channel liberal principles of the time. Initially, its major opponents, organized in the Liberal party, had few ideological differences with the Colorados. As the twentieth century wore on, however, the Colorados increasingly became interpreters of a highly nationalistic position, departing from their liberal orientation. After the Civil War of 1947, the Colorados emerged with strong internal differences, thus setting in motion a process of partisan fragmentation. Part of the reason for Stroessner's success in creating his own political doctrine rested in the confrontations that plagued the Colorados after 1947.[20]

The Civil War led to deep divisions within the leadership of the Colorado party. Earlier, Juan Mallorquín had helped maintain the unity of the party, but Mallorquín died during the war. In the end, Federico Chávez headed the democratic group, and its members proved to be interested in promoting democracy by accepting the need for compromise. They supported the coalition government created by President Morínigo wherein the Colorados shared cabinet posts with the Febreristas and two military men. The other wing of the party, the *guionistas*, was led by Natalicio González, a self-taught strongman of Indian background. González saw the negotiating skills of Chávez as a sign of weakness, and he decided to work his way into the presidency by harassing groups of party members, with the semisanction of Morínigo. The fights that this group provoked in union meetings, universities, and party rallies gave notoriety to González and his "Guión Rojo."[21]

The guionistas gained ascendancy over the *democráticos* by resorting to violence and rioting. They managed to create such chaos in the party convention of November 1947 that González was made the party's candidate. The defeat of the democratic faction was so overwhelming that many of the democrats opted for exile in Argentina or Uruguay. Clearly, the Guión Rojo was sympathetic to the pro-Nazi stand of Morínigo. The expectation of the guionistas was to continue the political ideology expressed during the Francia and López years: a strong stand against foreign intervention, an authoritarian style, and a tendency to redistribute income in favor of the poor.[22]

After 1947 the political life of the nation came to be defined more and more by two concurrent elements: the distinctive ideological factions within the Colorado party and the quest for leadership of the Colorados. Important men led the factions, and most of them were obviously running for the presidency. Two of these leaders were Edgar L. Ynsfrán and Epifanio Méndez Fleitas. They both exhibited the trademark of Paraguayan politicians—an exaggerated tendency to personalize themselves as authentic leaders—and they both had a strong impact on the rank and file of the party. How much their ideas conformed to popular notions of what the Colorado party ought to have been is not easy to ascertain, but each clearly attracted a large popular constituency. It was only after Stroessner cast them out of the party that he had irrefutable control over the party machinery, and only then was he able to enroll it in the new version of the Colorado ideals, his own stronista ideology.[23]

It is important in this old duel for ideological supremacy to understand what Ynsfrán and Méndez Fleitas actually represented, for beyond the efforts of Stroessner to replace them as potential challengers he was concerned with eliminating ideologues who could defeat him in his reorganizing of national politics and the state apparatus. Although neither man occupied the presidential seat, their ideas were the sources for the challenges of the democráticos and the guionistas.

Méndez Fleitas was a protégé of Federico Chávez, and hence he had been associated with the democráticos from the beginning. A self-taught, strong, and energetic man, he was appointed to head the police of Asunción during the administration of Felipe Molas López, a dissident guionista who took office in February of 1949. As a police chief, Méndez Fleitas displayed a highly astute political sense. His ability to reckon with the different groups within Paraguayan society won wide respect, just as did his tendency toward a brand of populism often tinted by socialist ideas. For a while, Méndez Fleitas served well as chief of police, a position he retained after Federico Chávez became president in February 1953.

The role as chief of police won Méndez Fleitas such a remarkable reputation that President Chávez decided to increase the domain of his power by seating him on the board of the Institute of Agrarian Reform and on the Executive Committee of the Colorado party. His major accomplishments during the administration of Molas López had been to abort several coups organized by guionista leaders, including one by former President Rolón, Eulogio Estigarribia, and other exiles. The most prominent prize Méndez Fleitas received for his efforts was the presidency of the Central Bank.

The political wit and accomplishments of this man soon translated into much more power than he was able to enjoy for long. He courted military officers, among whom the most prominent were Major Mario Ortega, the new chief of police, and General Stroessner, the new commander in chief of the armed forces. Méndez Fleitas had strong support from cabinet members like Guillermo Enciso Velloso and Tomás Romero Pereira, and moreover he was a popular leader with working-class Paraguayans. Opposition to him materialized especially in the Sociedad Rural, because of his stand against raising the price of beef, which would, he thought, spur inflation and hurt the poor. He favored the masses through two wage hikes, which led members of the Sociedad Rural to ask Chávez to remove him from his post. On January 7, 1954, Chávez dismissed Méndez Fleitas, Enciso Velloso, Romero Pereira, and Major Ortega.

The political ideology of Méndez Fleitas was unique within the ranks of the party. Although he had been a Febrerista when young, he had also served the Colorado party for many years. He was somewhat charismatic, certainly energetic, and had enthusiastic followers among Paraguayan workers and in the lower strata of society. At the same time, his politics were much more progressive than the democráticos said them to be, and he was a great admirer of Peronism, always flirting with populist positions. Having seen that too much emphasis on populism had not served him well, Méndez Fleitas gave his support to General Stroessner. He was the author of the plot that brought Stroessner to the presidency, forcing Chávez out of office. Thinking that Stroessner would be a good interim president, Méndez Fleitas saw his hopes dashed when, in May 1956 he was ousted from the party, exiled from the country, and declared persona non grata by the new administration.[24]

The circumstances that forced Méndez Fleitas out of Paraguay are indicative of Stroessner's ability to maneuver his opponents from the scene. A crisis developed when General Juan D. Perón, ousted by the Argentine military in September 1955, took refuge on Paraguayan soil. Caught by the embarrassment of protecting him, by the pressure from Buenos Aires, and by Perón's liking for Méndez Fleitas and his supporters, Stroessner decided to intern Perón in the interior in order to please all the parties involved. He did so while Méndez Fleitas was out of the country on a government mission, and once Méndez Fleitas returned, a confrontation with Stroessner was unavoidable.[25]

Stroessner initiated efforts to reunite the party in October 1955, allowing several key figures to return from abroad. Among them were various guionistas, including one very young and violent leader, Edgar Ynsfrán. Méndez Fleitas established a connection with Ynsfrán and found him a job with the police as chief of the investigative division. In this way, Méndez Fleitas assured obtaining political information for himself. Even if both Méndez Fleitas and Ynsfrán had ultimate ambitions for the presidency, Ynsfrán still used his position in the police to help Stroessner discard Méndez Fleitas. In the ensuing crisis, Méndez Fleitas and his *epifanista* supporters were exiled, thus eliminating them from contention.[26]

The ousting of Méndez Fleitas resulted from his and Stroessner's different orientations. Méndez Fleitas was more a *caudillo* in the Latin American style, although skillful and well prepared. His command of guaraní made him a prominent figure with workers, students, and intellectuals, and his ability to manage the Central Bank won him influence in business circles and in international financial centers. But

Méndez Fleitas was a rather special breed of nationalist-populist, one who certainly also posed a strong challenge to Stroessner, who then was a leader without much popular appeal.[27]

Once Ynsfrán was promoted to chief of police, he became crucial for Stroessner. He had long collaborated with Natalicio González, so that he qualified as a fervent guionista. With wit and a violent temperament, he seemed well suited for the position in police headquarters, and by 1956 his power had increased considerably. Ynsfrán's desire to achieve a more prominent position prompted Stroessner to give him the Interior Ministry, an important political position from which Ynsfrán could control not only the police but grass-roots organizations as well.

Ideologically, Ynsfrán was the antithesis of Méndez Fleitas. A brilliant politician, Ynsfrán had supported the violent activities of the guionistas and was also a strong anticommunist. His views seemed perfect for the job of persecuting the opposition, and according to Méndez Fleitas, Ynsfrán's efforts at eliminating potential dissidents prompted him to create communist insurrection anywhere he saw fit. Not being politically able to stand for ideological principles other than Stroessner's, Ynsfrán's political career depended almost entirely on his own leadership skills.[28]

Given his orientations, Ynsfrán became key to the containment of potential challengers. Exiled groups were organizing excursions into Paraguayan territory, trying to undermine the power base of the Stroessner administration. But Ynsfrán, who before had helped Stroessner to get rid of Méndez Fleitas and the Colorado epifanistas, obtained considerable peasant support himself in the process of receiving information with which to control guerrilla warfare.[29]

Concerned with internal problems and external threats, Stroessner saw that a change of direction would be beneficial in the long run. He concluded that a period of liberalization would be conducive to better management of internal politics and would also promote a better image abroad. Stroessner allowed a wing of the Liberal party to return to the Paraguay, to organize a party convention and to run in the elections of 1963. The liberalization of the political scene was to be the death sentence for Ynsfrán, however, who had become a strong ideologue with popular ascendancy over sectors of the Colorados.[30]

As in the earlier case of Méndez Fleitas, the removal of Ynsfrán was again helped by a national event that called for little effort by Stroessner. A crisis occurred among the police in Asunción involving the police chief and several other Ynsfrán protégés. In bringing the corruption to light, Stroessner disposed of most of Ynsfrán's political supporters, and Ynsfrán was forced to resign in November 1966. He was dropped from the governing junta of the party and effectively gave up any future political role.

Although the confrontations between Stroessner and Méndez Fleitas and Ynsfrán can be understood on one level as mere competition for the presidential job, the two competitors also represented strong ideological positions within the party. The real intention of Stroessner was to eliminate all opposition rooted in different ideological orientations. Méndez Fleitas represented a populist, progressive ideology that the government could not tolerate. Ynsfrán, on the other hand, supported more repressive measures; he was a hard-liner who was likely to add more infighting than intellect to the ranks of the Colorados. Stroessner settled the matter by eliminating both. Without the democráticos, the epifanistas, the faction led by Méndez Fleitas, and the guionistas around, the only plausible scenario was for everyone to become stronistas. The president at last imposed his own new brand of politics upon the Colorado power base.

Just as Paraguayan history and the constitutional tradition provided the framework for a strong presidency, under Stroessner this tendency was matched with a strong bias toward the persona of the president himself. Loyalty to the ideas presented and pursued by the president mattered more than the ideological consistency of the major party or the military. The orientation of party politics shifted toward personal politics, in which a single individual once again defined the character of the political system. Stroessner became the president, the ideologue, and the architect of his own system, molding the authoritarian tradition to his own purposes and designs.

The Stronista Doctrine

The new stronista doctrine became the hallmark of the regime. Everyone in the administration, in the Colorado party, and in the military came to understand that one's support for the president was to be equated with allegiance to the system. Because political control rested solely in the hands of Stroessner, Paraguayan political processes became reorganized around the principles that he sanctioned as the cornerstone of his doctrine. Although his own intellectual contributions to the doctrine are not particularly important, his actions and his leadership style clearly focused on reinforcing the underlying principles through which his regime functioned. Building upon this example, the ideologues of the Stroessner entourage created a complex array of ideas that conveyed to the populace notions about value systems, belief systems, political organizations, and the desirable goals and means of politics.[31]

In dealing with these ideas, several themes help us to understand the nature of the stronista doctrine. Its crystallization was the program followed by the government in its effort to institutionalize political change. Among its key elements were, first, the tacit approval of practices that maintained the population in a constant state of fear. Although fear for one own's personal security was not prevalent throughout the entire population, the Paraguayan people became hesitant about their own thinking, their own values, and their freedom of thought and speech. Second, Paraguayans came to see government as an institution that works pragmatically in pursuit of measurable goals, and this orientation tended to minimize the level of political controversy within the nation. The Stroessner regime promoted an administrative style that obviated discussion of values, goals and orientations. Third, the regime emphasized the need to maintain peace and order. For Paraguayans who remembered the instability of previous administrations, the idea of a strong and stable government had much appeal.

At first, in the late 1950s, much of the stronista ideology seemed little more than a distinguishable brand of neofascism.[32] Some members of the guionista movement had an obvious liking for fascist ideologies, and some of them had personally witnessed the development of fascism in Europe. Stroessner seemed to favor the idea of dominating the domestic population, and the need for domination was fiercely defended during the first phase of his regime. The population was deemed unprepared for more participatory politics. Only a few members of the elite were supposed to command the affairs of state. The military and the influential rallied around the president, reassuring his "sense of mission." With the civilian politicians discredited, an elite of wealth, position, and ideological self-assurance held sway over the numerically large sectors of the lower and middle classes.

Evidence of neofascist tendencies during the Stroessner government showed up in the amount of protection provided to former members of the Nazi government in Germany. For a long time Paraguay was a haven for those who had escaped the war crimes trials. Joseph Mengele, the notorious Nazi doctor responsible for so many deaths, lived in Paraguay under a new identity. It is possible today to go into the hinterlands of Paraguay to meet former SS members now living as Paraguayan citizens. A *New York Times Magazine* article recounted considerable information about other fascists who had found refuge in Paraguay. Perhaps the most compelling evidence came from a witness to the provision of a Paraguayan passport for Mengele who had personally been given an honorary officer's commission by Stroessner to keep the secret.[33]

The neofascist orientation provided more than a rationale for domination. First and foremost, Stroessner attempted to convert the Colorado party into a movement with extensive lines into Paraguayan society. Remaining careful and concerned about the risks involved, he organized a network of support that flowed from the population to the highest ranks of power by pursuing a mass-line approach. The movement gave useful information to the authorities about people and organizations that criticized the government. In reality, the apparent mass-line never incorporated sectors of society more directly into politics or provided better avenues for participation. Instead, the objectives were to gain political intelligence and to allow Stroessner an opportunity to identify himself with the masses.[34]

The effort to promote the mass-line for the party gave the regime's doctrine a distinctive populist character. The brand of populism represented by the administration was also unique because it rested on no charismatic elements. Stroessner was not a particularly eloquent public speaker; he could not use forceful oratory, and most of the time he appeared to be rather dull, uninteresting, and reserved. Yet, his desire to appear close to his people prompted him to use every possible opportunity to show his affection for them. Paraguayans generally accepted his paternalistic orientations for what he claimed them to be: part of his effort to guide the nation to a brighter future.

To demonstrate his concern for Paraguayans, Stroessner appeared constantly in public. He could be seen presiding at ribbon-cutting ceremonies, distributing graduation diplomas, and inaugurating private and public buildings around the country. On occasion, he would reach out to people and talk informally in typical campaign style. The activities of the presidency received daily coverage on evening television and the radio networks, and sometimes even the most prosaic visitor would be reported as part of the daily agenda. The media often portrayed simple foreign guests as high-ranking international figures, further boosting Stroessner's public image. The intense exposure achieved total visibility for Stroessner within his political system. No other political personage appeared more identified with the needs of the people than did the president himself.[35] One of the major reasons that Stroessner ousted political opponents, such as Epifanio Méndez Fleitas and Edgar Ynsfrán, was because they commanded popular support. Stroessner had a deep liking for General Juan Perón of Argentina, but his political ideology and performance were strikingly different from Perón's. Perón emphasized redistribution efforts in favor of the poor; Stroessner defended an elitist, closed-minded group of political leaders who benefited economically from his staying in power.

The attempt to portray Stroessner's rule as popular exposed a number of situations that indicated the class bias of the stronista doctrine. His deactivation of the popular sector was carried out in a limited fashion, for example, and on one particular occasion, Stroessner referred to General Augusto Pinochet in Chile as incompetent because of his inability to create within the population at least a sense of participation. In

Paraguay, stronismo contrastingly provided that sense, so threats to the regime did not develop from the lower sectors.

Stroessner's policies, however, benefited only small sectors of Paraguayan society, essentially those that lent their unconditional support to the regime. Economic evidence indicates that the gap between the rich and the poor widened during the Stroessner era.[36] When Catholic church leaders complained about this unjust situation, a score of private businessmen rushed to defend the regime. Their basic explanation was that the trend found in Paraguay was not different from that found in other countries, such as Brazil, Chile, or Mexico. Further, they also criticized the church for meddling in affairs of the state.[37] Those who supported the regime understood the reality around them, and in that situation it remained far easier to sanction than to confront.

Another indication of the orientation of the regime is the composition of the cabinet. Ever since he assumed power in 1954, the president had been surrounded by a few select men, most of them very well educated. Stroessner stressed the need for loyalty and made no changes of consequence in the group of his collaborators. He made some shifts on occasion, but his closest advisers remained members of the party or the military and close friends. Some were members of previous administrations, and the elite benefited so greatly from his regime, that it became impossible to dissociate the regime from these public figures. Their loyalty to the principles guiding the administration was beyond question.

Stroessner also defended law and order to such an extent that order sometimes seemed the most important achievement of his administration. His speeches revealed a constant preoccupation with maintaining order, reassuring the population that the past experiences of instability and confrontations would not be repeated. In his yearly message to Congress of April 1, 1974, Stroessner pointed out that

> we dedicate ourselves without rest to consolidate peace in the Republic. This peace we must preserve at whatever cost because without it we will return to the abominable days of political regression, of fraticide fights and of unmerciful violence that is today affecting human coexistence and that destroys, irremediably, the fundamental structures in which freedom and democracy rest.[38]

By comparing the situation of Paraguay to that of other nations, and to that of earlier periods within Paraguay, he sought to provide Paraguayans with a sense of tranquillity. Quietness and peacefulness were major traits of the Guaraní populating the region in the sixteenth century. Given this image of a shared past, and given the tearing apart of Paraguay by international wars and internal unrest in the nineteenth and twentieth centuries, Stroessner's message was a very powerful one. Even if the regime used brutal forms of social and political control to achieve the goal, the goal itself still seemed worthwhile. Given the lack of sophistication of most of the population, and given the political messages to which it had been exposed, it could, rather ironically, appreciate the physical brutality of the regime and still see the regime as committed to principles of law and order.

Alternatively, another part of the governmental preoccupation with order stems from a concern with security. Following closely the ideas developed by the Brazilian military, the Stroessner regime defined security threats as any activities carried out with the expectation of change in the current order. Members of Congress were accused of subversive acts because they stood against some of the ideological principles upheld by the administration. In this sense, the military became a regressive rather than a modernizing institution. By inhibiting pluralistic views, this orientation resulted in a homogeneity of ideas that represented apathy more than support.

The *stronista* doctrine emphasized the role of the leader as a crucial element of the new political system. The *doctrina* defended by the regime revolved around the persona of the leader himself. All acts of government, all ideological constructs, all material well-being were said to come from the work and the creative thinking of the leader. In this regard, there centered on Stroessner a demicult of total and complete adulation. By carefully gaining and then exercising superiority over his subordinates, Stroessner received constant recognition for everything that happened in Paraguay. The Colorado party and the military became secondary institutions that, in the public mind, existed only as a reflection of the role that Stroessner played. With a strong tradition of centralized government, defended by the Constitution and sanctioned by a myriad of laws, the president also made himself appear to be at the center of the ideological principles that guided his actions. This tendency toward presidentialism reinforced the cultural legacy of the 1800s, when power was centralized for almost a century.

Pragmatically, the doctrine of the *stronista* movement further defined itself according to its accomplishments, such as the creation of infrastructure, the elaboration of new organizations and buildings, and the allegedly modern character given to public administration. Few other governments claimed credit for so many civic and public works, even works that were somehow remote from the actual sphere of government itself. The population was encouraged to judge the quality of the government by the number of achievements that could be seen. Stroessner's political philosophy was epitomized, almost caricatured, in its preoccupation with public works. In a country with a tradition of low political participation, the bulk of the population saw politics in terms of increases in aggregate welfare. Public works reflected a new standard of living that many Paraguayans equated with the quality of their leadership and the successful political environment in which they lived.[39]

Other traits of the administration further reinforced this commitment to authoritarian politics. The Stroessner regime was staunchly anticommunist, going to the extreme of labeling almost any unsanctioned political activity as connected in some way to communist expansionism in the area. This tendency to exaggerate the security dimension of Soviet expansion in the Southern Cone was used to justify higher levels of political repression as a mechanism for preventing social and political change. The end result is a *doctrina* that opposes any kind of political change, thus perpetuating the status quo and accepting very little contribution from nontraditional sources.

Authoritarian Paraguay: The Stronista Tradition

Stroessner created a brand of ideology that achieved two goals of particular importance. First, it displaced the traditional parties and made them almost totally irrelevant, at least for as long as he was in power, in upholding banners of ideological factionalism. Second, it replaced the old ideologies of the parties with a new mixture of Stroessner's own creation. It was far more relevant to talk about support and opposition to Stroessner than it was to define Paraguayan politics as a confrontation between the ideologies of different parties. Before 1954 distinctions were made among Colorados, Liberales, and Febreristas; after 1954 the distinction was between the *democráticos* and the *guionistas* within the Colorado party. But by 1967 everyone remaining in Paraguay had become, at least on the surface, a loyal *stronista*.

The turn to a personalistic type of ideology, however, did not reduce the complexity of the regime. On the contrary, the multifaceted doctrinal background with which Stroessner flavored the political life of Paraguay constituted one of the strongest elements of his successful tenure. The reduction to a single ideology reinforced the centralized nature of the entire system. The result was, then, a population that tended to talk very little in terms of goals and objectives, a society that passively accepted a consensual pattern of organization. However, the level of consensus in Paraguayan society was more apparent than real; now that the linchpin of the system is gone, Paraguayans may engage afresh in ideological and political discussions. Yet, the ideological foundations of the regime provided the lens through which loyalties were analyzed and judged. And even friends of the president who adopted critical positions were normally invited to exile themselves or were removed from public life without further ceremony.

The reduction of the entire ideological spectrum to a single set of principles sanctioned by loyalty to one leader created also a formidable political vacuum. Rather sadly, the premise under which stronismo functioned involved a conception of time that did not respect history. The ultimate outcome of this ideological vacuum manifested itself in confrontations within the Colorado party, but it eventually could cause conflict among the major parties, or even a general state of convulsion. The outcome of the regime's style may be Paraguay's return to a state of affairs prevalent when Stroessner first assumed power: the instability and chaos that he worked so steadily to prevent.

Notes

1. In his discussion of the authoritarian regime that ruled Spain, Linz indicated that he was following Theodor Geiger in his decision to use the term "mentality." See Juan J. Linz, "An Authoritarian Regime: Spain," in *Mass Politics: Studies in Political Sociology*, ed. Erik Allardt and Stein Rokkan (New York: Free Press, 1970), p. 257.

2. Bolivar Lamounier, "Ideologia em regimes autoritários: Uma crítica a Juan J. Linz," *Estudos Cebrap* 7 (1974): 69.

3. See Juan J. Linz, "The Future of an Authoritarian Situation or the Institutionalization of an Authoritarian Regime: The Case of Brazil," in *Authoritarian Brazil: Origins, Policies and Future*, ed. Alfred Stepan (New Haven: Yale University Press, 1973).

4. See Lamounier, "Ideologia em regimes autoritários," p. 74.

5. See Don Martindale, *The Nature and Types of Sociological Theory* (Boston: Houghton Mifflin, 1960), p. 415. The original conceptions of Mannheim were published in Germany in 1929 and translated by Louis Wirth and Edward Shils. See Karl Mannheim, *Ideology and Utopia* (New York: Harcourt, Brace, 1936).

6. For an excellent discussion of the role that national security doctrine played in the configuration of the Brazilian political order, see María Helena Moreira Alves, *State and Opposition in Military Brazil* (Austin: University of Texas Press, 1985). Moreira Alves elaborates on the relationship between the national security "state" as an example of political "order" and the dependent status of Brazilian society. Her work borrows from the contributions of Peter Evans concerning Brazilian national development and Alfred Stepan in regard to the role of the military in politics.

7. See John Hoyt Williams, *The Rise and Fall of the Paraguayan Republic, 1800–1870* (Austin: Institute of Latin American Studies, University of Texas, 1979), p. 37.

8. The Triple Alliance War had devastating effects on Paraguay, and these effects have been open to various interpretations. For example, one prominent Paraguayan writer and politician argues that the war set in motion a process of

denationalization and introduced foreign-owned companies into Paraguay. See Domingo Laíno, *Paraguay: De la independencia a la dependencia* (Asunción: Ediciones Cerro Corá, 1976).

9. For a detailed discussion of the constitutional convention that proclaimed the 1870 charter, see Harris G. Warren, *Paraguay and the Triple Alliance: The Postwar Decade, 1869–1878* (Austin: Institute of Latin American Studies, University of Texas, 1978), pp. 88–91.

10. For a strong defense of the liberties proclaimed by the Constitution and its support for democratic principles, see F. Arturo Bordón, *Historia política del Paraguay*, vol. 1 (Asunción: Orbis, 1976).

11. A commission directed by Cecilio Báez wrote a draft of the new constitution, which was an obvious effort to save the Liberal Constitution of 1870 by introducing some necessary changes. Although the draft was the result of Báez's personal effort and not really that of the commission, it was considered by the writers of the final draft of the 1940 document. On the Báez draft, see Justo J. Prieto, "El anteproyecto de constitución de Cecilio Báez," *Estudios Paraguayos* 9 (June 1981): 119–56.

12. For a complete text of the Estigarribia Constitution, see "Paraguay" in *Constitutions of Nations*, ed. Amos J. Peaslee, vol. 3, 2d ed. (The Hague: Martinius Nijhof, 1956), p. 111.

13. See José F. Estigarribia, "Comments on the Constitution of Paraguay," in *Constitutions of Nations*, ed. Amos J. Peaslee (The Hague: Martinius Nijhof, 1956), p. 125. The article was written by Estigarribia at the request of the editor of the volume.

14. Article 173 of the 1940 Constitution indicated that the president could be reelected for another period, consecutively or alternatively. In 1977 a second constitutional convention introduced a modification in the same article, stating simply that "the President can be re-elected." See Editorial Comuneros, *Constitución de la República del Paraguay* (Asunción: Editorial Comuneros, 1984), p. 34.

15. Although I have raised only the issue concerning the separation of powers, during the Stroessner regime Paraguay did not do well on the other dimensions of democracy suggested by Robert Dahl and Arend Lijphart. Issues like freedom to join organizations, freedom of expression, and free and fair elections are also problematic in this context. For a detailed discussion of the dimensions of democratic government, see Robert A. Dahl, *Polyarchy: Participation and Opposition* (New Haven: Yale University Press, 1971), pp. 1–5, and Arend Lijphart, *Democracies: Patterns of Majoritarian and Consensus Government in Twenty-One Countries* (New Haven: Yale University Press, 1984), pp. 4–36.

16. I learned about this concept in several conversations with Dr. Adriano Irala Burgos. Although not a political scientist by training, Irala Burgos displays an acute understanding of Paraguayan politics. I have been impressed by his concern for the future of Paraguayan politics as well as by his profound respect for the history and tradition of Paraguayan culture. An article explaining some of his ideas appeared in an edition of *ABC Color*, on December 30, 1979.

17. Professor Luis Resck, in a conversation with me on June 23, 1985, in Buenos Aires, expanded on the problem of the three powers. His prolific work in support of civic liberties in Paraguay has extended beyond the Southern Cone.

18. Paul Lewis indicates that by 1967 everyone in the administration had converted to *stronismo*. I believe that the year can be utilized as a milestone in the life of the regime. The legal recognition of the Liberal party ended the period of "challenges and confrontations" and began the period of "towards the consolidation."

19. I gained a good understanding of the ideological differences between *coloradismo* and *stronismo* in conversations with Epifanio Méndez Fleitas in Buenos Aires during the month of June 1985. To an extent, the argument that I develop here is a consequence of our discussions. My encounters with Don Epifanio were intense. He displayed very detailed knowledge of the inner workings of Paraguayan politics. I regret that he died in October of 1985, for we had planned to continue our talks in December of that year.

20. For a discussion of the Civil War and its implications for the Colorado party, see Paul H. Lewis, *Paraguay under Stroessner* (Chapel Hill: University of North Carolina Press, 1980), pp. 35–37.

21. J. Natalicio González wrote his personal view of the role that Paraguay plays in the region, capturing the character of the Paraguayan people with impressive accuracy. See "Meditaciones actuales," in J. Natalicio González, *Cómo se construye una nación* (Asunción: Editorial Guarania, 1949).

22. See Lewis, *Paraguay under Stroessner*, p. 40.

23. It is important to note that Méndez Fleitas had been one of the few *democráticos* who chose not to go into exile and who decided to fight back. The opposition of Méndez Fleitas to the González nomination was the first indication of the differences between Ynsfrán and Méndez Fleitas; Ynsfrán, though young, was closely associated with González.

24. The "official" explanation for the expulsion of Méndez Fleitas from the party was his management of the finances of the Central Bank. The discussion is documented in Epifanio Méndez Fleitas, *Diagnosis Paraguaya* (Montevideo: Editorial Prometeo, 1965), and a pamphlet supposedly published by the government under the authorship of Veritas, *Epifanio: El mago de las finanzas* (Asunción: N.p., 1970).

25. At the time of the confrontation, Méndez Fleitas had the support of loyal *epifanistas*. The situation was delicate because Stroessner had to avoid a clash with the epifanistas and had to satisfy the demands of the Argentine government as well. By "exiling" Perón to the interior, Stroessner prompted the former Argentine leader to leave Paraguay. The showdown between Stroessner and Méndez Fleitas came when a plot to oust Stroessner was discovered, although Méndez Fleitas denied ever conspiring against Stroessner. Epifanio Méndez Fleitas, in a conversation with me in Buenos Aires, June 12, 1985.

26. The events of December 20, 1955, prove the respect Méndez Fleitas and Ynsfrán had for each other. During the very controversial uprising against Stroessner by some of Méndez Fleitas's supporters in the military, the two men were said to have spent the evening together "listening to music" in Méndez

Fleitas's home. Having disconnected the telephone, Méndez Fleitas was isolated from the events. Méndez Fleitas's denials of conspiring against Stroessner suggest that the idea was possibly Ynsfrán's, whose plot was probably to oust Méndez Fleitas so that the competition was limited to himself and Stroessner.

27. The extensive writings of Méndez Fleitas testify to his solid preparation. See Epifanio Méndez Fleitas, *Ideologías de dependencia y segunda emancipación* (Buenos Aires: Editorial Emancipación, 1973); Epifanio Méndez Fleitas, *Lo histórico y lo antihistórico en el Paraguay: Carta a los Colorados* (Buenos Aires: N.p., 1976); Epifanio Méndez Fleitas, *Psicología del colonialismo: Imperialismo yanqui-brasilero en el Paraguay* (Buenos Aires: Instituto de Cultura Pane-Garay, 1971); Epifanio Méndez Fleitas, *El valor social de la historia* (Asunción: La Colmena, 1951); Epifanio Méndez Fleitas, *El orden para la libertad* (Asunción: Editorial Cultura, 1951); Epifanio Méndez Fleitas, *Desatinos y calumnias al descubierto: Cartas polémicas* (Buenos Aires: N.p., 1957); Epifanio Méndez Fleitas, *El reencuentro partidario* (Montevideo: Editorial Firmeza, 1958).

28. For examples of Ynsfrán's writings, see Edgar L. Ynsfrán, *Tríptico republicano: Democracia, agrarismo, paraguayidad* (Asunción: Editorial América-Sapucai, 1956); and Edgar L. Ynsfrán, *La irrupción moscovita en la Marina Paraguaya* (Asunción: By the author, 1947).

29. Ynsfrán had been under pressure because of his role as interior minister. In a confrontation with Chávez, he reacted violently to charges that the police were using brutality. The resulting tension was part of Ynsfrán's own doing; he had convinced the military of the threat of insurgency, and he had also devised his own way to deal with it.

30. Ynsfrán proved to be effective and useful to Stroessner during the early phase of his regime. Much opposition was exercised during the first seven years of the administration, and Ynsfrán may have been the right man for "cracking down" on the opposition's efforts. His special utility was reduced, however, when Stroessner adopted a more conciliatory attitude. The need for Ynsfrán and the role that he played were both gone.

31. The concept of the *stronista* doctrine should not be confused with the Colorado doctrine. In essence, during Stroessner's tenure the latter gave in to the former. Paraguayans argue that Stroessner "saved" the Colorado party from deeper crisis. His attempt to replace party principles by his own may have come about as a result of a realization after 1954 that further instability would result from internal party problems. Méndez Fleitas, in a conversation with me in Buenos Aires, on June 10, 1985, said that Stroessner in reality became president on December 21, 1955, when he took full control of the process of reconciliation within the Colorado party.

32. Nazist and fascist movements in Paraguay were already active in the late 1930s. The ideological background found support in certain circles of the army during the Morínigo administration. A detailed analysis is found in Alfredo M. Seiferheld, *Nazismo y fascismo en el Paraguay*, 2 vols. (Asunción: Editorial Histórica, 1986).

33. See John Vinocur, "A Republic of Fear," *New York Times Magazine*, September 23, 1984.

34. The key institution in helping the regime gain mass support was the *seccional*, for it brought down to the neighborhood level the benefits of the Colorado party. It organized social activities, helped people who had specific problems in employment or health, and aided party members to deal with the government. Observers differ as to whether the *real* role of the seccional was to encourage participation or to keep the population at bay, but somewhat paradoxically, it did both at the same time. On the role of the seccional, see Frederick Hicks, "Interpersonal Relationships and Caudillismo in Paraguay," *Journal of Interamerican Studies and World Affairs* 13 (January 1971): 89–111.

35. The president traveled extensively throughout Paraguay in an effort to keep informed by local leaders and party members, and Lewis notes that his ability to keep informed was one of the bases of his long tenure. See Lewis, *Paraguay under Stroessner*, p. 107.

36. See Aníbal Miranda, *Desarrollo y pobreza en Paraguay* (Asunción: Comité de Iglesias e Inter-American Foundation, 1982).

37. Examples of the support were reproduced in the daily *ABC Color* on June 14 and 15, 1979. Several entrepreneurs, among them Atilio Seppe, Alirio Díaz, and José Yaryes, attacked the Catholic church document produced by the Bishops Conference in June of 1979. See "Moral Healing of the Nation: Paraguay," *LADOC* 10 (November-December 1979): 1.

38. Presidencia de la República, Subsecretaría de Informaciones y Cultura, *Mensajes y discursos del excelentísimo Señor Presidente de la República del Paraguay, General de Ejército Don Alfredo Stroessner,* vol. 4 (Asunción: Subsecretaría de Informaciones y Cultura, 1981), p. 230. The translation is mine.

39. Examples of this concern are the yearly messages with which the president opened the session of Congress on April 1. Rather than spelling out political objectives and plans, he listed all the achievements of his administration during the previous year. For examples of the messages, see Presidencia de la República, Subsecretaría de Informaciones y Cultura, *Mensajes y discursos del excelentísimo Señor Presidente de la República del Paraguay, General de Ejército Don Alfredo Stroessner* (Asunción: Subsecretaría de Informaciones y Cultura, 1981). Five volumes include speeches delivered between 1954 and 1981.

Limited Mobilization and
the Politics of Control

5 The ideological structure of the Stroessner administration was reinforced by stiff mechanisms of control that attempted to limit the role of the opposition at the same time that they safeguarded the integrity of the regime. Not only was the stability of the entire system assured but its bases of apparent legitimacy were also strengthened, for no real opposition was allowed to exist within a nation where so much coercion and control was exercised.

To understand the nature of the existing order, it is important to focus on the interrelations among three levels of political control. Policies were directed toward the party structure, which only formalistically allowed for political dissent; toward interest groups, which did indeed represent the needs and perceptions of various sectors of society; and toward individual dissidents who openly challenged the regime. Although the record of the Stroessner regime was best known in terms of its highly publicized violations of human rights, even more important for the consolidation of the regime was the systematic undermining of opposition groups to eliminate discontent, dissatisfaction, and dissent. In placing limitations on the functioning of these basic political groups, the regime sharply diminished the likelihood that it could be seriously challenged.

Although ideological and historical elements were constant, the pattern of political control underwent periodic changes. The shifting nature of the control mechanisms allowed the regime to adjust its level of coercion according to particular situations, to meet both temporary and permanent threats. The same can be said about the pattern of co-optation, for these two patterns constituted the dynamic elements in the system that sustained the authoritarian regime over long periods of time. The Stroessner regime mixed appropriate levels of control with sustainable levels of co-optation in order to maintain its hegemony.

The amount of control exercised by a regime is in direct relationship to what Guillermo O'Donnell calls "the level of threat" perceived by the regime in a precoup situation. In the case of an authoritarian regime that is more personalistic than bureaucratic and that is long-standing, the fear of an immediate coup becomes less, but the level of threat as perceived by the regime's leadership remains a major determinant of how much control is exercised. At times a regime may utilize a supposed high level of threat as justification for its actions. Pressures to anticipate possible challenges mount to the extent that threat situations become artifacts rather than facts. The difference between the actual level of threat and the perceived level of threat affects the amount of political control and repression that are applied at any point in time.[1]

The extent of control in an authoritarian regime operates in the social as well as the political arena. Informally, patterns of control can be established through social mores and customs that inhibit participatory tendencies within the population. In Paraguay, an entire informal system prevented the people from developing high expectations about a participatory system wherein social and economic demands from all sectors of society would be honored. At the same time formal mechanisms were firmly established to allow the regime to control groups, institutions, and individuals without limitations.[2] The regime used a mix of informal and formal means to achieve its goals. The legislature provided all the needed legal instruments to guarantee the functioning of the control apparatus.

The Legal Framework of Political Control

Many of the activities of control undertaken by the Stroessner administration were possible because of the constitutional and legal provisions that had been created for this particular purpose. The Constitution of Paraguay, approved in 1940, reflected the authoritarian nature of the system in its articles that provide the executive with extensive powers.[3] A revised version of the 1940 Constitution was sanctioned by the constitutional convention of 1967, which passed an amendment allowing Stroessner to extend his tenure as president.[4]

Article 79 of the Constitution established the state of siege as a means of protecting the Constitution and the authorities invested in it. Although the article limited the occasions when a state of siege could be imposed, it left considerable room for political maneuvering and was clearly designed to dampen and/or deter internal unrest.[5] The article also placed limitations on the right to meet. Decree 181 provided the president with the authority to institute the state of siege,[6] although the Constitution established in Article 40 that the executive should abstain from creating special situations under which he would have control over the life, liberty, honor, and property of citizens. This same article stated that "dictatorship is outside the law."[7] Although almost entirely limited to the capital, the state of siege was maintained in effect for decades except on election days, when to satisfy constitutional requirements, it was lifted for twenty-four hours. In 1987 it was lifted permanently because of pressure from the United States.

The extent to which the state of siege was important in Paraguay during the Stroessner regime centers in the overall constitutional context from which it was derived, and this suggests that the principle was an exceptional rule. Although the temporary enactment of such a legal principle may be necessary in many countries, the consistent return to this practice in Paraguay showed that Stroessner's leadership was unable to solve its problems by resorting only to the normal instruments of coercion.

Among the powers provided the president by the state-of-siege article were those of arrest, confinement, and the prohibition of public meetings and demonstrations. The article also stated that the executive must report to Congress within five days of institution of a state of siege. The legislature gave up its constitutional mandate to approve the creation of the state of siege in exchange for simply being informed, thus placing the entire process in the hands of the executive.[8]

The decree stipulated that the state of siege must be specific in three regards: (1) the reasons for the state of siege, (2) the guarantees that are suspended, and (3) the geographical areas in which it will be enforced. The first issue, causation, appears to be the most difficult to evaluate. In a typical decree, the government alluded to the existence of "organizations and clandestine groups whose activities are geared toward altering the legitimate order by using violent means to destroy the fundamental bases upon which our society rests."[9] Without naming the organizations, the third item in the decree declared that the existence of the organizations was "public knowledge."

The issue of guarantees was also a delicate one under the state of siege. The decree did not attack directly the right to personal freedom; it merely said that this right cannot be guaranteed in all situations. But, by conditioning the right, the government could handpick when and where the principle would apply. The third issue, containment of a state of siege to a particular area, meant, at least theoretically, that the areas in which no state of siege existed enjoyed all the guarantees protected by the Constitution.[10]

With legal, supposedly protective procedures firmly in place, the judiciary continually excused itself from litigating cases having to do with alleged denials of freedom because of the state of siege. The judiciary also denied citizens the writ of habeas corpus on the basis that it did not fit the particular situation of the state of siege. To allow habeas corpus would require ascertainment by the judiciary of whether or not an action of the regime under the state of siege was reasonable according to the particular circumstances. And the judiciary simply refused to determine whether the institution of the state of siege was justifiable, so that, in effect, the restrictions that the decrees imposed on Paraguayan citizens were total.[11]

Although the state of siege lies at the heart of Paraguayan authoritarianism, several other laws gave the administration further legal claims against a large number of opponents. The first law that reinforced the state of siege was passed by Congress on October 17, 1955. Ironically entitled In Defense of Democracy, Law 294 concerned persons who propagated the doctrine of communism or any other political ideology that would alter the political structure of the nation. It extended protection to members of the government, and curtailed meetings, the distribution of information, and the use of the media. Although the law was geared to constraining the Communist party and its sympathizers, its latitude was such that any other oppositional organization or doctrine could also be included under it.[12]

The most useful legal instrument was Law 209, Defense of the Public Peace and the Freedom of Individuals, which was passed by Congress on September 10, 1970. It allowed the sanctioning of people who planned to commit crimes or break the law, especially laws against "public institutions." It also prohibited preaching "hate between Paraguayans" or "the destruction of the social classes." Its Article 8 made it a crime to belong to the Communist party or any other organization that might attempt to injure the ruling regime and described the Stroessner regime as democratic and republican.[13] In practice, the law was even used against dissident Colorados, as it was on May 11, 1984, in the arrest of three leaders of the Movimiento de Autenticidad Colorado (MAC), a wing of the official Colorado party that was trying to establish a dialogue with some of the Colorados in exile.

The legal framework provided by Article 79 of the Constitution and Law 209 were utilized mostly to harass opposition leaders. The heads of the major opposition parties were constantly brought to the Asunción police headquarters for interrogation under the guise of upholding the Constitution and the law. Many were confined for extended periods without trial, and the judiciary declared itself incompetent to rule on such matters, which were defined to be the exclusive responsibility of the executive. The consequence of this organizational scheme was paradoxical. The regime was able to create laws that served as a foundation for its activities of control, arguing all the while that everything that was done for the sake of preserving the democratic order was done in accordance with the law. The regime thus underscored its crude disrespect for human and civil rights.

The Party Structure and Political Control

The structure of political representation can also become a useful mechanism for political control in an authoritarian system. Most autocracies place extensive limitations on the activities, memberships, and social influence of political parties. Even under such circumstances, however, the party structures still allow for some expression of different positions and for the defense of particular interests.

In regard to party systems, the single-party system appears to predominate in long-standing authoritarian arrangements.[14] The role of the single party is different from the role of a dominant party, for the single party is the only channel through which citizens can make known their political interests. In the dominant-party system, smaller parties may offer alternatives; in the single-party system, political demands can be articulated only within the one party.

Beyond these limitations on articulation, the single-party system makes it very difficult for organized groups to present alternative visions of the best patterns of social organization, or of different political paths by which to achieve social goals. The perspective of the single party is the only avenue open to the population, and this reinforces the assumption that other parties should never be allowed to become genuine challengers. In Paraguay, because one of the major objectives of the Stroessner regime was to maintain its monolithic structure, parties were seen as channels through which organized opposition could undermine the pillars of that structure.

The situation of Paraguay during the Stroessner years in this context was remarkable. Although the Colorado party could be thought of as the dominant party within a competitive party system, in reality it was the only effective channel through which to articulate political demands in the country as a whole. Yet, the party leadership was unwilling to accept criticism even from within its own ranks, thus making policy articulation outside its boundaries impossible.

This monolithic approach to political organization was rooted in the effort of the regime to crystallize its political ideology. Therefore, loyalty to the regime required not only allegiance to the organizational party but also ideological conformity, the unquestioning acceptance of the political goals and means that the regime defined. According to this vision, other political parties were to be either eliminated or undermined because of their ideological differences or because of their representation of particularistic sectors of society.

The party structure was a constant source of conflict for the Stroessner regime. The reason is rather complex: the political parties arose during a troubled historical period and have always represented consistent political ideologies.[15] During the course of the twentieth century, the parties strengthened their constituencies, creating several supporting groups with very different political expectations. Internal divisions within the major parties produced a wide spectrum of partisan positions, but they did not lead to a competitive system. Instead of constituting a multiparty system, the parties became instruments by which to achieve personal power, power that was ultimately utilized to control the opposition.

The Stroessner administration masterfully used internal party fragmentations and the party structure at large to assure its dominance. Secure in knowing that a strong relationship between the Colorado party and the armed forces had virtually assured its continuity, the regime played up to other parties' situations and centralized the activities of the "official" party around the administration. The result was a structure of representation sharply limited in scope, one that could not provide a foundation for open competition.

The Limited Opposition

The political parties acting as opposition forces to Stroessner were few. The usual party role had been subsumed by the political system, and they only very weakly represented the interests of their constituencies. The regime saw to it that some degree of opposition existed, so that a functional democracy could operate. This manipulation divided the opposition parties into two groups: the officially approved opposition parties and the unwelcomed opposition parties. The narrow scope of the first group's activities contributed to the stability of the regime and reinforced its control over the entire political system.

The effort to create an organized opposition party rested mainly in the hands of the traditional Partido Liberal. The Liberal party came into being after the nation had experienced authoritarianism under Francia and the Lópezes. It was built up at about the same time that General Caballero founded the Colorado party. Amidst the political differences existing after the Triple Alliance War, the options represented by the two parties were a matter of tendencies. The Colorado party was somewhat more populist; the Liberal Party stood more behind ideas necessary for a liberal democracy, such as the freedom of suffrage. Both parties, however, pursued basically the same political agendas.

The earliest representatives of the Liberal party were the Legionnaires. They were members of the upper class who during the administrations of Francia and the Lópezes had been exiled to Argentina, where they had organized the Paraguayan Legion. The legion was attached to the Argentine army during the Triple Alliance War and fought actively against Francisco Solano López. Concerned about the socialist and populist overtones of the autocratic rule imposed by the authoritarian administrations, the Legionnaires gathered strength and in 1887 founded the Centro Democrático, which later changed its name to the Liberal party. They were basically opposed to the more authoritarian tendencies of the Colorados, and supportive of positions fostering free enterprise and liberal democratic principles.

Although both parties were organized along social-class lines, they actually had no meaningful ideological differences. The Liberals were prone to receiving help from abroad and to selling public land in order to improve the economic conditions of the country. They managed to do both in the Liberal era but were totally unable to install a democratic system. They were more concerned with personalistic confrontations with the Colorados than with reforming the political institutions of the nation. The internal divisions in the Liberal party produced a civil confrontation in 1922, reflecting its inability to maintain order. During the thirty-two years of Liberal rule, there were twenty administrations. When Stroessner became president in 1954, the Liberals were the only opposition party with some popular support, and they acted as the opposition in the unicameral Congress.[16]

The Liberal party split into two factions in 1963 because of a dispute over Stroessner's invitation to participate in the elections. The Renovationists were a small group, but they kept the banner and name of the original Liberal party. The majority of the old party's members went over to the new Radical Liberal party, which achieved legal status after 1967. The Liberal party was then seen as a collaborationist group because it supported many of the government positions in Congress.[17]

The Radical Liberals joined the Febreristas and became the organized opposition, but in 1971 they split again, as different tendencies and leaders fought for control of the party. The crisis that affected the Radical Liberals lasted until 1975, when Domingo Laíno, a member of Congress and leader of the party was jailed and lost his congressional seat. The division of the Radical Liberals demonstrated once again the talent of the Stroessner administration for meddling in the internal affairs of the opposition.

The Radical Liberals attempted to overcome their differences at several party conventions. At hand was always the subject of reunification with the Liberals, but the party remained divided between a more conservative and a more radical wing. Once the more radical wing gained control of the party, its members looked for an arrangement with the Liberals so as to present a unified front to the Colorados and to the regime during the party convention of 1977. They called this unification the United Liberal party, and suggested that unless the state of siege was lifted and political prisoners were released, they would abstain from participating in the 1978 election.

The administration was in need of a quick fix that would help to settle the issue, and one appeared in Justo Pastor Benítez, an old leader of the more conservative faction within the Radical Liberals. Failing to understand that the goal of the United Liberal party was strong opposition to the administration, Benítez sued the party, alleging that it lacked legal standing. The courts quickly declared him to be the legal leader of the Radical Liberal party, and assigned to him the party's assets and control of its headquarters and newspaper. At one stroke, the administration had done away with the challenge presented by the potential merger of the Radicals and the Liberals.

The divisions among Liberals affected the ways in which they could effectively become an organized opposition to the regime. The left-wing Radicals went on to form the Partido Liberal Radical Auténtico in February of 1977, but their leader, Domingo Laíno, was exiled in 1982 and allowed to return only in 1987. He tried five times to reenter Paraguay, only to be violently repulsed at the port of entry, even when escorted by foreign dignitaries.[18]

The fissiparousness of the Liberals illustrated the Stroessner regime's ability to manipulate the opposition and thereby retain its strength. The issues that divided the Liberals were to a large extent governmentally created: election participation, the Itaipú vote (congressional disputes concerning the signing of the Itaipú Treaty) and the legal reunification of the party rejected by the government. By imposing so many limitations on the activities of the opposition, the regime solidified its position as a unique power holder, resting in effect on the performance of a single party.

The Febreristas were no different from the Liberals in respect to inner disarray. The party had developed after the Revolution of 1936 under Colonel Rafael Franco, and his charismatic leadership proved to be the basis of the party. Since his departure from office a year later, the Febreristas have struggled with issues of unity and organization. Even in the beginning, however, Franco allegiants comprised two groups: backers of "febrerismo neto" and backers of "febrerismo revolucionario." The former group had been members of the Liberal party and supported ideas that were rooted in the old Liberal ideology. The latter group was more progressive, adhering to the ideas and principles of the Communist party. According to Antonio González, the ideology of Franco was between the two, and his personal leadership was a sign of the mystique of the party.[19]

Differences between the Febreristas and the other parties limited the Febrerista role in politics. They were committed to revolutionary principles, to going very far beyond the scheme offered by the Colorados and the Liberals. But soon after the party's creation, Febrerista leaders recognized that its revolutionary character forced Febrerismo to accept people with very different ideological orientations. The party brought together radical activists whose origins had been communist, nationalist, and even liberal. The Febreristas' tendency to pursue extreme positions became their legendary *raison d'être* as well as the reason for the party's demise. The ideological differences between the Marxist and non-Marxist wings within the party were a constant source of friction.[20]

Differences also existed between the young members and the old guard of the party. After some discord was settled by ousting the party's left wing, the old Febreristas struck a deal with the Stroessner regime and participated in the 1967 elections.[21] Their showing was so poor that party members finally recognized that they had left the mainstream of politics. With discontent intensifying among the more progressive young militants, the party did not participate in general elections against Stroessner after 1973.[22]

The challenge presented by the Febrerista party to the Stroessner regime was a limited one. After decades in exile, the party had lost its popular appeal within Paraguay. Old members joined ranks with the Radical Liberal party and its several factions. The Stroessner regime, however, continued to accept the Febreristas as a legitimate form of opposition, albeit ineffective because of its decision to bypass elections. Actually, the Febreristas served more as a pressure group than as a party. Further, because most of its more radical members had been sent into exile early in the life of the Stroessner regime, a potential source of bitter opposition had been eliminated.

The Unwelcome Opposition

The Stroessner regime also presents a different case concerning the role of political parties because it constitutionally allowed a structure of limited opposition by some groups and no opposition by others. Political parties were circumscribed by requirements antecedent to legal recognition. Legal rules also denied political existence to other types of organizations, thus minimizing the growth of an effective opposition.

Law 204 defined various matters relating to electoral procedures. Its Article 21 declared that to receive legal recognition, a new party must present a petition with signatures of no fewer than ten thousand members.

The same law established that if only one party participates in an election, it will receive all the positions to be filled. It also stated that if a party fails to gain legal recognition, it can appeal the decision to the Supreme Court.[23] Law 204 resulted in three parties being denied political participation: the Christian Democratic party, the Communist party, and the Movimiento Popular Colorado (MOPOCO).

The Christian Democrats organized as a party in the early 1960s. They have no formal relationship with the Catholic church, although most are members of faculties at the Catholic University and middle-class professionals who advocate positions close to the social teachings of the church. Their party was denied legal recognition as a result of application of Law 204, although they maintained that they had secured the required number of members' signatures. In a never-ending quarrel with the Stroessner administration, which refused to have a case in this regard heard in court, the Christian Democrats continued to denounce the excesses of the regime but with limited impact.[24]

The Communist party of Paraguay was founded in 1928, and was initially active among the labor unions. Many of its members are former radicals of Febrerismo, and since it has not been legal in Paraguay during the Stroessner regime, its activities have been rather limited. All together, it is said to command the support of about three thousand constituents. The party was not allowed to present candidates for any political position. Its members were jailed time after time, and their situation received considerable attention in international forums due to their extensive contacts outside Paraguay. Their leaders Miguel A. Soler and his successor, Antonio Maidana, have both been missing since their disappearances in 1977 and in 1980, respectively. Although banned from political activity, the Communist party managed to remain very active within Paraguay through the combined efforts of students and labor leaders.[25]

MOPOCO was the largest opposition party to the Stroessner administration, but it was in exile for most of the time between 1954 and 1986. Its membership comprised mainly former members of the *epifanistas* and *democráticos*, the two factions exiled by Stroessner early on. The leaders of the MOPOCO were Waldino Lovera and Miguel González Casabianca. The group denounced the support given to the Stroessner government by the United States and was against Brazil's role in Paraguay.[26] Méndez Fleitas headed the Asociación Nacional Republicana en el Exilio y la Resistencia until his death in 1985. Other prominent Colorado democráticos exiled in Argentina and Uruguay have also been closely involved with the Movimiento Popular Colorado.[27]

In addition to the curtailment of opposition parties, the structure of political representation under Stroessner was organized to meet the needs of the regime. In consequence of the difficulties of presenting an opposition front, the opposition leaders formed a National Accord in February 1979, an alliance of parties striving for the liberalization of political competition. Remarkably, only one of the parties involved in the agreement had legal status as far as Stroessner was concerned; the others were illegal, exiled, or not allowed to function. Although the Acuerdo Nacional achieved greater success only during the mobilization that brought the Stroessner regime to an end, it had in general raised the level of consciousness about the deteriorating situation. In the beginning it lacked popular support, and experienced severe fragmentation among its members. Help from the administration of U.S. President Jimmy Carter, however, provided enough political space so as to convert it into a strong political presence.[28]

The Role of the Single Party

One of the distinctive characteristics of the Stroessner regime in Paraguay was the dominant role of the Colorado party. The party acted as what Robert Tucker calls a "movement-regime," an ideal type elaborated in Tucker's description of nationalistic and revolutionary regimes that deserves closer comparison with communist and fascist forms of political organization. Tucker writes that

> the leadership of the authoritarian movement-regime insists that it is also democratic in a "new way" (i.e., not the liberal Western way). This mode of thought, in which the dichotomy of "dictatorship-democracy" is rejected, is an outgrowth of the original concept of the revolutionary struggle as a mass movement for national or supra-national objectives under guidance of a disciplined political elite organization.[29]

The creation of a movement-regime under Stroessner was intertwined with the development of a particular brand of political leadership that rejected the possibility that the system may not be a democratic one. The regime exercised control over the structure of party competition, and also provided for the existence of a mass movement under a single party that acted as an instrument of control. The Colorado party changed its internal organizational structure as a result of Stroessner's rise to power: the Asociación Nacional Republicana (Colorado party) became a mass movement party, one with strong ties to neighborhood and grass-roots organizations. Patterned after the Peronist party and the authoritarian parties of Europe, it was a formidable political machine that penetrated all sectors of Paraguayan society.[30]

The role of the Colorados was complex. They served as one of the administration's most important pillars, providing, together with the armed forces, the political backing it needed to remain strong. Yet, at the same time, they also lent a certain balance to the distribution of power, especially standing against any possible outburst by the military. The Colorados' role was not only to limit the activities of the organized opposition but also to make sure that no internal threats were posed to the regime. In this regard, the party stretched the power base of the regime beyond the typical spheres of the upper classes and the military into the lower spheres. Stroessner's ability to reach deep down into these pockets of support through manipulation and clientelism gave the regime its populist flavor, one that was so crucial to the creation of its own brand of authoritarian doctrine.

The party was organized along the principle of *verticalismo*. The hierarchy allowed no possibility of democratic participation within its ranks, and internal dissent was seen as treason. The party's most important unit is the Junta de Gobierno, which administers the party and fosters its continued growth. Members of the Junta de Gobierno were close collaborators with the administration and also with the Colorado representatives in Congress. Several committees dealt with specific issues, such as labor, peasants, women, youth, law, and propaganda. Beyond these groups, the junta drew strong support and counsel from professional organizations made up of party members.[31]

Political matters are the province of the Committee on Party Organization. It oversees policy changes that should be carried out within the party, and it also established connections with party committees throughout Paraguay. It is active during elections when delegates to the national assembly are chosen nationwide. At the neighborhood level, *seccionales* represent the interest of the party, and *subseccionales* are sometimes created to subdivide the areas where seccionales are active. The committee and the seccionales were the channels through which the national party line flowed down to the grass-roots level during the Stroessner years. They also were an additional avenue for making sure that national policy found no challenge within the party itself.

The organizational scheme that supported the role of the single party was reinforced by a strong grass-roots movement that mobilized peasants for the party. After the Civil War of 1947, the Colorado party enjoyed the backing of the *py-ñandí* (barefooted ones), peasants who unequivocally upheld the government and provided excellent information about opposition factions. They were crucial in helping Stroessner control the Frente Unido por la Liberación Nacional (FULNA) in the countryside in 1960; in defeating the Ligas Agrarias in Coronel Oviedo in 1973; and in backing Stroessner in 1974 against some military officers who were critical of his policies.

The actions of the py-ñandí proved to Stroessner that he could count on his party organization for impressive demonstrations when needed. The party was run from the top down with a clear bias toward the more privileged classes but with wide and strong support from popular sectors as well. Low-income Paraguayans valued the performance of the regime in terms of the stability that it assured, and they refused to argue about costs involved. Membership in the Colorado party became a prerequisite of political favors, government jobs, access to the judiciary. Each member of the party who worked for the government contributed 5 percent of his or her salary to the party.

The party served as an instrument of control through neighborhood organizations, and it profoundly influenced the bureaucracy and the cabinet. All members of the cabinet are party members, with some also belonging to the armed forces. The ability to control the bureaucratic apparatus and influence appointments to key government positions rendered it the centerpiece of politics. It reinforced the personalistic power of the executive. The dominant situation of the Colorados contributed to the order existing under Stroessner. The party set the rules by which everyone could understand what was politically feasible. In this respect, the party acted as a moderator of the political game. The control exercised by it made it the cornerstone of the entire regime. When a major crisis affected party unity, the regime weakened, thereby creating favorable conditions for a transition to a more open political system, initiating the democratization of Paraguayan politics.

Interest Groups and Political Control

One of the most important distinctions between authoritarian and totalitarian regimes is often said to lie in the way that the former exercises control at the institutional level rather than at the individual level.[32] In most Latin American countries, authoritarian regimes have tended to subordinate individual rights to institutional needs. In this regard, however, extensive political control can sometimes be exercised equally over institutions and citizens, blurring the distinction between authoritarianism and totalitarianism in some countries.[33]

Political control under Stroessner was not limited to individual citizens or to the political parties; several groups were also targeted, groups that represented values, activities, or goals not desired by the administration. When institutions openly challenged the system or injustices of the regime, they made themselves targets, as did people who voiced their opposition. The Catholic church, labor unions, student organizations, and intellectual circles were ever-present sore points for the regime, which tried to limit their ability to educate the public more widely on selected political issues.

The Catholic Church

The problematic relationship between the Paraguayan Catholic church and authoritarianism is a long one, dating back to the governments of Francia and the Lópezes. The Stroessner regime found in the church one of its most bitter critics, and the relationship became one of mutual distrust. Withal, the government and the church needed to find ways to coexist. The government supported Catholic education in public schools, did not tax church buildings, and paid subsidies to the church and its priests. In return, the president had some say in nominations to high Catholic posts, and he also allowed the church a seat in the Council of State. These arrangements exerted additional pressure on both sides of the partnership, so it was not surprising that any amount of conflict had serious implications for the life of the regime.[34]

Paraguay is certainly a Catholic country. Its population has particular devotion to the shrine of Caacupé, to which pilgrims regularly travel. The best educational facilities are church controlled, and the Catholic university is a major cultural and intellectual center outside the sphere of government influence. For many reasons, Paraguayans constantly look to the church for guidance and strength, and therefore the relationship that Stroessner maintained with it for so very many years, bumpy as it may have been, was always understood as crucial for the continuity of the regime.[35]

The first crisis in church-state relations during the Stroessner tenure took place when a young priest from a poor parish in Asunción publicly criticized the government for its lack of respect for human rights. His objective was to enlist popular support to resist the dictatorship, but on the very day that he spoke out, he was taken into custody. The ensuing troubles involved Father Ramón Talavera and his parishioners and the entire Catholic church of Paraguay. Stroessner ordered the hierarchy of the church to silence the priest, only to find that the hierarchy would not accept such direction, even from the president. The government next ordered the parish evacuated, to make way for the construction of a military building. Talavera disappeared, but was found two days later with evidence on his body that he had been beaten. The government declared that he had suffered a nervous breakdown, and the church hierarchy decided to send him to Uruguay. The government never allowed him to return.[36]

The Talavera episode set in motion a series of face-offs between the Catholic church and the regime. Other priests took up the cause initiated by Talavera, and at the same time the Catholic University of Asunción was created. Given the intellectual ferment at the institution, the church was now able to enlist student support, becoming the most visible center of discontent within the nation. With the advent of a more social approach to evangelical issues as a result of the conferences of Medellín and Puebla, and in consequence of the documents of the Second Vatican Council, the church became involved in social and political activities. In 1962 it organized the Christian Agrarian Leagues, which attempted to raise the level of political consciousness of the peasant communities. By offering educational programs, the church slowly spread its message of opposition to the dictatorship.[37]

The criticisms that emanated from the church, its organizations, and personnel brought a harsh response from the administration. Priests were closely watched, brought in for interrogation, imprisoned, and expelled from the country. The Agrarian Leagues suffered unending harassment, and were finally rendered unable to fulfill their mission. Many activities were assumed to be subversive, and only some segments of the church managed to maintain a position of intransigence. The more radical priests continued to decry the regime's actions, but the hierarchy learned to accept the situation. Monsignor Ismael Rolón was a strong critic of the government, but sufficiently moderate to be tolerated and gain President Stroessner's acceptance.[38]

The activities of the Agrarian Leagues and of the many priests who advocated social change were alleged by the regime to be part of the communist infiltration. The author of an anonymous article published by the Archdiocese of Asunción complained that priests were labeled as Communists in order to discredit them in the eyes of the peasant population. The author wrote that "a leading Catholic man said he could not see how the Bishops Conference of Paraguay dared ask for the return of two Communists like Father Oliva and Father Ramallo." He added that Paraguayan peasants were normally told that the *pa'i* (fathers) were all Communists.[39]

The regime's violence also touched the lives of many peasant families, who had little more than their religious faith to sustain them in the oppressive environment in which they lived. For instance, on July 17, 1976, Father Demetrio Aquino, the bishop of Caacupé, wrote to Sabino Montanaro, the minister of the interior, to complain about the death of Arturo Bernal. Bernal had been arrested, brought to prison in Asunción and killed by government authorities. Aquino held the minister personally responsible for the death of another Paraguayan.[40]

Organized Labor

Labor unions, too, were government targets. After having called a general strike on August 27, 1958, the Confederación Paraguaya de Trabajadores (CPT) became a government organization. It received part of the budget allocated to the Interior Ministry and the Labor Ministry, and operated under the guidance of those two arms of the government.

The extent of intervention in the affairs of the labor organization was important. No union could be created without the consent of the Ministry of Justice and Ministry of Labor, and bargaining was replaced almost as a matter of course by ministerial arbitration. By such means the regime enjoyed total control of urban and rural workers from the early 1960s onward, thereby doing away with an earlier source of political opposition. A free labor movement operated only in exile; it was recognized by the General Confederation of Free Labor Organizations.[41]

The repressive efforts of the administration in regard to labor gained added strength through the character of Paraguayan commerce and industry. Because the country did not embark on import-substituting industrialization, largely depending on agricultural products for its national income, an urban working class never materialized. With the lack of policies to encourage large industrial enterprises in urban areas, the Stroessner regime curtailed both the size and the potential influence of the labor movement. Beyond efforts at institutional opposition articulated through the Catholic church, the labor movement was of little significance to the politics of Paraguay.

The Indian Population

An inability to affect the political process also characterized peasant and Indian groups, which were similarly subjected to isolating policies. Most peasants had supported Stroessner, but the Indian communities had demonstrated their discontent on numerous occasions. In consequence of their temerity several tribes were decimated, and others were subjected to arbitrary government controls.

A major international controversy developed in wake of the treatment that the Stroessner administration accorded the Aché Indians of eastern Paraguay. The Aché were brought onto reservations, where the government worked to exterminate them. An investigation was launched by Mark Münzel of the Ethnology Department of the University of Giessen (Germany). He reported on his findings in a 1973 publication of the International Group for Indigenous Affairs in Copenhagen,[42] and later described the three-pronged government approach to the Indian problem in Paraguay: the Indians were successively hunted, enslaved, and then deprived of their culture. Eyewitness accounts detailing the use of military vehicles and troops as part of the entire operation, led Münzel to conclude that the government of Paraguay was actively involved in genocide.[43] Another description of the major Indian reservation depicts the policies of the Stroessner regime. One visitor saw Indians tortured, mistreated, and left without food until they finally willed themselves to die. Young Indian women were sold as prostitutes, and young Indian boys were used as household servants. Apparently with tacit cooperation of some of the fundamentalist American missionaries in the region, the Indian population was deprived of its most basic rights.[44]

Individual Repression and Human Rights

The ability of the regime to manipulate the politics of the nation demanded control exercised not only at the systemic and institutional levels but at the individual level as well. Efforts in this regard were conspicuous and ongoing. The record of human rights violations in Paraguay is not as extensive as in some other nations of Latin America because the repressive activities of the Stroessner regime were purposely carried out behind the scenes to deny the world access. Violations of human and civil rights were a constant during all of the Stroessner's years. After Congress passed the Law for the Defense of Democracy in October 1955, when the regime went after members of the Liberal and the Febrerista parties, most members of the opposition went into exile.

At the end of the 1950s, the idea that an armed insurrection could depose the regime gained widespread credence within the ranks of the younger generation of the opposition. Guerrilla activism flourished along the border. The group 14th of May was created, combining former Liberal activists and the Vanguardia Febrerista under the leadership of Arnaldo Valdovinos, and it obtained support from abroad. Leadership disputes later split the Vanguardistas from the 14th of May. Part of the organization made an unsuccessful attempt to invade Paraguay in December of 1959, only to be beaten back by the army. In April 1960 a second unsuccessful attempt sealed the fate of the 14th of May forever.[45] The United National Liberation Front (FULNA) emerged then with strong backing from the Communist party of Paraguay and also with support from Cuba. Its members managed to cross the border into Paraguay in May 1960, but military and police units repulsed them. A second invasion resulted in another disaster; FULNA made a last attempt in December of 1960 with similar results. The efforts to bring the regime down through armed confrontation had failed dismally.

The elimination of FULNA and the 14th of May did not prevent other groups from organizing attacks on the government or on Stroessner. After a November 1974 attempt on Stroessner's life, the regime unleashed a new wave of repression. In April 1976, police forces destroyed the Organización Político Militar (OPM), whose supporters included exiled Argentine guerrillas and whose active leaders, according to government reports, were members of the Paraguayan Jesuit order. Government officials broke into the Jesuit-run Cristo Rey School searching for evidence that could connect the organization to the religious order, and Minister of the Interior Sabino Montanaro accused the Jesuits of spreading communism and supporting terrorist activities. Two leaders of the movement were killed, and many students and peasant leaders were arrested in the aftermath.

Armed challenges to the regime only stiffened its back. Crackdowns were incessant and opposition leaders were harassed, interrogated, intimidated, and jailed. In 1966, an Amnesty International report said that in Paraguay "torture had been a usual means of extracting confessions from prisoners."[46] In 1973 Amnesty International found that both "the Ministry of the Interior and the Department of Crimes and Vigilance in Asunción carry out tortures in their respective centers."[47] During this period, the bodies of many prisoners who allegedly had died while in the hands of the police turned up on the shores of Uruguay or Argentina. The practice of throwing them into the Paraná and Paraguay rivers was meant to have a "demonstration effect" on the entire population.

The Organization of American States (OAS) also investigated human rights in Paraguay as a result of information received by the Inter-American Commission on Human Rights (IACHR). Several reports prepared by the commission were discussed during sessions of the OAS.[48] In 1978 the IACHR released a lengthy appraisal of the situation, concluding that "the majority of human rights recognized in the American Declaration of the Rights and Duties of Man, and in other similar instruments, not only are not respected in a manner in keeping with the international commitments assumed by that country, but also have become the object of a practice of constant violation."[49]

Evidence of the human rights violations by the Stroessner regime also reached the U.S. Congress. On July 28, 1976, the House of Representatives Subcommittee on International Organizations held hearings on the situation in Paraguay. Three witnesses who provided accounts were Ben Stephansky, Robert Alexander, and Frisco Gilchrist. The first two were members of a team sent to Paraguay by the International League of Human Rights; Gilchrist had been a member of the Disciples of Christ Church mission in Paraguay from 1952 to 1976.[50]

Professor Alexander spoke about the general historical background of the regime, but was quick to point out that the regime was peculiar even in the way that it had replaced the military to some extent by a strong police force. He suggested that the pattern of individual repression in Paraguay was random and used to instill fear among the population rather than to obtain information. Stephansky spoke along the same lines, stressing that dictatorships of the Stroessner variety were not fighting communism but preventing democracy. He suggested that they resorted to the same type of coercion practiced in communist regimes. The Gilchrist testimony was of a different nature. Having served as a missionary, Gilchrist described several situations where the work of his church was under siege. He called many of the government's stories fabricated, adding that his church had never supported terrorist activities. His account of how the police raided several offices of the mission and detained most of its members confirmed what the other two witnesses had said about the excesses of the government.

Some individual cases of repression in Paraguay have become widely known. One concerns Joelito Filartiga, the son of a well-known medical doctor who ran a private clinic for peasants in rural Paraguay. (Ironically, it was called The Clinic of Hope.) The seventeen-year-old was found dead in the house of a police inspector in Asunción on March 29, 1976.[51] Filartiga had been taken to the police station in Asunción, where he was interrogated about the activities of his father. After repeating that he had no information to share, he was subjected to electric shock torture and died after going into cardiac arrest. Attempting to cover up the misdeed, the perpetrators carried his body to Police Inspector Américo Peña-Irala's home, and laid it on the bed of the daughter of Peña-Irala's mistress. Because she was married, they arranged the room as a typical crime-of-passion setting, making it appear that Filartiga had been found *in flagrante delicto.* When the young woman's husband was called to the scene, they beat him and told him that he must confess to the murder.[52] Four hours later the torturers brought in Filartiga's sister and told her to take the body and bury it immediately. The supposed adultress attempted to speak to Dr. Filartiga, but before they could meet, she disappeared. A member of the Filartiga family who attempted to locate her has also disappeared. Peña-Irala continued to torment the Filartiga family and their lawyer by filing a lawsuit in Asunción.

The Filartiga case received worldwide attention when Mrs. Filartiga, having received political asylum in the United States, learned that Peña-Irala was also living in the United States. This provided an opportunity to expose the repression in Paraguay through the U.S. courts. The decision favored the Filartigas, but by the time it came down Peña-Irala had been expelled from the United States because he held an expired tourist visa. One of the culprits escaped justice, but the sordidness of Paraguayan repression was made known to a far wider audience.[53]

Consolidation Through Political Control

The pattern of political control exercised by the Stroessner administration revealed the nature of the political system itself. The imposition of a uniform political ideology and the ability of the regime to reign with total impunity prompted several organizations to criticize publicly its activities and policies. But speaking out was an unavailing effort. The regime had managed so to cow the population that almost all Paraguayans accepted, at least tacitly, the rule of fear institutionalized by the rule of law: strong-arm tactics that were supported by legal principles, which themselves had been established by one-sided courts, conventions, and legislative bodies.

But the regime was not satisfied with eliminating the potential competition inspired by democratic principles. It also created procedures by which challengers both from above and from below became disinclined to intervene. This eventuated in a two-tier policy: on the one hand, advocating terror and fear to silence challengers, and on the other hand, working to co-opt those who could benefit in some measure from the status quo. When the regime resorted to co-optation, potential challengers concluded that the most safe, convenient, and profitable strategy was to accept things the way they were. At the crossroads of these two dimensions of policy, the regime managed to establish and to maintain a political culture that was vivid and distinctive, deeply entrenched so long as its founder did not depart the scene, one that remained narrowly elitist in economic benefits yet was able to generate a surprising degree of acceptance and even support among the rank and file.

Notes

1. Elaboration of the concept "level of threat" as suggested by O'Donnell can be found in David Collier, "The Bureaucratic-Authoritarian Model: Synthesis and Priorities for Future Research," in *The New Authoritarianism in Latin America*, ed. David Collier (Princeton: Princeton University Press, 1979), p. 387. Collier calls "level of threat" an "intervening" variable affecting a larger variable used by O'Donnell, namely, the strength of the popular sector.

2. An example of the informal mechanisms of control is described by the guaraní word *mbareté*. The word originally meant strong, and there is no one word that captures its meaning in English. The closest analogy is "superior power over others." A report produced by the International League for Human Rights indicates that "when 'mbareté' conflicts with the rule of law, it is 'mbareté' which governs." See David M. Helfeld and William L. Wipfler, *Mbareté: The Higher Law of Paraguay* (New York: International League for Human Rights, 1980), p. 6. The report says that the term is used to refer to the direct action taken by a political boss who wants to circumvent the law. Implicitly, it also means the fear of the consequences if one does not comply.

3. The first Constitution sanctioned by the Paraguayan nation was written in 1870 and was largely the result of the Triple Alliance War. In that document liberal principles were articulated, and the nation survived until 1940 with a liberal Constitution. The initiative of President Morínigo was, only nominally,

to "bring the democratic system to perfection," and the initiative produced the Constitution of 1940. In the context of Latin America's constitutional tradition, the charter of Paraguay was actually formulated according to historical and cultural traits in line with the authoritarian tradition of Francia and the Lópezes.

4. The 1967 Constitution was not different in spirit from the document drafted in 1940. It sanctioned a strong executive, with powers extending within and outside the government. Article 173 declared that the president of the republic could be reelected for only one additional period, either consecutively or alternatively. A convention on March 10, 1977, sanctioned an article declaring that the president could be reelected. See Justo J. Prieto, *La constitución Paraguaya concordada* (Asunción: Biblioteca de Estudios Paraguayos, 1981), p. 83.

5. For a revision of the article itself, see ibid., p. 44.

6. Ibid., p. 90.

7. Ibid., p. 27.

8. The International League for Human Rights gives an example of how the state of siege is used by the regime. Of a list of 236 state-of-siege prisoners detained as of July 1977, 195 had been released without having been tried, in some cases after a jail term of eighteen years; 36 were prosecuted for violation of Law 209, of whom 4 were convicted and 32 were let go. See Helfeld and Wipfler, *Mbareté*, p. 26.

9. Decree 24.025, March 23, 1981. See Justo J. Prieto, "El estado de sitio en la constitución Paraguaya," *Estudios Paraguayos* 9 (December 1981): 364.

10. Ibid., p. 365.

11. The president of the Colegio de Abogados of Asunción revealed the way in which the judiciary operates under the tutelage of the regime. Dr. Rubén Bassani indicated that from a liberal state with minimal legislation, Paraguay became a nation with total social control, one without respect for human and individual rights. See Pepa Kostianovsky, *28 entrevistas para este tiempo*, 2d ed. (Asunción: Universidad Católica de Asunción, 1985), p. 39.

12. See Oscar Paciello, *Código penal Paraguayo y leyes complementarias actualizadas* (Asunción: Ediciones Comuneros, 1981), p. 194.

13. Ibid., p. 174.

14. See Samuel P. Huntington and Clement H. Moore, eds., *Authoritarian Politics in Modern Society: The Dynamics of Established One-Party Systems* (New York: Basic Books, 1970).

15. On the historical and ideological background of the major political parties of Paraguay, see Graziella Corvalán, "Ideologías y origen social de los grupos políticos en el Paraguay," *Revista Paraguaya de Sociología* 9 (January-April 1972): 106–18.

16. Most of the unrest during the Liberal era had its origin in the army. There were constant uprisings led by military men who wanted to achieve prominent positions. The unrest of the military finally produced the revolution of February 1936, when Colonel Franco ousted Eligio Ayala from the presidency.

17. The split divided the party between those who wanted to remain on good terms with Stroessner and those who challenged the legitimacy of the regime. The division between the Liberals and the Radical Liberals was evident

in 1973 during the Itaipú vote, when the Liberals voted with the official party and against the opposition. See Paul H. Lewis, *Paraguay under Stroessner* (Chapel Hill: University of North Carolina Press, 1980), p. 203.

18. See "Paraguayan Police Beat Exile," *New York Times*, June 25, 1986, p. A3.

19. See Antonio González, *La rebelión de Concepción* (Buenos Aires: Editorial Guarania, 1947), p. 37.

20. On the ideology of the Febrerismo, see Paul H. Lewis, *The Politics of Exile: Paraguay's Febrerista Party* (Chapel Hill: University of North Carolina Press, 1965), p. 89. Lewis shows the different tendencies within the party, concluding that the effort to react against the Liberal state did not create a socialist position, although it did manage to restore the state's supremacy within a position of extreme nationalism, possibly influenced by Nazism and fascist developments in Europe.

21. The problems of leadership within the party are discussed in Paul H. Lewis, "Leadership and Conflict within the Febrerista Party of Paraguay," *Journal of Inter-American Studies* 9 (April 1967): 283–95.

22. On the role of Febrerismo in Paraguayan politics, see Roberto Céspedes Ruffinelli, *El febrerismo: Del movimiento al partido, 1936/1951* (Asunción: Editorial Luxe, 1983); Víctor Salomoni, *Fundamentos ideológicos del Partido Revolucionario Febrerista* (Asunción: EMASA, 1981); and Juan Speratti, *Los partidos políticos: Orientaciones, esfuerzos y realidades del adoctrinamiento Febrerista* (Asunción: EMASA, 1967).

23. See Universidad Católica de Asunción, *Legislación Paraguaya* (Asunción: Facultad de Ciencias Jurídicas, 1981), p. 65.

24. The party was also internally divided between a more progressive and a more conservative faction. In the 1984 party elections, the candidate from the conservative group gained control of the party. Alfredo Rojas León indicated that the Christian Democratic party was the party of the "democratic future of Paraguay and the best guarantee against a dictatorship of the left or of the right." See Comité de Iglesias, *Apuntes Trimestrales* 8 (Asunción: Comité de Iglesias, 1984): 34.

25. An account of the activities of the Communist party in Paraguay is Reynaldo Marín, "The Masses Will Decide the Outcome of the Battle," *World Marxist Review* 18 (December 1975): 21–35. Marín was the first secretary of the Communist party in 1975, and he called for the creation of an "anti-dictatorial front . . . open to all."

26. See Asociación Nacional Republicana (Partido Colorado), Junta de Gobierno del Exilio y la Resistencia, *Declaración de principios y programa mínimo* (1973).

27. The position of Méndez Fleitas and his opinions about members of the government are clearly depicted in Epifanio Méndez Fleitas, *Diagnosis Paraguaya* (Montevideo: Editorial Prometeo, 1965).

28. The Acuerdo Nacional increased its activities as a result of the democratic processes of several southern nations, most notably Argentina. Its members received strong support from the Radical party of Argentina as well as other organizations in Venezuela and Perú.

29. See Robert C. Tucker, "Towards a Comparative Politics of Movement-Regimes," *American Political Science Review* 55 (June 1961): 285.

30. On the early history of the Colorado party and its later developments, see Paul H. Lewis, *Socialism, Liberalism and Dictatorship in Paraguay* (New York: Praeger, 1982), pp. 31–34, 54–61.

31. On the membership and role of the Junta de Gobierno of the Colorado party, see Asociación Nacional Republicana, *Acta de fundación del Partido Colorado y estatutos* (Asunción: Ed. Universo, n.d.).

32. Within the now-vast literature on the concept of totalitarianism, among the most important studies remain Carl J. Friedrich, ed., *Totalitarianism* (New York: Grosset & Dunlap, 1954); Hannah Arendt, *The Origins of Totalitarianism* (New York: World, 1958); Carl J. Friedrich and Zbigniew K. Brzezinski, *Totalitarian Dictatorship and Autocracy*, 2d ed. (New York: Praeger, 1965); Raymond Aron, *Democracy and Totalitarianism*, trans. Valence Ionescu (New York: Praeger, 1965); Paul T. Mason, *Totalitarianism: Temporary Madness or Permanent Danger?* (Boston: Heath, 1967); and Carl J. Friedrich, Michael Curtis, and Benjamin R. Barber, *Totalitarianism in Perspective: Three Views* (New York: Praeger, 1969).

33. The idea that authoritarian regimes portray institutionally oriented constraints on society is taken from Kalman H. Silvert, ed., *Essays in Understanding Latin America* (Philadelphia: Institute for the Study of Human Issues, 1977), p. 56.

34. Archbishop Aníbal Mena Porta succeeded Monsignor Juan Bogarín and had little trouble accepting the benefits of "co-optation" into the regime. The government provided him a car with a chauffeur, and Stroessner awarded him a medal in recognition of all the services that he provided for the nation.

35. Useful information about the troubled relationship between Stroessner and the church is included in Penny Lernoux, *Cry of the People* (New York: Penguin Books, 1982). She indicates that the church has struggled to provide a sense of identity to the Paraguayan poor by resorting to symbolism, as at the shrine at Caacupé (p. 379).

36. The Talavera episode was covered in several issues of the *Hispanic American Report*. However, Turner has found that some of the information contained in those issues was not correct. For a detailed explanation of the episode, see Frederick C. Turner, *Catholicism and Political Development in Latin America* (Chapel Hill: University of North Carolina Press, 1971), pp. 116–21.

37. The strong stand of the church on social issues was documented by the Conferencia Episcopal Paraguaya. The Equipo Nacional de Acción Social was in charge of organizing activities for the peasant and Indian population. See Conferencia Episcopal Paraguaya, *Tierra y sociedad: Problemática de la tierra urbana, rural e indígena en el Paraguay* (Asunción: Equipo Nacional de Pastoral de la CEP, 1984); Conferencia Episcopal Paraguaya, *Fe cristiana y compromiso social* (Asunción: EDIPAR, 1984); and in issues of *Sendero*, the church's newspaper.

38. The transition from Monsignor Mena Porta to Monsignor Ismael Blás Rolón Silvero was not a smooth one. Even under the guidance of Mena Porta, the church had polarized itself vis-à-vis the government. On December 8, 1969,

priests refused to march to the shrine of Caacupé and organized a silent march instead. The reaction of Stroessner forced Mena Porta out. The government attempted to push the Vatican into appointing a priest of Stroessner's liking, but the Holy See refused to cooperate. Rolón Silvero had been a critic while he was a bishop of Villarica, but he was the most "reasonable" choice, given the circumstances. See Lewis, *Paraguay under Stroessner,* p. 194.

39. Father Oliva was expelled in 1969 after he preached against social injustice in Asunción. See "It Is Calumny," *LADOC* 5 (August 1970): 1. There are also well-documented expulsions of Catholic priests from Paraguay. On February 22, 1972, Father Vicente Barreto was seized and left in Posadas, Argentina, with the warning that he would be shot on sight if he attempted to return to Paraguay. Similarly, on May 5, 1972, Father José Caravias was abducted from his post in the countryside and left behind in Clorinda, on the Argentine side. See "Father Caravias Tells of His Deportation," *LADOC* 2 (June 1972): 38a.

40. The letter is reproduced in "Another Victim of Violence," *LADOC* 70 (September-October 1976): 14–15.

41. See Confederación Paraguaya de Trabajadores en el Exilio, *Los trabajadores Paraguayos frente a la tiranía de Stroessner* (Buenos Aires, 1975); and Confederación Paraguaya de Trabajadores en el Exilio, *Los trabajadores Paraguayos frente a la tiranía de Stroessner* (Buenos Aires, 1983).

42. Mark Münzel, "The Aché Indians: Genocide in Paraguay," IWGWIA Document No. 11 (Copenhagen, 1973).

43. See Richard Arens, ed., *Genocide in Paraguay* (Philadelphia: Temple University Press, 1976), p. 20.

44. See Norman Lewis, "The Camp at Cecilio Baez," in *Genocide in Paraguay,* ed. Richard Arens (Philadelphia: Temple University Press, 1976), p. 58.

45. On the role of the different guerrilla movements, see Lewis, *Paraguay under Stroessner,* p. 180.

46. See Amnesty International, *Prison Conditions in Paraguay: Conditions for Political Prisoners; A Factual Report* (London: Amnesty International, 1966).

47. See Amnesty International, *Report on Torture* (New York: Noonday, 1973), p. 216.

48. Human rights in Paraguay were first discussed during the 3d session of the Inter-American Commission on Human Rights, at the end of 1961. A second report was brought for consideration at its 9th session, in October 1964, which resulted in a visit by leaders of the commission to Paraguay during August of 1965. At its 30th session, the commission adopted a resolution requesting information on the whereabouts of several political figures in Paraguay. During the 31st, 36th, and 38th sessions, the commission requested the government of Paraguay to report on particular abuses of human rights. Receiving no answer to the several requests, the commission concluded the violations to be confirmed. At the 40th session the commission decided to send an investigative team to Paraguay to monitor developments.

49. Organization of American States, *Report of the Situation of Human Rights in Paraguay* (Washington, D.C.: Inter-American Commission on Human Rights, 1978), p. 86.

50. See U.S. House of Representatives, Committee on International Relations, Subcommittee on International Organizations, *Human Rights in Uruguay and Paraguay* (Washington, D.C.: Government Printing Office, 1976), p. 31.

51. For a detailed account of the case, see Richard Pierre Claude, "The Case of Joelito Filartiga and the Clinic of Hope," *Human Rights Quarterly* 5 (1983): 275.

52. The U.S. media played an important role in making the Filartiga case known to the world. See, for example, Richard Alan White, "In New York a Key Paraguayan Murder Suspect Faces U.S. Justice," *Los Angeles Times*, April 15, 1979, part 5, p. 3; Lee Lescaze, "Paraguayan Police Figure Is Arrested in New York," *Washington Post*, April 5, 1979, p. A17; and Selwyn Raab, "Paraguayan Alien Tied to Murders in Native Land," *New York Times*, May 15, 1979, p. B4.

53. For the decision of the trial, see *Filartiga v. Peña-Irala*, 630 F.2d 876 (2d Cir. 1980). The case helped establish a precedent that abusers of internationally recognized human rights who may find themselves in the United States can be tried for damages by former hostages. The court ruled that the Filartiga family was entitled to $10.4 million in damages. However, in January of 1984, the Supreme Court in Paraguay dismissed the case presented by Dr. Filartiga, awarding substantial damages to the former inspector general of Asunción, Américo Peña-Irala.

Economic Development and the Pattern of Co-optation

6 With control mechanisms limiting the extent of political participation, most authoritarian regimes center their policy efforts on the economy. In the past autocrats have increased their legitimacy by promoting strong national economies. Brazil after 1964 provides a good example of policies set up during a period of authoritarian rule that helped the country to achieve great increases in economic growth, albeit at the expense of a more skewed distribution of income. In other Latin American countries, notably Argentina between 1976 and 1984, the fates of authoritarian governments were sealed when economic policies resulted in increased instability, social unrest, and political alienation. In Paraguay during the Stroessner era, economic achievements became fundamental to the consolidation of the regime.

Economic policies are very important to the life of authoritarian regimes, and the reasons for this are highly revealing. First, most such regimes comprise military officers who, at least in Latin America, have a solid technical education. They tend to understand social and political problems purely in technical terms. They see economics as a relatively nonpolitical area wherein discussions of ideology, policies, and alternatives are not necessary. When they draw policymakers from the civilian sector, they tend to look to the technocracy, professionals with high levels of expertise in their respective fields. As a result, military officers trust and respect economists more than they do political scientists, sociologists, and other social scientists.

A second reason that economic policy is important to authoritarian regimes is that autocrats can exercise full control over the economic system without worrying about political implications. In societies that are making significant efforts to develop and modernize, only a few planners can understand the details of national economic policies. Everyday citizens are removed from the technicalities of economic decisions, and this reinforces the regime's belief that it can make such decisions based on its own interests and objectives. In societies where subsistence is difficult, the citizenry is preoccupied with assuring its own livelihood.

Third, economic policy receives attention in authoritarian regimes because of the reduced political expectations of the population. A characteristic of authoritarian regimes is low political participation. When people recognize that they are to receive few political benefits in terms of institutional gains, coalitions, party organization, or interest group formation, their expectations turn to economic issues. The quality of the leadership furnished by the regime is then defined in terms of its economic performance. A high standard of living, low unemployment, low inflation, and availability of government support services are seen as adequate substitutes for increased political participation and the provision of political space for different groups.

The fourth reason that economic policy is important to the life of an authoritarian regime is that, when successful, it yields a sense of well-being and accomplishment—albeit false—to both the citizenry and the leadership. The best way to keep a country together is by seeing to the economic needs of its people. Contemporary autocrats in Latin America are aware that nothing is a stronger argument in their favor than a considerably improved economy. When the stakes are so high, they attempt to make economic policy the cornerstone of their governance.

The case of Paraguay is useful in highlighting the ways in which economic decisions can shape political developments. Landlocked and strikingly poor, Paraguay in the 1950s impressed visitors with its relative tranquillity, the quality of its people, and its beauty. Outsiders called it a "heaven on earth" even in the absence of modern facilities and conveniences. But nature's gifts and its human assets did not relieve Paraguay from crushing poverty and grim economic prospects.

Through shrewd political maneuvering, President Stroessner delivered Paraguay from the economic ostracism it once suffered. Surely, the Paraguay of today is markedly different from the Paraguay that appealed to visitors three decades ago. Per capita income is much higher, consumption has increased, and a general sense of well-being compels Paraguayans to believe that the days of debilitating poverty are over. Yet, a sense of uneasiness is present within many areas of the country. The economic boom of the 1970s gave way to uncertainty in the 1980s as Paraguay prepared to usher in the post-Stroessner era.

Economic development policies were the cornerstone of the Stroessner dictatorship, which proudly displayed its economic achievements as evidence of what political stability can bring. And, it must be conceded that impressive economic transformations took place subsequent to the inauguration of Stroessner in 1954. We cannot evaluate the economic policies solely in terms of the purple prose of his administration, however.

The complexities of the Paraguayan case force a more complete analysis of the evidence, especially because it is through the well-lubricated economic machinery that the support for authoritarian institutions was built and sustained. The economic co-optation of those who could have challenged the regime from above and from below has been another trademark of Stroessner's ability to manipulate his country's destiny.[1]

The Structure of the Paraguayan Economy

The structure of the Paraguayan economy has been affected since independence by the country's mediterranean situation. The colonial history of Paraguay indicated no great wealth waiting to be extracted. After a series of territorial wars, Paraguay's boundaries were delineated by its inability to obtain access to the Atlantic or Pacific. Landlocked and unable to expand its commercial relations with the major centers of international trade, Paraguay continued in its agricultural production.[2]

The economy suffered during confrontations with neighboring countries over territory. The Triple Alliance War devastated Paraguay in terms of economic and human resources. Although accounts vary, the decrease in males was substantial. The country was not stable enough to foster business, although a few ranchers managed to prosper. The nation was dependent on agriculture for a way out of its distress.[3] The 1930s territorial dispute with Bolivia over the Chaco, although ending in victory dissipated more of Paraguay's meager resources. With roughly 36,000 dead and more than $125 million spent, Paraguay was again in shambles. Prior to the Chaco War, Paraguay had managed under the guidance of Eligio Ayala to increase its holdings of foreign exchange by expanding its sales of yerba mate and leather abroad. The Ayala administration provided better military resources during the conflict with Bolivia, but its effort to change the Paraguayan productive structure was unavailing.[4]

Internal disputes also affected the performance of the economy. The civil war of 1947, for example, caused further instability and curtailed possibilities for additional growth. Between 1938 and 1946 the GDP had grown at an average rate of about 3.5 percent; between 1947 and 1954 growth was 0.8 percent.[5] With population rising at about 2.7 percent annually, the economy was barely keeping pace. External demand for Paraguayan products fluctuated, and many Paraguayans chose to emigrate. With a large balance of payments deficit, efforts to revive the economy by increasing the money supply backfired, spurring inflation on to high levels.

The Stroessner administration inherited a nation tragically affected by its geographical location, its foreign wars, and its economic misman-agement. Since independence, Paraguayans had feared absorption by their neighbors, and they had been unable to break out of their isolation and expand economically. But, the leadership of Stroessner gave Paraguay the chance to relieve its oppressive poverty by resorting to a carefully planned economic development policy that changed the course of the country's future.

After assuming power in 1954, Stroessner promptly signed an agreement with the International Monetary Fund, and instituted a stabilization plan to bring inflation down, increase the volume and diversity of exports, and attract foreign investment. By limiting the chances for domestic revolt, Stroessner imposed his austerity measures without occasioning much resistance from the population. He only eliminated the challenge presented by the democratic wing of the Colorado party, and expelled Epifanio Méndez Fleitas from the leadership of the Central Bank.

The economy picked up quickly. Foreign investment rose, exports increased, and inflation lessened. At the same time Stroessner committed himself to a centrally planned economy with strong state intervention. The development policy of his administration became the hallmark of his success. Building on basic characteristics of the Paraguayan economy, Stroessner stressed three key sectors of the economy: agriculture, foreign trade, and infrastructure. Efforts in these areas, together with a tight foreign exchange policy, brightened Paraguay's prospects.

The Agricultural Sector

Paraguay has always been an agricultural nation. Its soil and climate have reinforced a predisposition of Paraguayans to make their living from the land. The agricultural sector was unusual in several ways. First, there was virtually no large-scale production, due to the size of most holdings and the lack of technology. Second, the work force was highly mobile; internal migration is of the rural-rural type, a situation quite different from that of the other Latin American nations.

The first element to consider in discussing the character of Paraguayan agriculture is the disparity between the eastern and western regions. The western region, or the Paraguayan Chaco, extends to the boundary with Bolivia; it is isolated and there is little reason to use land for agricultural purposes. The eastern region is the area of the *minifundio;* holdings are relatively small but of excellent quality for agricultural purposes. Population distribution reflects the scarcity of infrastructure in the western section and the nature of the land, contributing to the difference between regions.[6]

The eastern region comprises 159,827 square kilometers, and its population increased from 1,274,175 in 1950 to 2,969,170 in 1982. The western region comprises 246,925 square kilometers but its population has risen negligibly, from 54,277 in 1950 to 56,995 in 1982. The western region, with about 60 percent of the total area of Paraguay, has only about 1.8 percent of the total population, proof of the inhospitable environment of the Chaco. In the eastern region, the situation is the reverse: 40 percent of the country's area is inhabited by more than 98 percent of the population.[7]

The disparities between regions have important implications for agricultural policy. Land under cultivation is mostly located in the eastern region, whereas forests constitute most of the western region. In 1962 about 60 percent of Paraguay was forested; about 35 percent was utilized mainly for livestock; and 2.1 percent was farmed for crops. Understandably, then, the pressure on the agricultural sector was rather intense when the Technical Secretariat for Planning elaborated its first Social and Economic Development Plan for the 1965–1966 period.[8]

Traditionally, Paraguay has been an important producer of field crops and tree crops. Field crops are mostly mandioca, sugar cane, beans, peas, rice, sweet potatoes, onions, potatoes, peanuts, wheat, and alfalfa, which for the most part are consumed internally. Among field crops, cotton and tobacco are produced for export. Tree crops are citrus fruits, yerba, bananas, oilseeds, and coffee; most of these are exported.

One of the problems confronting the Stroessner administration was relatively low crop yields per hectare, which generally remained relatively constant between the Agricultural Census of 1942 and the Sample Agricultural and Livestock Census of 1960. Of nineteen products, only sugar cane and tung registered sharp increases during this eighteen-year period; others remained stable or even decreased.[9] Even so, the agricultural sector's output made Paraguay self-sufficient in agriculture. The Stroessner administration encouraged production through a land reform program and gave additional incentives to farmers who planted particular crops. Although the results of the land reform program were mixed, for some time Stroessner kept the peasants quiet and allowed them to practice subsistence agriculture on their own plots.

The most remarkable characteristic of the agricultural sector is its pattern of landholding, a pattern that created substantial difficulties. For the most part, production occurs on family units that are too small to be economically feasible as independent units. Most families practice subsistence agriculture, remaining at low income levels because of poor productivity. The agricultural sector has traditionally employed most of the labor force, but a large proportion of these workers are either unemployed or underemployed.[10] The pattern of landholding has affected the distribution of population as well. Most Latin American countries have large urban populations, but Paraguay has remained virtually rural. Between the censuses of 1960 and 1982, the urban proportion of the population stayed the same. The process of rural-rural migration reinforced the character of Paraguayan society by discouraging people from looking for employment in the cities.[11]

Agriculture, then, was the key sector in the Paraguayan economic structure, but it was based on self-sufficient household units that mainly produced for themselves; only a few large agricultural enterprises utilized modern technology, most of them owned by foreigners. Within this dichotomy, the economic policy of the Stroessner regime attempted to increase the amount of land under cultivation and raise production levels in crops that carried high prices in the international market.

The Industrial Sector

Several elements have conditioned the evolution of industrial development in Paraguay. Paraguay is far from major world markets. More important, the size of the domestic market has not occasioned enough demand to support a consequential industrialization program. And until two decades ago, Paraguay lacked the infrastructure precedential to industrial development. Notwithstanding these limitations, the economy has made progress toward industrialization.[12]

Relevant data obtained in the early 1960s indicated that Paraguayan industry comprised three kinds of manufacturing systems: rural artisans, urban artisans, and mechanized factory production. The first two catered to the lower-income brackets, and their production was accomplished in family-owned shops with very simple tools. The distinction between the more mechanized and the family-oriented types of manufacturing created a problem in the industrial sector that has remained constant: there are few interrelations among manufacturing facilities in Paraguay.

Of all industrial establishments recorded in 1963, 84.5 percent were individually owned, and 63 percent had only two to four employees. Tooling was certainly a problem, for 68.7 percent of the installed shops had no access to mechanical power. The more advanced enterprises controlled most of the sector: 3 percent of the industrial enterprises accounted for 74.9 percent of total output and for 70.5 percent of the value added in manufacturing. Industries were confined to particular areas, and 57.4 percent of the shops were located in urban areas. Corporations were for the most part located in and around Asunción.[13]

Industrial production in Paraguay was not very diverse. Only five major kinds of products were manufactured. Food products accounted for 42 percent of the total, with most of the plants involving meat processing, sugar production, flour milling, and baking. Chemicals accounted for 12.2 percent, producing mainly industrial oils and animal fats. Textiles accounted for 11.5 percent, producing yarns, fabrics, and finished products. Electric power production accounted for some 6 percent. Beverages accounted for 5.3 percent, primarily alcoholic beverages and beer.

The country has limited mineral resources. Most mineral production is centered on clay, related products, and limestone for the production of cement, talc, and glass sand. There are some small iron deposits, and a very little manganese, copper, and mica or beryl. Petroleum reserves are scarce, and except for wood and water, few energy sources are readily available. Although some mining looked promising in 1960, the contribution of that sector to the development of a strong industrial base was marginal at best.

With a scanty resource endowment and an inability to compete in international markets, the economy of Paraguay faced a stiff fight against underdevelopment. Furthermore, its human capital was more dispersed than that of other nations—such as Taiwan, Singapore, or the Republic of Korea—that were to grow rapidly in per capita income from the 1960s to the 1980s. In 1960 most of the Paraguayan population lived in rural areas, had very low incomes, and generated little domestic demand. With few industrial products produced domestically, Paraguay was always at the mercy of its dominant neighbors. The dynamic trade between Brazil, Argentina, and Paraguay fostered the belief that there was no reason to embark on industrialization at home.

Yet another variable affecting industrialization was government policy. The country has remained largely agricultural due in part to decisions made by the authorities. With little industrialization, the Stroessner regime did not face the rise of an industrial working class that could have made demands of the government. Making little effort to industrialize, Stroessner avoided institutionalized unions, a major source of potential political conflict. The regime controlled the small unions that emerged as a result of the little industrialization it did promote. The Executive Board of the Confederación Paraguaya de Trabajadores (CPT) was closely monitored to assure the election of pro-Stroessner men. The CPT came under the government's wing in 1958, when it organized a nationwide strike for a wage increase. One year later, on April 13, 1959, the leaders of the CPT founded the Confederación Paraguaya de Trabajadores en el Exilio, but they were not able to affect events or policies undertaken by the regime.

Infrastructure

Because infrastructure is basic to development of an integrated economy, it is normally one of the first priorities of policymakers in developing countries. For Paraguay, this problem has had special implications because the nation is landlocked. Roads and transportation facilities are vital to the country's integration into the regional economic system of the Plata region and its trade with Brazil and Bolivia. Paraguay is blessed in this respect with a very useful system of internal navigation, one that acts as a channel for economic communication. The population first settled along river banks, and it was not until the advent of a railroad in 1861 that people began to migrate to other parts of the country. In 1960 the only existing infrastructure was composed of railroads, a few roads, and the rivers.[14]

Rail communication had grown up with the help of the British at the end of the nineteenth century. By 1961, the major competition was between automotive and railway transportation. After 1950 the ability of the railroad system to meet Paraguay's transportation needs diminished. The number of passengers carried in 1950 was five times that in 1965, and the amount of tonnage transported per kilometer dropped by about 50 percent in the same period. Responsibility for moving people and goods shifted to automobiles and trucks, especially once roads reached towns on the frontier with Brazil. Joseph Pincus notes that beyond the decrease in passengers serviced, the railroad system operated at a loss from 1958 to 1965. Given the increased use of paved roads, especially in the eastern region, the railway system was already obsolescent more than two decades earlier.

Creation of a road network was not very difficult in Paraguay due to the gentle nature of the terrain. Costs were high, however, because of elevated prices for asphalt and petroleum, and the expense of construction in the rainy climate. Nonetheless, Stroessner built roads: "all-weather" roads in 1955 measured only 711 miles; in 1960, 1,330 miles; and in 1966, 3,000 miles. Most roads go to the Brazilian border, and the Trans-Chaco Highway extends almost 500 miles into the western region to neighboring Bolivia. The network was one of the most publicized accomplishments of the regime.

Telecommunications were not extensive when Stroessner came to power. The census of 1966 indicated only 149 offices of the Administración Nacional de Telecomunicaciones, with a total of 9,896 subscribers—8,456 in Asunción and 1,440 in the interior. Paraguay received a low-cost loan from the United States in 1961 to modernize the system, and by November of 1965 the quality and range of services offered by the telephone company had improved considerably.[15]

The infrastructure that Stroessner inherited was certainly meager in relation to the needs of a nation striving to overcome underdevelopment, but his regime created several National Development Plans that provided the bases for the economic transformation that the country witnessed in the following three decades. The professed motive for economic development was to raise the standard of living; the unspoken motive was to win political acquiescence. If the performance of the Paraguayan economy was remarkable, so was its serving as recompense for the political price paid by the people. The co-optation scheme worked to the advantage of the administration, which convinced most Paraguayans of its superior leadership.

The Politics of Development Planning

Creation of the Technical Secretariat of Planning put in motion a new process of economic policy-making in Paraguay. The goal was to achieve social and economic modernization through development policies based on national resources. The strategy called for expansion of the agricultural sector, more hydroelectric energy production and the maintenance of fixed rates for the *guaraní* against the U.S. dollar.[16]

The three-pronged approach was successful in helping the country to achieve high rates of economic growth. When viewed from a more global perspective, however, the impressive performance of the economy did not change its fundamental nature. Income distribution did not improve, and pervasive poverty remained an intractable problem. After a dynamic decade, the economy entered the 1980s showing signs of strain. The achievements of the 1970s sprang from an economy that had been flooded with outsize investment and that had not incorporated structural changes during its expansion. The recessions of 1982 and 1984 clearly indicated that, although the economy had theretofore responded to external stimuli, it remained unable to generate stability if left susceptible to internal market conditions.[17]

The New Role of Agriculture

The agricultural sector was the most important area subject to the policy-making of the Technical Secretariat of Planning. The Institute for Rural Welfare (IBR) was created in 1963 as part of the Agrarian Statute (Estatuto Agrario). Its main purpose was to bring about land reform. Extensive titling efforts delivered lands to individual families who used the acreage for their own consumption. Agricultural policy became geared to helping the economy grow and to maintaining the structural configuration of the agricultural sector. The IBR created enough programs for subsistence farmers so that a process of rural-urban migration never developed. Titling efforts were quite impressive. In the Agrarian Census of 1956 owners accounted for only 36 percent of the total, with 49 percent of farmers occupying land, but in the Agrarian Survey of 1977 the proportion of owners was 69 percent and that of occupants 20 percent. The number of renters (or lessees) remained stable during this period at about 12 percent.[18] With larger political considerations directing the efforts, the administration then concentrated on improving production in agriculture.

Land redistribution has followed several colonizing vectors that departed from Asunción toward the north, the east, and the west. Of the 42,000 families that the IBR assisted between 1960 and 1973, about 30 percent settled in the eastern region. The strong pole of development established in the eastern region was also in line with the several hydroelectric projects being constructed along the Paraná and Paraguay rivers. Families had improved their economic situation because of the colonization, and their salaries had increased about threefold to tenfold compared with those of their original residence.[19]

The impact of resettlement on agricultural production was important because the eastern region contains the most suitable soil for agricultural activities.[20] Between 1971 and 1975, production rose for corn, manioc, beans, cotton, soybeans, rice, and tobacco, and decreased only for wheat. In several cases, harvests were staggering: soybeans jumped from 75,253 tons in 1971 to 220,086 tons in 1975; cotton from 17,461 to 99,615. Paraguayans pushed exports of their key agricultural products that were doing well on the international market. The export price of soybeans, for example, increased 71.7 percent from 1970 to 1974. Expanded production fortuitously matched very favorable market conditions.[21]

It was not the Paraguayans, however, who benefited the most from these circumstances. The eastern border area was colonized by a large number of Brazilian farmers. R. Andrew Nickson advances several reasons for the expansion of the Brazilian presence. One was the neglect of the area in the Paraguayan economy before the 1960s. In 1962, the Eastern Border Region (comprising the states of Amambay, Canendiyú, and Alto Paraná) was home to only 3.2 percent of the national population. The influx of Brazilians was influenced by the fact that Brazilians could sell their holdings in Brazil high and buy land in Paraguay low.

Nickson also points out that lower taxation and greater credit opportunities lured Brazilians to the eastern region. The soybeans grown there were not taxed upon exportation, and credit conditions were favorable due to help from international agencies. In sum, profits could be maximized. Nickson notes, too, that the IBR sold land to members of the Paraguayan armed forces and the Colorado party from 1967 to 1977 at official prices, that is, below market level. The buyers, in turn, sold the land to real estate firms in São Paulo and Curitiba, Brazil.[22]

The colonization programs and the expansion of Brazilians into the region divided the agricultural sector into two well-defined groups: commercial producers and farming families. The family units resulted principally from the IBR colonization effort. However, the IBR programs provided very small plots that sometimes were even subdivided by recipient families. The commercial producers, mostly Brazilians, owned larger plots of land and were able to improve productivity through mechanization. Even though new land was cleared and new roads were opened, small Paraguayan farmers did not receive adequate support from the government. Insufficient credit, too few distribution facilities, and lack of mechanization, meant that the goal of raising rural family income could not be reached.

The Hydroelectric Potential

The second reason that the Paraguayan economy achieved impressive records of growth in the 1970s was the large hydroelectric projects completed in partnership with neighboring countries, part of the effort of the Stroessner regime to capitalize on the hydroelectric potential of the region. Several small dams were put up along the Paraná River on the eastern border, but the most important was the Itaipú dam, a joint venture with Brazil, and the Yacyretá dam, currently being built with Argentina.[23]

The economic and social impact of the construction effort was substantial and complex. Paraguay stood to gain in the short and in the long term. It immediately received large benefits without investment of its own funds. The financing came from external sources guaranteed by the Brazilian and Argentine governments, and Paraguay received in compensation approximately half of the energy produced. Given the limited energy needs for its own industrial development, by the mid-1990s Paraguay will be the largest hydroelectric energy exporter in the world.[24]

Socially, the boost to the construction industry created a growth pole around Ciudad Presidente Stroessner in the eastern state of Alto Paraná. The urbanization was of considerable magnitude, and a new web of services was created. About $1 billion had gone into the Itaipú dam by the end of 1977, about 25 percent of which was spent on the Paraguayan side of the border. The construction contract was awarded to a consortium of Brazilian and Paraguayan firms, but Paraguayan subcontractors were also actively involved. The large influx of foreign exchange allowed the banking system enough liquidity to increase available credit significantly and to discourage an upward trend in the rate of exchange.

Unfortunately, the Paraguayan manufacturing sector could not meet the demand generated by the project. Domestic production of materials required did not increase because of the inability of the binational commissions to assure to domestic industries a consistent demand. To illustrate, Paraguay was forced to import cement in 1977. There were no efforts to materialize the externalities of the projects, and the Paraguayan economic elite channeled funds into areas such as real estate that did not contribute to major economic improvements.[25]

Another area where the Paraguayans did not meet the challenge of the Itaipú dam was labor. With each side expecting to contribute about half the total manpower, Brazilians dominated in the higher echelons. At the peak of construction in 1978, workers numbered more than 31,000, and only 43 percent were Paraguayans. Some 57 percent of the Paraguayans were in the lowest skill category, and they were mostly displaced urban workers and a few Paraguayan emigrants resident in Argentina who had returned to take advantage of the job availability. Still, the challenge for the Paraguayan economy was to reabsorb the newly trained workers because after completion of the project, the labor requirements of Itaipú were sharply reduced.[26]

As a result, the construction of Itaipú generated an outsize demand that was unrealistic, given the conditions of the economy. With the availability of credit and the abundance of foreign exchange, Paraguay was flooded with foreign goods. As Baer and Birch indicate, the lack of domestic production met by foreign imports, and the excessive liquidity placed pressures on the economy such that inflation finally reached 28.2 percent in 1979. Once the construction of Itaipú slowed, the Paraguayan economy took a serious downturn, showing important signs of strain and suffering a series of minirecessions.

Although it is easy to see the benefits that Itaipú wrought for the economy of Paraguay, the treaty with Brazil brought considerable political controversy. Members of the opposition alleged that the conditions under which the partnership had been conceived were more favorable to Brazil. Heated debate in the Senate raised crucial points concerning the price to be paid by Brazil for the unused Paraguayan energy and the length of time during which the Paraguayans would be required to turn over excess energy to the Brazilians. The more radical groups saw construction of the dam as part of Brazilian expansionism and as an attempt to incorporate Paraguay into the international capitalist economy.[27] Others saw a potential geopolitical conflict in the making: Paraguayan nationalism would be hurt by excessive transfer of benefits from the Paraguayan to the Brazilian side.[28]

The old debate continues today at a reduced level of passion, but contemporary critics argue that Paraguay will have excess hydroelectric energy unless it embarks on energy-intensive industrialization. A study conducted by a German group concluded that there are several industries, such as construction products and steel products, where the utilization of low-cost hydroelectric energy would make international competition possible. The Stroessner regime did not decide to implement an industrialization plan, however, probably because of the political price that it perceived it might have to pay in urban strife for doing so. The resulting situation is enigmatic: Will Paraguay be able to cash in more fully on the benefits of the dam projects and thus provide for expanded public investment and a higher standard of living?[29]

Financial Policy and Development

One of the cornerstones of the Stroessner regime's economic performance was its monetary and fiscal policy. After a long period of financial instability and a constant need to devalue the guaraní, the government suggested to the Central Bank that a long-run fiscal plan be created to curtail inflationary pressures. The program was initiated in August of 1957, and it remained a key element in the development process.

The effort came as a response to the severe crisis that had affected Paraguay in the period between 1946 and 1956. The crisis originated in a combination of financial policies orchestrated by the Central Bank. One was the unlimited increase in the money supply; the circulation of guaraní had increased from 65 million in 1946 to about 1,656 million in 1955. The excess money supply created pressures for the Central Bank to offer extensive credit. Another policy regarded the use of multiple exchange rates to subsidize budget deficits. These policies plunged the economy into turmoil as the cost of living rose at an annual rate of 51 percent between 1950 and 1955 and the guaraní decreased in value at an annual rate of 87 percent.[30]

The reform reversed the direction in which the Paraguayan economy was moving. It was successful in achieving its objectives: to halt inflation, to increase exports, to raise import capacity, and to strengthen the economy. Abandoning multiple exchange rates and exchange rate controls, the bank instituted a single exchange rate. Although the rate was assumed to fluctuate freely, the Central Bank intervened in the market after October 1960 to maintain the rate at 126 guaraní to the U.S. dollar. The stability of the foreign exchange market was an important part of the successful development pattern followed in the 1960s and 1970s. Although domestic price levels remained unchanged, the fixed exchange policy was still subject to pressure from exchange rates in neighboring countries. Because of the amount of foreign trade and the high levels of inflation recorded in Argentina and Brazil, Paraguay suffered some regional economic instability despite its own monetary policy.

Until the 1970s, Paraguay continued to abide by its fixed exchange rate, which in reality was undervalued, given the important fluctuations taking place in the region. The rate made exports more competitive, and also increased the cost of imports. When in the early 1970s the currencies of neighboring countries became even more undervalued, the Paraguayan situation changed to one of overvaluation, making imports cheaper and exports more difficult. Wisely, however, Paraguay had expanded its agricultural base and concentrated on exports of products that recorded substantial increases in price worldwide. Income from exports rose during the 1970s, thereby helping to offset the cost of overvaluing the currency.

A dramatic rise in imports also took place, although the greatest growth occurred in the undeclared trade. Contraband—long a key sector of the Paraguayan economy— became much more widespread, partially because of the relatively low cost of foreign goods and because of the demand during construction of the Itaipú dam. As the government heavily burdened the import-export trade with tariffs, permits, and other bureaucratic red tape, contraband activities flourished.

The Pattern of Co-optation

With an expanding economy and better chances for using resources, the government converted its economic gains into political benefits. The co-optation scheme created by the Stroessner administration achieved several goals concurrently. One was to keep the military at bay, without fostering challenging attitudes in the ranks. Another was to provide a sense of well-being to the middle class by incorporating several thousands of its members into government positions in and around Asunción. The third was to relax the pressure on the lower classes by institutionalizing the transfer of land ownership to rural families and by accepting the existence of a large informal sector within the urban economy. All of these policies taken together created the impression that the government was fair and that options for improvement were plentiful.

Co-optation from Above

Potential challengers to the system were co-opted by being given some of the benefits that the regime created. The most important co-optation took place at the top; military officers became heavily involved in the thriving contraband trade. By now, it is common knowledge in Paraguay and elsewhere that illegal trade went well beyond what could be carried out merely by the poor families who reside along the border. Its type, scope, and amount necessitated the conclusion that it took place with strong support from the Stroessner regime.

The Paraguayan military maintained important links to the financial and economic community. In many respects, a convergence of interests produced a decrease of interelite conflict and therefore served as a foundation for the stability of the regime. President Stroessner himself acknowledged that many military men devoted themselves to other activities, which, although legal, were quite outside their purview. The officers' ability to receive economic benefits from two different sources certainly diminished their desire to become involved in politics. They lived beyond their military means, certainly not in congruence with the simple lifestyles of most of Paraguayan society. As a U.S. military officer who had spent years in Paraguay pointed out, the military in Paraguay was a profit-making institution. Low-ranking officers also pursued activities that supplemented their incomes, sometimes even on the bases.

Paraguay is a hub of the regional undeclared trade. In the international web of illegal commerce, it stands at the center of Latin American contraband activities. This is in part due to strategic location, size of the country, and characteristics of its borders, as well as, of course, to the important institutional support that the Stroessner regime accorded the trade. With Argentina and Brazil stumbling through years of high inflation, recessions, and inadequate production, Paraguay has become a paradise for interested buyers from neighboring nations.

The pattern of smuggling within Paraguay is consistent with the premises under which illegal trade prospers worldwide. In an excellent review article, Jorge Domínguez argues that Paraguay fits the classification of intermediary smuggling, the benefits of which are clearly seen in the balance of payments. Paraguay levies a rather insignificant "in-transit" tax on goods that are to be traded with other countries in the region, a tax that is well below the protectionist measures instituted by those countries. The large amount of U.S. cigarettes smuggled into Paraguay illustrates the case.[31]

Two additional types of smuggling operations also take place in Paraguay. One concerns goods brought into the country for internal consumption; the other, drugs. In the first case, the merchandise is geared to small consumers. The smugglers pay no duties on these products, and because protection of the contraband trade is such an important priority, the legal duties on them are kept exceedingly high so that honest competition cannot prosper.

Evidence of the regime's involvement in contraband is hard come by. Around Asunción, much of the information that circulates is in the form of common knowledge. One can ask any Paraguayan citizen about the role of smuggling, and he or she will normally have a number of examples at hand. There is, however, a case in which the involvement of the Paraguayan officials was unquestioned. A notorious Frenchman, André Ricord, masterminded an organization to bring heroin and cocaine into the United States from Latin America. His base of operations was Paraguay, and he was under the tutelage of high-ranking officials of the military.[32] One of the officers involved in the drug traffic scheme was Stroessner's successor, General Andrés Rodríguez. Accounts indicate that he rented out his ranch for use as an airstrip. The case was closed by U.S. authorities only when extradition of the leader of the ring was linked to further U.S. military and economic aid in 1972. Ricord was convicted in a federal court in New York City although he was subsequently released from U.S. prison.

Evidence of the magnitude of the smuggling is also quite revealing. No analysis of the economy can omit the external sector, and even Paraguayan analysts feel compelled to include a category for undeclared trade. Juan Carlos Herken concludes, for example, that the amount of undeclared trade has been far greater than that calculated by the World Bank and the International Monetary Fund.[33] He provides a useful picture: undeclared imports increased from $30 million in 1972 to an estimated $170 million in 1981, and exports from $22 million to about $75 million in the same period. These data underscore a very important point: such smuggling simply could not exist without strong institutional support. The small-time smugglers who bring in illegal goods daily have such limited means that, acting alone, they could not possibly mount such operations.[34]

The data also indicate that at the same time that the Stroessner regime was consolidating itself, smuggling was increasing. With such large profits to be realized—cigarettes and Scotch were real moneymakers—no member of the military would have ever entertained the thought of challenging the regime. At the same time, the government's collusion in the military's off-the-books schemes required it to wink at the smuggling of the lower sectors as well.

The Co-optation of the Middle Sectors

Co-optation also worked at the level of the ordinary citizen. The strongest efforts of the Stroessner regime were, perhaps, geared toward incorporating the middle class. In this respect, the activities of neighborhood organizations were important because they conveyed the range of options open to the general public through membership or nonmembership in the official party. The middle class in Paraguay, the shopkeepers, wage earners, and small professionals, came to value the stability of the regime and its promotion of sound economic policies. Members of the business class supported the regime because of the better economic situation that allowed them to increase their incomes.

Stroessner's concern for the middle class was actualized especially in the creation of public jobs. Many members of this class saw the opportunity to work for the government as a sign of the new order emerging in

Paraguay because of Stroessner's policies. A pattern of patron-client relationships evolved around the official party, and membership in the Asociación Nacional Republicana (Colorado party) became a prerequisite for a government job, a teaching position, and other government work. Masked by the expansion of the economy, the public sector offered some people an opportunity to increase their standard of living and to learn of the benefits associated with the regime.

Changes in the labor force reveal the extent to which the government absorbed the middle class. José Nicolás Morínigo's analysis suggests that the increase in services affected all government operational units. Between 1962 and 1972, the service sector registered an annual growth rate of 3.7 percent, and by 1972 was 16.9 percent of the total labor force. Morínigo suggests that the increase is due to the larger work force employed by the government.[35] Employment in the government sector increased from 20,416 in 1972 to 52,240 in 1982. This is the greatest increase in any of the industries constituting the service sector.[36]

The creation of employment opportunities in the urban service sector obviously won over to the Stroessner regime many people from within the middle class. The emergence of urban white-collar workers provided the regime with widespread middle-class backing. Developing countries trying to escape structural problems of underdevelopment see employment opportunities as of paramount importance. Even for persons who do not enter the public employ, the expansion of other service industries furnishes additional job slots. The ability of an administration to open up employment within the government sector and elsewhere frequently translates into political support for its policies. This was certainly the case in Paraguay during the Stroessner era.

Co-optation from Below

The lower class was the least fortunate under the Stroessner regime. The distribution of the new wealth did not in any sense eliminate poverty, and members of the working class had little wealth and little political power. They were unable to unionize, and there were few industrial jobs. Co-opting the lower class seemed less urgent to the regime than co-opting those who enjoyed more political power through their organized efforts. Co-optation was directed to groups that were potential challengers to the regime, and the lower class was not such.

With few political resources and low mobilization, members of the lower class sought refuge in umbrella institutions. The Catholic church, for example, took up the cause of the the rural poor, and other relief agencies gave counsel and assistance to the poor. But the regime quite successfully maintained its intransigence concerning their plight. Stroessner skillfully allowed an informal urban economy to grow up, though, thereby increasing their economic options. He permitted the unrestricted exodus of lower-class citizens to neighboring countries, thus providing a safety valve for his political system as a whole. The potential threat of a mobilized lower class had been minimized.

A survey conducted by Aníbal Miranda, a Paraguayan economist, substantiates that the lower class had little access to the new economic opportunities. Comparing income-distribution data for 1974 and 1980, he concluded that income distribution became more unequal during this short period. The lowest 20 percent of the households received only 5 percent of the total income; the highest 20 percent, about 84 percent. Strikingly, the highest 5 percent of the households received 70 percent.[37]

The presence of an informal urban sector indicated the lack of employment opportunities, even in light of the higher growth rates and expanded economic activity of the 1970s. Souza and Tokman concluded that more than 80 percent of the informal sector in Asunción, excluding domestic service, did not receive a stable income.[38] The actual situation was probably worse, because the definition of informal sector involved people working for formal establishments with fewer than five employees. Given the structure of the Paraguayan economy, such a definition may leave out or obscure the situation of those who are economically marginal. In an effort to quantify the poor living in and near Asunción, Morínigo concluded that "the total number of people living in areas considered poor in Asunción has increased from 47,697 in 1972 to 68,313 in 1980."[39] He went on to suggest that 24,000 families in Asunción could be said to live in poverty because they lacked bare subsistence needs.

Given their situation generally, the poor of Paraguay were inclined to seek better fortune elsewhere. And, the government was relaxed about their doing so, encouraging people to move to Argentina or Brazil. The number going to Argentina has remained constantly high. Statistics indicate that in 1970 there were about 212,000 Paraguayans living in Argentina, or about 9 percent of the population of Paraguay.[40] A study concerning the reasons that Paraguayans depart for Argentina reveals that their number peaked during the 1960s. That decade 85,575 "voted with their feet," and during the 1970s, 75,367 did so. The 1980 National Census of Population and Housing tallied 262,799 Paraguayans living in Argentina.[41]

The policies of the Stroessner administration minimized the potential for the migrants or for those left behind to become politically organized. The expansion of the economy took place only in certain sectors, and could not accommodate the needs of the large rural sector operating at a subsistence level. But the regime's decision to offer limited opportunities in the urban economy to a few members of the lower class can be interpreted as a decision to emphasize their economic gain and to deactivate their political-action potential. As for the outmigrants, most of the leaders who went into exile were those who could have eventually emerged as catalysts of popular opposition. By attacking and neutralizing organizations like the Catholic church, which provided some help to the lower class, the regime minimized possible threats from this sector.

The Co-optation of Potential Challengers

The Stroessner regime had important accomplishments in the area of economic growth. Yearly increases in per capita income were among the highest for Latin America during the 1970s, but the policies that raised incomes failed to change the structure of the Paraguayan economy. Economic expansion peaked during the late 1970s, and signs of strain and recessions were consistent during the 1980s. In economic terms, the Stroessner legacy will be short-lived. Beyond the bonanza of Itaipú, the country lost a historical opportunity to realize more fully its potential in the region.

Furthermore, the main concern guiding the economic management style of the regime was to create enough economic resources to defuse potential political challengers. The way that the military operated within this scheme has even been reinforced by law. On December 19, 1980, a legal instrument was created through which members of the armed forces have access to other activities within the private sector. When Stroessner was questioned about the nonmilitary activities of some military officers, he dismissed the implications of wrongdoing by declaring that everything they were doing was within the law. Smuggling operations brought enormous sums of money into the pockets of key military figures, and they assured the stability of the Stroessner regime.

The distribution of economic benefits in a country struggling to achieve a better standard of living became a deciding factor in the consolidation of the regime. In a small country, one plagued by internal, personal contests for political power, the ameliorated role of the military was a key to longevity. As long as the members of the armed forces found their moonlighting lucrative, they supported the political system that made it possible. And if Stroessner co-opted the armed forces, he also co-opted the middle class through public-sector jobs. For the lower class, his policies combined to limit the size of the urban working class through rejection of industrialization; to allow an informal urban sector wherein the poor can scratch out a living; to encourage the class's more upwardly mobile members to emigrate; and to exile or silence the most articulate and effective spokesmen for the poor. Here, as in his deft treatment of the military elite and the middle class, Stroessner turned co-optation into a central mechanism of his political system.

Notes

1. A discussion of the political role of economic policy-making during the Stroessner regime is included in Paul H. Lewis, *Paraguay under Stroessner* (Chapel Hill: University of North Carolina Press, 1980), pp. 151–67. Lewis centers his discussion on the contributions made by private domestic capital, foreign capital, and the state in financing the process of economic development. He implicitly suggests that benefits provided to several key groups, among them entrepreneurs and the middle and lower classes, through increased public works and jobs have played a key political role. In pursuing this argument further, I have decided to discuss economic policy as a "co-optation pattern."

2. The lack of relations with the outside world was also the cornerstone of Francia's and the Lópezes' economic orientations. Geography thus initially prompted colonial development in a different direction from the rest of the Southern Cone, but after independence, the process of isolating the Paraguayan economy was certainly a matter of policy. See Christian Lalive D'Epinay and Louis Necker, "Paraguay (1811–1870): A Utopia of Self-Oriented Change," in *Self Reliance: A Strategy for Development,* ed. Johan Galtung, Peter O'Brien, and Roy Preiswerk (London: Bogle-L'Ouverture Publications, 1980), pp. 249–68.

3. Census figures indicate that the Paraguayan population reached 1,337,000 in 1857. Other accounts suggest, however, that Paraguay had no more than 600,000 inhabitants in 1865 at the outset of the War of the Triple Alliance. Indications also vary concerning the number of casualties, but most accounts agree that Paraguay lost about 65 percent of its total population. See Raúl Mendoza A., "Desarrollo y evolución de la población Paraguaya," *Revista Paraguaya de Sociología* 5 (August 1968): 11.

4. Paraguay had managed to pay for the war almost on a "cash basis." The sources were export proceeds, loans from Argentina, and the gold surpluses generated during the Ayala years. But the price plunged Paraguay into an abyss of poverty again. See David H. Zook, *The Conduct of the Chaco War* (New Haven: Bookman Associates, 1960), p. 241.

5. Delfín Ugarte Centurión, *Evolución histórica de la economía Paraguaya* (Asunción: Editorial Graphis, 1983), p. 143.

6. For a discussion of the differences between the geography of the eastern and western regions, see Adlai F. Arnold, *Foundations of an Agricultural Policy in Paraguay* (New York: Praeger, 1971), pp. 1–17.

7. The data are from Presidencia de la Nación, Secretaría Técnica de Planificación, *Diagnóstico demográfico del Paraguay, 1950–1977,* vol. 1 (Asunción: Secretaría Técnica de Planificación, 1980), p. 146; and República del Paraguay, Dirección General de Estadísticas y Censos, *Censo nacional de población y viviendas, 1982: Cifras provisionales* (Asunción: Dirección Nacional de Estadísticas y Censos, 1982), p. 4.

8. The data are from Presidencia de la Nación, Secretaría Técnica de Planificación, *Plan nacional de desarrollo económico y social para el bienio 1965-1966*, vol. 2 (Asunción: Secretaría Técnica de Planificación, 1965), p. 14.

9. Sugar cane yield increased from 21,600 kilograms per hectare in 1942-1943 to 30,000 kilograms in 1960. Tung increased from 1,800 kilograms per plant to 5,600 kilograms in the same period. See Joseph Pincus, *The Economy of Paraguay* (New York: Praeger, 1968), pp. 48-49.

10. Pincus and Arnold defined the way that size of plot affects the agricultural sector in Paraguay. Arnold indicates that the plots are "insufficient land resources to satisfy the social and economic needs of those who live on them," and Pincus mentions that Paraguay is a "classic case of low level equilibrium based on subsistence agriculture." See Arnold, *Foundations of an Agricultural Policy in Paraguay*, p. 85; and Pincus, *The Economy of Paraguay*, p. 34.

11. The land tenure system is only one of the reasons that the urbanization process in Paraguay has been weak. Other elements are the lack of industrial development, migration to neighboring countries, and the political context of Paraguayan development.

12. The problems affecting Paraguay's efforts at industrialization are discussed in Werner Baer, "The Paraguayan Economic Condition: Past and Current Obstacles to Economic Modernization," *Inter-American Economic Affairs* 29 (Winter 1975): 49-63.

13. Pincus, *The Economy of Paraguay*, indicates that opportunities for import substitution and export production existed in Paraguay in the early 1960s. Most of the industries where expansion was probable involved agricultural products. In a study concerning an investment program conducted by the Technical Secretariat of Planning in 1977, the government suggested areas of investment that were all linked to the agricultural or the mining sectors. See Presidencia de la República, Secretaría Técnica de Planificación, *Paraguay: Perfiles industriales* (Asunción, 1977).

14. Hindrances to utilization of the river system for economic purposes are falls in the Paraná River and the low levels of water in the Paraguay River. Ports in Paraguay are also inadequate, and the nation depends on help from the Argentine and Brazilian governments to gain access to the Atlantic.

15. An ambitious plan to equip the country with 37,000 new telephones was developed in 1968, of which 24,000 would be in Asunción. By 1983, the total number of subscribers reached 67,632.

16. The discussion on which I base this section is Werner Baer and Melissa Birch, "Expansion of the Economic Frontier: Paraguayan Growth in the 1970s," *World Development* 12 (August 1984): 783-98.

17. A discussion of the economic fluctuations experienced by Paraguay during the 1970s is Richard Lynn Ground, "El auge y la recesión de la economía Paraguaya, 1972-1983: El papel de la política económica interna," in *Economía del Paraguay contemporáneo*, 2 vols. (Asunción: Centro Paraguayo de Estudios Sociológicos, 1984), pp. 493-573.

18. Presidencia de la República, Secretaría Técnica de Planificación, *Diagnóstico demográfico del Paraguay, 1980* (Asunción, 1980), p. 294.

19. See Heriberto Alegre, "La colonización en el Paraguay: El eje este," *Revista Paraguaya de Sociología* 14 (January-April 1977): 135–55.

20. The results of the study are reported in World Bank, *Paraguay: Regional Development in Eastern Paraguay* (Washington, D.C., 1978). The eastern state of Alto Paraná had the largest portion of land suitable for intensive agricultural use, 2.79 million hectares.

21. Ibid., p. 48; data concerning the increase in price level appear on p. 9.

22. See R. Andrew Nickson, "Brazilian Colonization of the Eastern Border Region of Paraguay," *Journal of Latin American Studies* 13 (May 1981): 111–31.

23. The Treaty of Itaipú was subscribed to in Brasilia on April 26, 1973, by President Stroessner and President Emílio Garrastazu Medici. The Treaty of Yacyretá between the Republic of Paraguay and Argentina was signed in Asunción on December 3, 1973, by Stroessner and President Juan Domingo Perón of Argentina.

24. Reaction to the hydroelectric potential of Paraguay was reflected in the wide coverage that the North American media gave the case. See "The World Needs Energy—and Little Paraguay's Got It," *Miami Herald*, December 29, 1977; Ira Nambeil, "Hydroelectric Projects Seen Key to Economic Growth in Paraguay," *Journal of Commerce*, January 16, 1973.

25. A member of Stroessner's entourage made this point to me very strongly on several occasions. Dr. Federico Mandelburger, executive director of the Technical Secretariat of Planning, was able to anticipate the drawbacks of the process. His office suggested that benefits produced by the Itaipú project should have been invested in agro-industrial projects. In a conversation with me, in Asunción, January 13, 1984.

26. Baer and Birch, "Expansion of the Economic Frontier," p. 789.

27. For a detailed discussion of the technicalities involved in the agreement between Paraguay and Brazil and the controversy that followed, see Efraín Enríquez Gamón, *Itaipú: Aguas que valen oro* (Buenos Aires: Editorial Guadalupe, 1975).

28. See R. Andrew Nickson, "The Itaipú Hydro-Electric Project: The Paraguayan Perspective," *Bulletin of Latin American Research* 2 (May 1982): 1–20.

29. The report was the result of the visit made by the minister of industry and commerce to the Federal Republic of Germany in 1980. The German government commissioned two international firms to study the industrial potential of Paraguay. The report was published by the ministry in February of 1982 under the title "Plan Maestro para el Desarrollo Industrial del Paraguay." The study concluded that import substitution applied to seventeen groups of products and could be implemented before 1985.

30. A complete discussion of the serious financial problems affecting Paraguay prior to the advent of Stroessner appear in Juan Bautista Rivarola Paoli, *Historia monetaria del Paraguay* (Asunción: Editorial El Gráfico, 1982), p. 480.

31. Domínguez indicates that Paraguay conforms to the group of countries that "consumed" more than 250 cigarettes per capita in 1968. That figure is much higher than the actual consumption of cigarettes in most developed nations,

about the same as in Panama, but lower than that in Kuwait or the Netherlands Antilles. See Jorge I. Domínguez, "Smuggling," *Foreign Policy* 20 (Fall 1975): 88.

32. The case of André Ricord received wide coverage in the United States. He operated the "Latin American connection," and the U.S. government sought his extradition from Paraguay in 1972. The Paraguayan government tried to deny his release because of concern that he might implicate high officers of the army. General Patricio Colmán and General Andrés Rodríguez were said to have participated in the dealings. After the Nixon administration threatened to cut off aid, and after General Colmán died in a U.S. hospital because of complications from an old wound, Stroessner released Ricord. Details about the operation are in Nathan M. Adams, "The Hunt for André," *Reader's Digest*, March 1973, pp. 224–59. The trial received extensive coverage in the *New York Times*.

33. Juan Carlos Herken, "El sector externo en la economía Paraguaya," *Estudios Paraguayos* 6 (September 1978): 87–114.

34. Ibid., pp. 102–3.

35. José Nicolás Morínigo A., "El proceso de cambio en la estructura de la población económicamente activa en el Paraguay," *Estudios Paraguayos* 6 (December 1978): 128–39.

36. Oscar Corvalán Vázquez, "Recursos humanos y empleo en el Paraguay," in *Economía del Paraguay contemporáneo* 1: 169.

37. Aníbal Miranda, *Desarrollo y pobreza en Paraguay* (Asunción: Comité de Iglesias e Inter-American Foundation, 1982), p. 239.

38. Paulo R. Souza and Víctor E. Tokman, "Características y funcionamiento del sector informal: El caso del Paraguay," *Revista Paraguaya de Sociología* 31 (September-December 1974): 63.

39. José Nicolás Morínigo A., "Hacia una cuantificación de la población pobre en Asunción," *Estudios Paraguayos* 9 (June 1981): 192. The translation is mine.

40. República Argentina, Instituto Nacional de Estadísticas y Censos, *Anuario estadístico* (Buenos Aires, 1980), p. 127.

41. Donald G. Richards, "International Household Migration: The Case of Paraguay" (unpublished paper, Indiana State University, 1986), p. 4.

The Demise of
the Stroessner Regime

7 The process of consolidation made the Stroessner regime one of the most stable authoritarian political systems ever to have held power in Latin America. The ideological manipulation, extreme control of opposition groups, and co-optation through economic benefits created a foundation that seemed destined to last. However, in the early 1980s, the regime began to suffer a series of challenges that eventually led to its demise in February of 1989. The deterioration proved that Stroessner's ability to hold his detractors at bay was limited, and even though Paraguay must confront the reality of the post-Stroessner era before it can construct a stable democratic and competitive system, the continuity that Stroessner provided with the authoritarian past appears to have been broken. More important, Stroessner left the country in disgrace, when only a few years earlier he had been the object of adulation by most Paraguayan citizens.

The dawn of the regime came about as a result of changes in the Paraguayan economy, society, and politics. The Paraguay that Stroessner left in 1989 is certainly much different from the one he took over in 1954. And although he was in full control of the accelerated process of modernization during the 1970s, he eventually lost his grip and was overwhelmed by the changes themselves. Furthermore, his departure confirms the notion that no dictator can afford to create a political system based on corruption, hatred, and violence. When his ability to maintain ideological hegemony failed, when exercising control through policies based on civil rights violations could not keep the opposition quiet, and when the economic resources were not enough to keep the benefits of corruption coming, his system perished. Ironically, the very practices that helped Stroessner consolidate his power during the 1960s and 1970s brought about his departure in the late 1980s.

The political changes that ultimately sent Stroessner into exile began in the early 1980s, when conditions began to march against the regime:

economic deterioration, a deep cleavage within the Colorado party itself, and the mobilization of a lower class and middle class that had achieved new political clout after the Itaipú boom. The economy began to show signs of difficulties once the activities at Itaipú slowed down at the end of the 1970s. Without the influx of dollars from the construction project into the Paraguayan economy, recessions occurred. The adverse economic climate allowed the opposition to gain ground in light of new mobilization and strong dissent from different sectors of Paraguayan society. The momentum of the opposition and pressure from the newly emerged democratic regimes of the Southern Cone caused the official party to split into two groups: one in favor and one against a more democratic future for Paraguay. Once party unifier, Stroessner gave his support to the Colorado faction attempting to perpetuate his style, but the intervention of General Andrés Rodríguez forced Stroessner into exile.

From Boom to Crisis: Changing Economic Realities

The economic policymakers of the Stroessner regime were unwilling to recognize that a serious economic recession was in the making throughout 1981 and 1982. Officers at the Ministry of Industry and Commerce and at the Secretariat of Planning refused to acknowledge that with the slowdown of Itaipú and the uncertainty over the Yacyretá project, the economy had entered into a period of crisis.[1] But in the first quarter of 1983, the data released by the Central Bank confirmed what many people had anticipated: for the first time since 1966 the country's GDP had decreased, 2.0 percent during 1982. The strongest recessive tendencies were seen in agriculture (a decrease of 5 percent) and industry (4.5 percent); the service sector increased its GDP by 9.5 percent. The service sector had become overextended for a country strongly dependent on its agricultural sector and without significant industrial development.[2]

The most important consequence of the deep recession was unemployment, which climbed from 2.1 percent in 1980, to 4.6 percent in 1981, 9.4 percent in 1982, and 15 percent in 1983. It is remarkable that in 1980 the country had enjoyed the lowest unemployment level in its history—in part due to the hydroelectric projects, which drove the economy—but by 1982, the country had returned to unemployment levels reminiscent of the 1960s and even before, when economic conditions were much different.[3]

The severity of Paraguay's situation was exacerbated by international conditions unfavorable to its economic expansion. The second oil crisis had raised interest rates and curtailed demand for primary products worldwide. Unfortunately for Paraguay, the price of soybeans dropped about 1 percent in 1980, almost 3 percent in 1981, and 15 percent in 1982, and the price of cotton tailed off by 9.5 percent in 1981 and 14.6 percent in 1982. Even if these commodities were to rebound in 1983, the direct effect of the world recession was undeniable. Indirect effects came by way of Brazil and Argentina; growth rates tumbled and inflation soared in both countries, with severe repercussions for Paraguay's external and internal sectors. Tourism dwindled and the contribution of the hydroelectric projects slowed down the recovery effort of the economy itself.[4]

The attempt at recovery during 1983 was hampered by flood problems. Heavy rains in the upper Paraná and Paraguay river systems as well as in the Pilcomayo and Iguazú river basins caused extensive damage to the agricultural sector. The departments of Ñeenbucú and Presidente Hayes were the most affected; 40 percent of the former was under water, and about 10 percent of the latter. Roughly a million head of cattle died. Industry and business sustained crippling losses as well.

The fiscal deficit increased due to the need for external credit because the Itaipú project no longer contributed to the economy. The slowdown of economic activity prompted the regime to consider a less rigid foreign exchange policy. The Central Bank, during the first quarter of 1983, decided on an attempt to restore equilibrium in the balance of payments, which had shown a surplus of $45 million in 1981 and a deficit of $71 million in 1982. It restricted imports by raising the exchange rate from ₲126 to ₲160, which contributed to the general climate of crisis in the industrial sector. Industry was unable to compete without imports and was under excessive pressure from contraband and illegal international traders. Importers complained, for they had purchased equipment abroad assuming the earlier rate. The policy attempted as well to increase exports. Preferential treatment was given to meat (₲177 per dollar), and to soybeans and cotton (about ₲156 per dollar); other products received ₲143 per dollar.

Foreign debt was also deeply troubling. By the end of 1982 the total owed was more than $1,200 million; a total increase of 26 percent over the previous year. Payments during 1982 were 39.5 percent of the amount of total exports. The government had no alternative but to reach into its own reserves, for approximately $130 million, leaving a balance of $652 million.[5]

The recession left nothing and no one in Paraguay untouched. The most pervasive effect was a steep rise in the cost of gasoline. PETROPAR, the government monopoly jacked up prices on January 12, 1983, by 45 percent for *alconafta* (gasohol) and 45 percent for *supernafta* (unleaded gasoline). The purpose was to fill official coffers, but consumer resistance was such that sales fell by roughly 90 percent. The government lowered gasoline prices in the first half of March, showing a weak and incoherent economic policy. The price rise, of course, had also served to bring in more contraband gasoline from Argentina, as well as discourage potential investors in the industry who took note of the erratic policy-making.

The Central Bank reported that during the first half of 1984 inflation reached 11 percent, compared to 6.4 percent the previous year. The rise in prices during June alone was 4 percent due to the 15 percent minimum wage increase just put into effect. A significant factor fueling inflation was the cost of gasoline on July 18, 1984, prices at the pumps went up anywhere between 11 to 34 percent, and some distributors had jumped the gun on the official announcement.

Business groups protested the uncertainties regarding economic policy. The government called on business leaders to moderate their price hikes. By the end of the year both were pleased by a 3 percent increase in the gross domestic product, and a decline in the value of the dollar in the free market. The overflow of dollars into the open market was a reflection of the subvaluation policy of the government, which encouraged export transactions to be undeclared to allow for the exchange under black market conditions.[6]

Economic matters continued to plague the regime during 1985. In the early months of 1986 the government reported that the growth rate for the gross domestic product had reached 4.0 percent in 1985; most of the increase was attributable to agricultural exports. There were still strong recessionary conditions in the services and construction sectors. Most important, devaluations of the guaraní adversely affected per capita income. Even the World Bank urged that Paraguay achieve a more realistic exchange rate policy and abandon the official rate of 160 for government debt service and 240 for government imports. In essence the policy subsidized the public sector: Paraguay received foreign currency at a rate of 320 per dollar for exports, and introduced them into the public sector at 160 and 240, thus further weakening the already weak situation of the government, and adding to inflationary speculation. Total reserves had been reduced to about $400 million in 1985, with liquid assets reaching only about $200 million—this after having reached more than $800 million in 1981.

Adding to the general discontent, in June of 1985 the Central Bank announced that a mishandling of foreign exchange reserves had been uncovered. High-ranking government officials as well as private business firms had received dollars at the official exchange rate to be used for imports, imports that never arrived. After several investigations, the president of the Central Bank, César Romeo Acosta, was excused from having to appear in court, proving once more the absence of an independent judicial branch in Paraguay. Estimates of the loss ranged from $30 to $60 million.

With the elections of 1988 fast approaching, pressures continue to mount against the regime in 1986 because of the adverse economic conditions: the deepening recession, the rising inflation, and the decrease in real wages. The severity of the situation moved the government to attempt to deal with the crisis in more pragmatic terms. On May 2 the Interinstitutional Commission, composed of experts from the Central Bank, the Ministry of Finance, the Bank of Development, and the Secretariat of Planning, revealed the Plan of Adjustment (Plan de Ajuste). The commission's findings were not well received by many government officers, entrepreneurs, and even labor, but the plan revealed a new government attitude. The commission accepted that the rate of inflation had reached 40 percent, the rate of unemployment, 8 percent, and that the public debt was in part due to a subsidized exchange rate and recessionary tendencies. The plan called for a public-sector exchange rate of 320 guaraní to the dollar and a two-tier private sector exchange rate of 500 guaraní and 320 guaraní, the first affecting exports and preferential imports, and the second for oil imports.

In August, the minister of industry and commerce, Delfín Ugarte Centurión, announced that the National Economic Plan (Plan Económico Nacional) had been approved by the National Council of Economic Coordination. Even if the new plan was similar to the commission's plan, it differed substantially in solutions proposed. The National Economic Plan called for the introduction of relevant legislation within sixty days; the adjustment plan basically placed responsibility in the hands of producers, consumers, and the government. Approval of the National Economic Plan by the regime initially attracted considerable support to it from different economic sectors. But it was too ambitious; it required a reorganization of economic activity that went far beyond an adjustment effort. The key goals were to increase production and exports, to substitute imports, to reduce the federal deficit, to change the exchange rate system, to control inflation, to increase reserves, to attract foreign investments, and to promote stable wages and financial stability.

Government officials turned indecisive, and a state of uncertainty dominated economic circles. Some of the specific points of the program, such as a personal income tax, a value added tax, and the selling of government bonds were controversial innovations. Lack of movement on the plan on the part of the regime prompted the institutions most affected by the economic crisis to continue to request realistic policy measures. But by the end of 1986 public-sector finances were out of control and no adjustment plan could restore order unless a complete change in economic policy was implemented.

Improvements during 1987 were mainly because of agricultural exports. Gross domestic product grew at a rate of 4.2 percent, in contrast to zero growth in 1986 and 4 percent in 1985. Exports increased to $350 million from $233 million in 1986, but so did the foreign debt, which rose to $2.05 billion from the $1.85 billion the year before. Foreign reserves fell to $200 million from $305 million in 1986 and $385 million in 1985.[7]

The economic situation changed somewhat during early 1988, but without presenting a clear-cut profile. The Foro de Economía of the Centro Paraguayo de Estudios Sociológicos forecasted that the economy would grow at a rate of 6 percent. The same figure was predicted by the Technical Secretariat of Planning, based on a substantial expansion in agricultural output, in some cases reaching 30 percent (soybeans); increases in the price of cotton and soybeans; and the impact that agricultural output would have on the rest of the economy. A critical view of that forecast was voiced. In simple terms, the forecast was assuming a growth rate for agriculture of 17 percent, when in 1981 it had peaked at 14.8 percent. In any event, the agricultural sector recorded a modest increment in output, 2.6 percent, and much higher revenues, which for the first six months reached a record of $295 million according to the Central Bank. The 25 percent increase in revenues was due to prices on the international market. Partially to blame for the low output were bad weather, lack of agricultural credit, and a decline in the cultivation of maize and manioc.[8]

The economic problems of the 1980s prompted doubts about the policies pursued by the regime. For a system that had functioned on the basis of distributing benefits, continued economic growth was paramount to its continuity. And, although the economic condition of Paraguay at the time of Stroessner's departure was much different from the economic conditions of the early 1950s and 1960s, so were the expectations of the population. During the 1970s Paraguayans had grown accustomed to a higher level of consumption, stable employment at high wages, and an economic bonanza that could not realistically endure.

The Institutional Crisis

A second contributing factor to the demise of the regime was the institutional crisis that brought even backers of the regime to open questioning of the practices by which Stroessner had survived for three and a half decades. Although this type of participation had lain dormant for many years, the magnitude of the crisis brought key institutions into confrontation with the regime, articulating political demands never before heard by the dictatorship. The breakdown of the staunch support received from the Colorado party, the armed forces, and the business community placed the regime into an extremity from which it would not recover. In these circumstances the elections of 1988, even with Stroessner's victory, already signaled that he could no longer continue to maintain the system in place.

Looking Ahead: Intraparty Conflict

The first sign of the weakening of the regime was the inability of Stroessner to keep the official party unified by preventing a confrontation within its ranks. Although the Colorados had been divided before, this time the differences were not settled by Stroessner himself. He remained above the fray as the factions battled over his succession. Laboring under advanced age and critical health problems, Stroessner did not, or could not, prepare the country for his stepping down. With transition to the post-Stroessner era looming, jockeying for position was the hallmark of the political scene, both within the official party and outside it. Once again, personalismo was at the forefront as factions gathered around possible candidates, not around ideas or plans for a reorganization of the country.

The Colorados split into two groups: one favored continuation of the Stroessner system into the future, albeit with a different leader, and the other, the historical group, favored a more open political system. The former looked to Mario Abdo Benítez, Stroessner's private secretary, for whom Stroessner wanted a much more active role in the party ranks. The *marioabdistas,* who were also known as militantes (militants) or stronistas, claimed ascendancy within the party because of their loyalty to Stroessner. The tradicionalistas (traditionalists) argued that the Colorado party had existed before Stroessner came to power and they advocated loyalty to the party rather than to Stroessner.

A crisis occurred during the convention of September 15–16, 1984. The party junta, controlled by members of the traditionalist faction, prevented the Benítez faction from promoting its man to a vice-presidential post. Benítez had catapulted himself into prominence as a modernizer, one who was more populist in orientation. His supporters obtained the signatures of 339 of the 498 delegates in favor of his nomination for one of the three party vice-presidential posts. The junta members did not bring the issue to the assembly but voted on it themselves. The junta nominated Sabino A. Montanaro, Rubén Stanley, and Adán Godoy Giménez. The makeup of new party junta also reflected the resistance of the traditionalists to pressure from the militantes. Of the total forty-eight posts, twenty went to the traditionalists; six went to the military; and the rest to neutral or undecided candidates.[9]

The events of the convention served to split the party more deeply that it had been before. The Benítez faction proved its strength there, especially among the youngest groups. The quiet support from Stroessner could have also been due to his desire to increase his control over the party to facilitate a transition to his liking. The marioabdistas suggested that the natural heir was Gustavo Stroessner (Stroessner's son), a colonel in the Air Force with more active business interests than political ones. Others advanced the notion that the system should remain intact under a military or civilian president who would safeguard the system.

The other faction, the traditionalists, was led by Juan Ramón Cháves, who had been elected president of the Junta de Gobierno of the party in 1984. Although loyal to Stroessner, the traditionalists favored change and a more democratic political system. Many army officers backed this faction, and the consensus within the army was strong for a civilian candidate for the presidency, Luis María Argaña, president of the Supreme Court. The traditionalists used the power of the party board to curtail the activities of the militantes. They attempted to ban the inclusion of militantes as party candidates in the municipal elections of October 1985.

The traditionalists joined forces with the *éticos* (ethicals), or *críticos* (critics), who, being strongly opposed to the regime itself, supported democratic change but were not close to the regime. The éticos, under Carlos Romero Pereira, distanced themselves from the party because of the corruption rampant among government officials. Of all the Colorado factions, the éticos were the ones who grew closer to the opposition. In 1987, two additional factions developed: the Group of 34 and the Group of 52; they were unified later as the Movimiento de Integración Colorada (MIC), led by former Interior Minister Edgar Ynsfrán. The MIC joined the éticos in opposing Stroessner. The Movimiento Nacional y Popular, led by Leandro Prieto Yegros, joined the militantes in supporting Stroessner.

The confrontation between the militants and traditionalists reached a critical point during the August 1987 convention. Earlier that year Stroessner had called on both groups to put aside their differences. In reality, Stroessner was trying first to dismantle the éticos so as to deal later with the traditionalists. The éticos were driven to join the factions of the Colorado party that were in strong opposition: the MOPOCO and the Movimiento de Integración Colorada. By convention time confrontation was inevitable. Stroessner was expected to intervene to keep the party together, but he stepped aside.

Convinced that the traditionalists endangered his power base, Stroessner had skillfully manipulated the situation once again. By stepping aside, he let the factions air their differences during the convention. The militantes gained control and forced the traditionalists to walk out. The president

of the party and member of the Senate, Juan R. Cháves, was replaced
by Sabino A. Montanaro, a militant who was interior minister and who
supported devolution of the presidency to Stroessner's son. Stroessner
allowed the division to reach the point of confrontation, showing that
the regime no longer enjoyed its former strength.[10] He then suggested
that the traditionalists and the militantes unite on a single candidate to
present to the nominating convention of November 1987.[11] By more or
less forcing this truce, Stroessner managed to clear the scene of éticos
and traditionalists to assure himself more control during the elections
of 1988 and possibly in handpicking his successor. But he had gone too
far. With most of the military supporting the traditionalist position and
a possible civilian candidate in the elections, Stroessner had sealed the
fate of his regime.

The Armed Forces and the Transition

The political unrest was not limited to the Colorado party. The armed
forces, the pillar of the regime, began to sound off with its own ideas
concerning the transition. Given the strength of its relationship with the
Colorado party, the military would have a strong voice in determining
the Colorado candidate, assuming Stroessner could not take part.

As early as 1980, the names of several military officers began to
circulate as possible contenders for the presidency. General Andrés Rodríguez, then commander of the 1st Cavalry Division and later commander
of the 1st Army Corps, seemed a natural because he enjoyed considerable
military and economic power. Lack of connections within economic circles
negatively affected the chances for nomination of General Germán Mar-
tínez, commander of the 1st Infantry Division and close friend of the
president. General Guillermo Clebsch, commander of the presidential
guard and deputy chief of the general staff, was another possible contender.
Other figures mentioned included General Gerardo Johannsen, director
of the Francisco Solano López military school, and General Alfredo
Fretes Dávalos, chief of the general staff. General Benito Guanes Serrano,
head of military intelligence, enjoyed some support within the Colorado
party but his name had been associated with the death of Orlando
Letelier in Washington and the United States would have probably
opposed his nomination.[12]

The newspaper *El Pueblo*, of the Revolutionary Febrerista Party,
informed its readers in July of 1984 that General Johannsen had been
selected by the military as successor to Stroessner. According to the
newspaper, Johannsen had declined the nomination, suggesting that Luis
María Argaña, a civilian, head the transition. Although the leaders of

the Febrerista party in Buenos Aires denied the veracity of the report, speculation mounted. Should its handpicked civilian candidate win the presidency, the armed forces could retain control over the political process without having to assume the burden of managing through an economic and political crisis.

There was talk not only about who the next president would be but about how to steer Paraguayan politics in new directions. In April of 1985, General Amancio Pampliega, a member of the old guard and already in retirement, published his memoirs. A man of solid reputation, he had written a substantial work that was quickly sold out. The police confiscated whatever copies they could find because he had discussed the transition and the Communist party of Paraguay. On both scores he departed from the conventional positions of the army and the Colorados. Pampliega had not spoken with Stroessner since 1967 because of a personal rift between them, but in the book he advised Stroessner as he had advised Morínigo: enter history as a great leader by retiring at the right time. Otherwise, the country could find itself in the same tragic conditions it had found itself in in 1870, 1904, 1908, 1912, 1923, 1936, and 1947. He also showed concern over the Itaipú bonanza and the piling up of debt.[13]

External Pressures

Pressure from abroad played a substantial role in the deterioration that ultimately brought the regime to closure. The international isolation of Paraguay grew to unprecedented levels during the last five years of the Stroessner era, due in part to the changes sweeping through the Southern Cone of Latin America and also because of a change in attitude of the United States. Within Latin America, Paraguay had had to cope with the disadvantages attendant upon being one of the few authoritarian governments still in power. The transition to democracy and inauguration of Raúl Alfonsín as president of Argentina created problems for the regime. Stroessner had a natural affinity for members of the Peronista party of Argentina, and diplomatic relations between the two countries were strained. The Brazilians, on the other hand, were less attentive to the nature of Paraguayan governance and the imminence of change therein. Although they too moved toward democracy, in 1985, the closeness of the two national economies as well as collaborative foreign policy objectives steered the Brazilians toward a hands-off stance. The military had relinquished power in Uruguay in 1984, and General Augusto Pinochet in Chile remained as the only other example of dictatorial rule in the area. Stroessner was said to be ready to go to Chile in case of an unexpected end of his tenure, and Pinochet was said to have purchased a house in Asunción in case his fate turned out that way.

After years of providing formal and informal support to the Stroessner regime, the United States began to champion democratic developments throughout the region, urging Paraguay to move in that direction. Great concern was expressed about human rights violations. Robert White, ambassador to Paraguay under the Carter administration, started an active campaign to expose the regime's human rights policies, and the two appointees of the Reagan administration, Arthur Davies and Clyde Taylor, continued to play a vital role in promoting democratization.

The United States leaned on the Stroessner regime on several critical issues. One was freedom of the press because the regime became more and more hostile to journalists and media organizations who were reporting the deteriorating social and economic conditions. Another concerned labor; the United States wanted the Paraguayan labor movement to be able to speak freely. When Davies met with Stroessner on these two issues in late 1983, he was reportedly told by Stroessner that he was involved in defending subversives.[14]

Particularly troubling were Ambassador Taylor's experiences. After meeting with members of the Acuerdo Nacional in January 1986, he was accused by Interior Minister Sabino A. Montanaro of gross interference in the internal affairs of Paraguay.[15] Later that year, the United States protested the regime's actions taken when Domingo Laíno, exiled leader of the PLRA, attempted to return to Paraguay. In December, Taylor accused the regime of not trying to solve the problems of Radio Ñandutí— government jamming—and Montanaro threatened to declare the U.S. ambassador persona non grata in Paraguay. On February 9, 1987, Paraguayan police fired tear gas at a reception held in honor of Taylor outside Asunción. Although the Stroessner administration later apologized for the action, tension between the two countries continued to mount.

The United States suggested in 1987 that it might end all preferential tariff treatments of Paraguayan exports to the United States, but did not carry out the action. A few months later, in September, the United States expressed concern about the deteriorating human rights situation, especially the regime's treatment of the opposition.[16] Embarrassment affected relations with Germany as well. In 1985, strong objections voiced to the West German government by the Social Democratic and Green parties led to cancellation of Stroessner's planned trip to Bavaria to visit the birthplace of his father. On April 27, 1986, the Paraguayan police arrested the German press attaché in Asunción and four members of a German television crew during a demonstration outside of the home of Domingo Laíno, who was then exiled in Argentina.[17]

Social and Political Mobilization

Keeping opposition groups at bay was another critical problem for the Stroessner regime during the 1980s. After the 1983 election, and under intense pressure from the United States, the opposition as well as other social groups within Paraguay gained momentum in their quest for change. Some of their activities to bring about social change engaged different groups, some of which were key institutions of Paraguayan society, like the Catholic church and business associations, but others engaged the lower sectors, which accelerated the deterioration of the political situation. The regime, however, allowed some political activism even as it clamped down on reportage.

In March 1984 the Colorado party decided to close the newspaper *ABC Color*. Its editor, Aldo Zucolillo, was a prominent businessman with close ties to some members of the Paraguayan army. He championed the cause of freedom, and when his paper provided information about the worsening conditions affecting the economy, he crossed the line of permissibility. The order to close the paper, signed by Interior Minister Sabino A. Montanaro, declared infringement of Article 71 of the Constitution, wherein it was prohibited to "preach hatred between Paraguayans." The order also pointed out that *ABC Color* had promoted confusion within public opinion, thereby jeopardizing peace within the country and the stability of institutions. On May 28 *ABC Color* journalists attempted to publish a sports newspaper but managed to put out only a single issue before it was banned. Reaction to the closing of *ABC Color* was worldwide. The decision was a turning point in Stroessner's effort to maintain his grip in the midst of a deepening political and economic crisis.[18]

Given the magnitude of the economic changes that Stroessner wrought, the business community's support for the regime is not surprising. The boom times of the Itaipú decade in particular created many new opportunities. But, when the 1980s brought hard times, the business community quickly demanded that corrective measures be taken. One of the most important business organizations to show discontent with the regime's policies was the Federation of Production, Industry, and Commerce (FEPRINCO). Created in 1951 to represent several business associations, it began a campaign in the 1980s to bring the ailing economy to public notice. It released a document in 1981 calling the attention of the government to diminishing export revenues and the continued increase in imports, especially oil. The federation called for a reduction in export taxes at a time when the government was announcing exactly the opposite measure: a reduction in import taxes. The latter was designed

to provide additional revenue to the government by discouraging contraband goods from entering into the country.[19]

The ongoing crisis and the ineffectiveness of the government led
FEPRINCO to step up its criticism. A second document was released
in 1982; it called again for a reduction in export taxes, a more selective
import policy, the elimination of contraband activities, no new taxes,
and the use of private investment funds in productive areas. In June of
1983 the organization asked the government to allow free exchange rates.
In July of 1984 it released another document, this one informing the
Ministry of Industry and Commerce of the difficulties of several of its
members organizations.[20] In December of 1987, the new president of
FEPRINCO, Alirio Ugarte Díaz, spoke out against the regime's economic
policies, asking for their review and for the elimination of corruption.
The bill of particulars: reform of the exchange system, a reduction in
the fiscal deficit, more credit opportunities for private production, elimination of import privileges, and a halt to Taiwanese immigration.[21]

The regime also had to deal with a mobilized rural peasantry. Most
of the peasants owned very small plots of land, on which they were
unable to practice even subsistence agriculture. Trouble over land first
arose in the department of Alto Paraná in August of 1985; it was settled
by the government. Unrest soon appeared in other areas, and by October
there had been thirty-one cases of illegal occupation. The peasants in
most cases would peacefully occupy the land, and after being evicted
would return. Several newly created peasant organizations, like the
Asamblea Permanente de Campesinos sin Tierra (First Assembly of
Peasants without Land) and the Comité Coordinador de Productores
Agrícolas de Paraguarí y Caaguazú (Committee of Agricultural Producers
of Paraguarí and Caaguazú) brought the matter to the public's attention
through the support of some sectors of the Catholic church and the
Consejo de Iglesias (Council of Churches).[22]

Although Paraguay has had a long tradition of weak opposition activity,
the moves and countermoves of the Stroessner regime during the 1980s
provided several opposition groups with much-needed opportunities to
become active in the democratization process. The beginning of the
political mobilization process took place in early 1984 with the return
of the leaders of the Movimiento Popular Colorado (MOPOCO) from
exile.[23] A month later a protest organized by the Febrerista revolutionary
party, with support of members of the Acuerdo Nacional, brought about
two thousand people into Plaza Italia, downtown Asunción. The strength
of these moves prompted the belief that the regime was allowing some
degree of mobilization to counter the pressure from Buenos Aires and
Washington. But the leaders of the MOPOCO were jailed, harassed, and
constantly monitored by government authorities.

Another manifestation of the new political climate was the increasingly larger role of the Acuerdo Nacional. The Acuerdo Nacional was created in February of 1979 with the support of the PLRA, PDC, PRF, and MOPOCO. The members of the agreement had been actively calling for an end to the politics of fear practiced by the government, for amnesty for political prisoners, and for better human rights policies. Although only one of its members enjoyed legal recognition, the Acuerdo Nacional gained leverage after the transitions to democracy in Argentina and Brazil. Even if at first it was unable to play a very active role, its ability to mobilize public opinion grew as the crisis unfolded. The first sign of its mobilizing power came on May 14, 1985, at a rally demanding democracy. The Acuerdo Nacional joined forces with the Catholic church in calling for a political opening.

The Catholic church was the other focal point of opposition to the regime. The church had traditionally taken such a stance, although during the early years of the regime and while Archbishop Mena Porta was in charge, it did not do so openly. In the 1970s it became more radical after the founding of the Catholic University, especially when the Stroessner regime violated many human rights. During the 1980s the Bishops Conference became more outspoken, thereby aiding the change toward democracy. In May of 1985, the church condemned the government for calling on people to visit the shrine of Caacupé to pray for continued guidance for General Stroessner.[24] On May 28, 1986 for example, the Archbishop of Asunción, Ismael Rolón Silvero, urged Catholics to support antiregime protests. In June of 1987 the church called for a second round of national dialogue. The idea of the church's acting as an intermediary between the opposition and the government had been on again, off again due to the intransigence of Stroessner and the Colorado party. In October 1987 the church sponsored a silent march in which more than 15,000 people showed their anti-Stroessner feelings. Asunción's church bells rang each Friday afternoon during the month to remind people of their situation. In January of 1988, the bishops produced a document calling for a "change of mentality in order to establish the different laws that will allow the effective and real existence of a democratic system."[25]

Another element that has affected the potential for change within the Paraguayan political system is the role played by labor organizations. The Stroessner regime had traditionally sponsored the official union, the Confederación Paraguaya de Trabajadores (CPT), but economic realities brought even the CPT into open confrontation with the regime. Because of the rising costs of fuel in 1984, bus fares were slated to go up by 29 percent; the CPT leadership loudly declared that if the working class had to cope with depreciating income, so should the bus companies.

Since 1985 parallel organizations have offered an alternative to the CPT. Among the most influential was the Movimiento Intersindical de Trabajadores del Paraguay (MIT-P; Interunion Movement of Workers of Paraguay), calling for a free labor movement within the context of a pluralistic democracy. Other organizations were the Agrupación Independiente de Trabajadores (AIT; Independent Group of Workers) and the Coordinación de Trabajadores del Acuerdo Nacional (COTAN; Coordination of Workers of the National Accord). The COTAN was composed of the Movimiento Sindical Febrerista (MSF; Febrerista Union Movement), the labor wing of the Partido Demócrata Cristiano, and the MOPOCO. It did not include the Movimiento Obrero Liberal Radical Auténtico (MOLRA; Labor Movement of the Partido Liberal Radical Auténtico), which enjoyed support in the rural areas. In addition, the labor organization that was part of the Catholic church, the Movimiento Obrero Cristiano (MOC), promoted the mobilization of workers through parish membership rather than political organizations. In essence, the labor movement presented a range of viewpoints, with some promoting the status quo and others working for democratic change. A similar situation obtained in student politics: the Federación Universitaria Paraguaya, loyal to the regime, was paralleled by the Federación de Estudiantes Paraguayos in 1986. The opposition springing from business, church organizations, students, and labor suggested that an organized challenge to the Stroessner regime was taking shape.

Even in the new circumstances, the regime marched toward the February 1988 elections seemingly unaffected by the shifting climate within the country. It remained committed to a policy-making style that had endured more than three decades. Halfway through 1987, Stroessner even allowed Domingo Laíno to return to Paraguay, after he had made five unsuccessful attempts to do so, and lifted the state of siege to show the regime's commitment to more openness. But those were token gestures to mollify the intensely negative feelings about the regime that were prevalent in foreign countries, especially in the United States.

Mapping the Transition: Proposals for Change

The general social mobilization that began to bear on Paraguayan politics in the mid-1980s prompted several key political figures to advance their ideas concerning the inevitable transition to the post-Stroessner era. With the impending crisis within the Colorado party, the active opposition, and deep socioeconomic problems, the structure of the regime began to crack and alternatives began to be formulated as potential maps for change.

Many proposals emerged during 1986, when the regime resorted once again to policies of repression and fear. One that received wide consideration in Paraguay as well as abroad was put forward by Augusto Roa Bastos, a well-known Paraguayan writer in exile in France. In February his "Carta Abierta al Pueblo Paraguayo" (Open letter to the Paraguayan people) appeared in several newspapers and was circulated by human rights organizations. He described the situation in Paraguay and how he had attacked the regime through more than three decades of exile. He argued that "only through public consensus in its plentiful liberty and sovereignty will we be able to arrive at negotiations based on good faith that attain the passage to the necessary reconciliation of all Paraguayans in a process of transition toward a pluralistic democracy."[26]

Suggesting that the situation called for a national reconciliation, Roa Bastos proposed several conditions for a peaceful changeover, among them lifting the state of siege, elimination of all laws that sanctioned repressive activities, full respect for human rights, guarantees of all rights sanctioned by the Constitution, changing the electoral law, and creation of a transitional government that would call for all parties to participate in and sponsor an amnesty for all political prisoners. Roa Bastos believed that the two key institutions of Paraguayan society, the Catholic church and the armed forces could act as guarantors of the entire process, through to creation of a pluralistic democracy. He envisioned a larger role for the armed forces, and a lesser role for the opposition political parties. Although well intentioned, the Roa proposal came up short in laying out ways and means for bringing about his sweeping improvements.

Fernando Levi Rufinelli weighed in with a proposal in March. He put an almost exclusive emphasis on open and clean elections. His position was that although there was ample agreement among the opposition parties on the need for an active political fight because they were against the use of violence, elections were therefore the proper weapon in the battle that would accompany the expected transition to democracy.[27]

Levi Rufinelli explained his logic by saying that because the opposition continued not to accept the election conditions imposed by the regime, it was responsible for its inability to achieve political change. In essence, to promote political change, the opposition should unite on a single candidate and participate in the elections under the conditions sanctioned by the regime for the past three decades. It is clear that Levi Rufinelli leaned more toward providing further legalization of the regime rather than promoting change. He failed to see that the unification of the opposition that he projected was only a cosmetic improvement. Operating within the restrictions imposed by the regime, no opposition—unified or not—could manage a victory.

The leader of the Partido Liberal Radical Auténtico (Authentic Liberal Radical party), Domingo Laíno, presented his "Bases para un Proyecto de Transición de la Dictadura a la Democracia" for the first time in August of 1985 in Buenos Aires during an international conference. Laíno called for the active participation of the people, and emphasized that the popular mobilization affecting different sectors showed the exhaustion of the dictatorship. Laíno wanted the transition to be peaceful, quick, democratic, and open, and to have a high degree of popular participation.

Laíno expanded on the institutional actors that would be involved in the transition. The opposition would unify in a consulting body called the council of political representatives comprising members from all parties who would have equal representation and powers. A provisory military junta would be in charge of the transition while conducting a process of reinstitutionalization of the armed forces. The Catholic church would act as a mediating institution between the opposition and the junta. Other economic, social, and cultural organizations would contribute to the transition through the appointed institutional channels or through open participation in the media.

A more elaborate proposal that went further into explanation of the crisis appeared in November under the title "Manifiesto Democrático."[28] Its authors were Euclides Acevedo and José Carlos Rodríguez. First, it correctly stated (1) that the authoritarian tradition of Paraguay antedated Stroessner; (2) that the crucial problem confronting Paraguay was the power vacuum that Stroessner's departure would occasion; (3) that because of the dictatorial nature of the regime, no mechanisms to deal with the power vacuum had been put into effect; and (4) that Paraguay should allow a political pact to bring about democracy and displace dictatorship.

Acevedo and Rodríguez also indicated that democratization would involve the contributions of professional, religious, and cultural institutions, the social movements, the political parties of the opposition and the official parties identified with democratic principles; the bureaucracy; the members of the legislative and judicial branches; and the international community. The transition could be accomplished in three stages: the first would involve the recovery of basic freedoms; the second, the political pact; and the third, the establishment of new norms and democratic powers. In the first stage, the proposal called for the abolition of laws and practices that endangered basic freedoms. In the second, the pact required a new electoral law and constitutional reform that would promote a more independent judiciary, a military without political affiliation, a less powerful executive, and the protection of human and civil rights. In the third stage, the new institutions of the state would engage in their specific activities: the constitutional assembly would be responsible for constitutional reforms, and the three independent branches would be the foundation of a democratic republic and a democratic state based on the rule of law.

The Revolutionary Febrerista party also provided a map for the transition to democracy. Although not as elaborate as other proposals, the document of the PRF provided a synthesis of the conditions extant in Paraguay at the time of the transition. The document highlighted the socioeconomic conditions affecting the agricultural sector, the industrial sector, foreign trade relations, the public debt, the impact of Itaipú, and other critical social problems. In light of the situation, the party proposed a political-institutional reorganization to reestablish the rule of law, after which emergency solutions for each of those areas could be implemented. Further, the document indicated that the authoritarian state no longer served Paraguay well. Social differentiation, an increase in per capita income, and dynamic urbanization were signs that the regime faced more than an economic crisis; it was a crisis of the entire social system.

Even though the Febrerista party did not provide ample details regarding the transition, it demanded that the regime recognize its limited role in the midst of changing conditions. More specifically, it suggested that the government eliminate smuggling and administrative corruption, constrain government budgets, impose taxes on individuals who had accumulated gains during the regime, and create an independent justice system.[29]

The Catholic church contributed to the transition process by organizing a national dialogue, the result of a series of proposals to improve the moral tenor of governance and bring to light the economic difficulties of the less privileged groups. The church had called for a dialogue that would include the opposition parties, the government, and several interest groups. Its proposal stemmed from its serious concern with public issues and the lack of unity between sectors of society, which the church deplored.

The Paraguayan Conference of Bishops was buoyed by a request from the National Accord to act as mediator between the opposition and the government. After the closing of the newspaper *ABC Color* in 1984, the church had stepped up its criticism of the Stroessner regime. On April 25 the bishops had released a document in which they "called for the unity and reconciliation of all those who live in this soil." Furthermore, the church had already pointed to dialogue among sectors as the only way to deal with the impending crisis. The bishops formally acceded to the request of the National Accord in March of 1986, but the Colorado party turned down the bishops' invitation to participate in a dialogue, saying that the proper place for national dialogue was the parliament, not a conference that included opposition parties not legally recognized.

Still, the church remained committed to a dialogue and patiently continued to press for it.

The various proposals show the complications attendant upon restoration of democracy subsequent to well-entrenched authoritarian rule. In the case of Paraguay, the range of suggestions indicated that the strong relationship between the Colorado party and the armed forces would be hard to break. Given the role of the military, it was obvious that the military would retain considerable leverage in determining the future of Paraguayan politics. The identification of the Colorado party with the military made the transition in prospect even more daunting unless a thoroughgoing rebuilding of key institutions was to be attempted.

While the mobilization of society was proceeding apace and as proposals for change multiplied, the Stroessner regime tried to dismiss the severity of the situation, hoping it could resort to the solutions of the past: repression and control. But the instability of the Colorado party was of concern to the military, and internal dissent acted as a catalyst to bring about a general consensus for change.[30]

The Coup and the Rodríguez Surprise

In the midst of so much speculation and pressure for an opening up of the political process, the Stroessner regime won the February 1988 elections, but without convincing the electorate of its legitimacy. The period prior to the election saw a speeding up of the mobilization of social and political groups, but elections during the Stroessner years had always been pro forma reaffirmations of the limited space given to the opposition and other groups. The expectation that a period of quiet politics would follow did not materialize this time because of the coup led by General Andrés Rodríguez, second to Stroessner in the line of command and one of the heirs apparent of the regime.

That Rodríguez would oust his former boss came as a surprise but was not wholly unexpected. The close relationship between the Colorado party and the military had been brought to a critical point by the divisions within the party. Allegiance to Stroessner had been the institutional position of the armed forces, but when Stroessner seemed unable to control the party, the military foresaw further struggles in the future. The ousting of the traditionalists from the August 1987 convention, together with controversial positions assumed by some of the pro-Stroessner men, prompted the military to agree with the traditionalists on a coup to oust the strongman. Pivotal in this process was the former president of the Supreme Court, Luis María Argaña, who, after having established a close relationship with Rodríguez, became one of the staunchest advocates of the traditionalists. Rodríguez used some of the decisions made by Stroessner concerning promotions and reassignments, which had alienated several military officers, to gain more support for the traditionalists.

The coup came about as a result of Stroessner's demand that Rodríguez accept the post of minister of defense or go into retirement. Rodríguez was an unlikely candidate to accept either of the two suggestions. He enjoyed the command of the largest share of troops as he led the army's 1st Cavalry Division and the 1st Army Corps; the position of defense minister would have carried substantially less power. Rodríguez was not likely to go into early retirement just to assure the continuity of Stroessner's tenure.

Relations between the two men were also complicated by feuding about money and personal matters. Rodríguez, a wealthy man who has been linked to smuggling and drug trafficking, controlled several businesses in Paraguay. The *Washington Post* reported that in late January 1989, Stroessner ordered the closing of all foreign exchange firms but allowed one of his sons to open a foreign exchange division in a bank. Rodríguez is said to own Cambios Guaraní, one of the largest foreign exchange companies in Paraguay. But, even if disharmonious personal relations precipitated the coup, the underlying reason that brought Rodríguez to power was the deterioration of Paraguayan politics.[31]

The coup took place the evening of February 2, 1989. It began in the Comando de Aeronáutica (Air Force Command) but was carried out by the Regimiento de Caballería Motorizado (Motorized Cavalry Regiment—RC2) with support from the Regimiento de Infantería "Cerro Corá" (1st Infantry Division—RI14) from Tacumbú, a unit of the 1st Army Corps. The Motorized Cavalry Regiment attacked the Presidential Escort Battalion, a small unit of about four hundred men who protect the president, the police headquarters, and the presidential palace. By early morning February 3, the forces led by General Rodríguez were in total control of the police headquarters and had taken Stroessner into custody at the 1st Army Corps in Asunción. Later on that day, Rodríguez assumed the presidency, closed down Congress, and restored Juan Ramón Cháves to the presidency of the Colorado party, a post he had lost in August 1987 to Sabino Augusto Montanaro, leader of the militant pro-Stroessner faction.

Rodríguez played to the sentiments of the nation by assuring Paraguayans that democracy would be restored, that human rights would be respected, and that the Catholic church would once again enjoy the institutional prerogatives negatively affected during the Stroessner regime. Rodríguez was effective in distancing himself from the regime he had helped strengthen over more than three decades. He recognized that a democratic order would replace the authoritarian state created by Stroessner. He also recognized the role of opposition groups by accepting their participation in a more open political arena. And he promoted respect for the Catholic church, which in recent years had adopted a more militant anti-Stroessner position and had grown closer to the opposition. The Rodríguez message brought hope and the expectation that a new era was about to begin.

Dissolution of Congress created a serious obstacle for the democratization process because according to the Constitution, elections would have to take place within three months. Immediately upon taking over the presidency, Rodríguez invited all political parties to participate in new elections on May 1. With only a few weeks to get ready, the challenge was substantial for the opposition, especially after so many years of absolute dictatorial rule. Even so, the opposition parties accepted with enthusiasm.

The New Election:
The Transition from Within

The elections of May 1, 1989, marked the end of the Stroessner era. General Andrés Rodríguez became the new president of Paraguay, in the freest elections that Paraguay has known. In a sense, the end of Stroessner's rule was ironic: he lost his seat to one of his closest associates, who had gained political momentum by bringing into the open the uncertain future looming for post-Stroessner Paraguay.

The election also marked the beginning of the democratization of Paraguayan politics. Just as in the case of Portugal in 1974, the army, after having provided ample support to a dictatorship, confronted an aging dictator and a severe institutional crisis, and became the path to a new political order. What that order will be in Paraguay remains uncertain. Although reform of the electoral laws, the participation of all political parties in the elections, and the relative freedom brought back by Rodríguez are very positive signs for the future, the real challenge remains embedded in the nature of Paraguayan society. A process of socialization will have to be initiated if a more democratic political culture is to emerge, and a redistribution of power among the executive, legislative, and judicial branches will have to be arranged through constitutional reform.

The quick pace of Stroessner's leavetaking confirms that authoritarian regimes based on the distribution of ill-gotten gains, corruption, and fear cannot sustain themselves in power forever. On the other hand, his longevity at the top shows that when enough resources are available to the elite, that when enough repression ensures a weak and ineffective opposition, and that when a cult of personality is built around the persona of a leader, authoritarian regimes can take tenacious hold. Long-lasting dictators do not promote effective political development in the Third World. Now that the eyes of the world are on events unfolding in Paraguay, the nation will try once again to move toward democracy, and with it, toward a more fulfilling and dignified life for all its citizens.

Notes

1. In two conversations with me, members of both of these organizations recognized the severity of the situation in early 1983 but were unwilling to discuss any economic data that involved the post-1981 period.

2. See Richard Lynn Ground, "El auge y recesión de la economía paraguaya, 1972–1983. El papel de la política económica interna," in *Economía del Paraguay Contemporáneo*, ed. Carlos Fletschner et al. (Asunción: Centro Paraguayo de Estudios Sociológicos, 1984), p. 522. See also Comité de Iglesias, Departamento de Estudios, *Apuntes Trimestrales* 1 (January–March 1983): 34.

3. Ground, "El auge y recesión de la economía paraguaya," p. 523.

4. Ibid., p. 526.

5. Comité de Iglesias, *Apuntes Trimestrales*, 1: 43.

6. "Economic uncertainty rises in Paraguay," *Latin American Regional Reports Southern Cone*, RS–84–06, 2 August 1984.

7. "Higher 1988 budget approved by senate," *Latin American Regional Reports Southern Cone*, RS–88–01, 4 February 1988, p. 3.

8. "Controversy over growth figures," *Latin American Regional Reports Southern Cone*, RS–88–08, 13 October 1988, p. 7.

9. "A victory for tradition," *Latin America Weekly Report*, WR–85–30, 2 August 1985, p. 3.

10. "Militantes gain control of party," *Latin America Weekly Report*, WR–87–31, 13 August 1987, p. 3.

11. "Stroessner orders Colorados to unite," *Latin America Weekly Report*, WR–87–06, 12 February 1987, p. 9.

12. "Stroessner's heirs jockey for places," *Latin American Regional Reports Southern Cone*, RS–80–06, 1 August 1980, pp. 3–4.

13. Amancio Pampliega, *Misión Cumplida* (Asunción: El Lector, 1985), pp. 207–12.

14. "Stroessner defends the past," *Latin American Regional Reports Southern Cone*, RS–83–10, 23 December 1983, p. 6.

15. "Losing friends north & south," *Latin America Weekly Report*, WR–86–04, 24 January 1986, p. 3.

16. "Colorado tactics get more violent," *Latin America Weekly Report*, WR–87–39, 8 October 1987, p. 5.

17. "Bonn denies Stroessner visit," *Latin America Weekly Report*, WR–86–17, 2 May 1986, p. 2.

18. For a compilation of the articles that *ABC Color* published, see Alcibiades González del Valle and Edwin Brítez, *Por qué clausuraron ABC Color* (Asunción: Editorial Histórica, 1987). See also "Death of *ABC Color* is grim warning,"

Latin American Regional Reports Southern Cone, RS–84–03, 13 April 1984; "Stroessner checks Colorado dissent," and "Media scored for ABC Shut down," *Latin American Regional Reports Southern Cone*, RS–84–05, 29 June 1984.

19. The document was entitled "Apreciaciones sobre la economía nacional." See "Feprinco sounds a warning note," *Latin American Regional Reports Southern Cone*, RS–82–01, 29 January 1982, p. 7; and Pablo Alfredo Herken Krauer, *Vía Crucis Económico: 1982–1986* (Asunción: Editorial Arte Nuevo, 1986), p. 33.

20. In 1983 the organization criticized the existence of multiple exchange rates for exports and imports. The 1984 document was signed by Tito F. Scavone, and it included reports from organizations outlining their export receipts and the cost of importing the products they needed for manufacturing. See Herken Krauer, *Vía Crucis Económico*, pp. 81–84, 158–61.

21. "New Feprinco boss outlines reform," *Latin American Weekly Report*, WR–87–48, 10 December 1987, p. 5.

22. Some of the confrontations were very violent. The army together with landowners burned ranchos in Curuguaty, ejected squatters in Concepción, and arrested peasant leaders in Caaguazú. The peasants feared a repression similar to the one in 1981, when twelve were killed and several others disappeared because of having taken a bus to ride to Asunción to protest against the government.

23. "Signs of opening for opposition," *Latin American Regional Reports Southern Cone*, RS–84–01, 3 February 1984.

24. "Acuerdo Nacional riding high," *Latin American Regional Reports Southern Cone*, RS–85–04, 24 May 1985, p. 7.

25. "Clergy announce protest campaign," *Latin America Weekly Report*, WR–87–42, 29 October 1987, p. 3; "Thousands join silent march," *Latin America Weekly Report*, WR–87–44, 12 November 1987, p. 3; "La Iglesia exhorta a un nuevo modo de convivencia política," *Sendero*, 15 January 1988, p. 8.

26. José Luis Simón G. et al., *Paraguay: Transición, Diálogo y Modernización Política* (Asunción: El Lector, 1987), p. 184. The translation is mine.

27. The document circulated in Asunción was entitled "Nuevo Planteamiento de Lucha Cívica Activa: Coalición Electoral de la Oposición. Fundamentación y Desarrollo del Planteamiento."

28. Euclides Acevedo and José Carlos Rodríguez, *Manifiesto Democrático: Una propuesta para el cambio* (Asunción: Editorial Araverá, 1986).

29. The text of the Febrerista proposal is reprinted in Simón et al., *Paraguay*, p. 233.

30. See John Hoyt Williams, "Paraguay's Stroessner: Losing Control," *Current History* (January 1987): 25–35.

31. "Paraguay's New Ruler Had Disputes with Stroessner," *Washington Post* February 4, 1989, p. A19.

The Stroessner Era

8 The experience of Paraguay under Stroessner provides a special opportunity to examine the process of consolidation in an authoritarian regime in Latin America. For nearly three and a half decades the tenure of the Stroessner administration went on unchallenged. The stability achieved by the regime invites a simple conclusion: authoritarianism in Paraguay worked well and has proven useful in guiding the modernization process of the nation. Additional elements need to be considered, however, to appreciate more fully the Paraguayan process of political development.

In fairness to the history of Paraguay and in order to draw accurate inferences applicable to other countries from the Paraguayan experience, a careful discussion of the additional elements is in order. Stroessner clearly understood the history of the nation, and he emphasized symbolic elements and traditions that reminded the population of its authoritarian past. The reason for such constant referral to historical events was that the Paraguayan people see their history as a struggle against internal and external opponents. They view their past as benign, and praise José Gaspar Rodríguez de Francia and Carlos Antonio López for their contributions to the creation of the nation. The struggle for independence is seen not so much as liberation from the Spanish but as an effort to resist the integrationist efforts of Buenos Aires. Hence, Paraguayans grant heroic stature to men whom they perceive as dedicated to protecting the nation from external threats and internal subversion.

The strong presidencies of Francia and López made firm the belief that personal leadership is best. During the early half of the nineteenth century, Paraguay achieved impressive economic results and maintained a stable political environment. The ascetic Francia provided the guidance necessary for the country to prosper, and citizens learned early the benefits flowing from strong, centralized leadership. When Carlos López succeeded Francia, few Paraguayans questioned his resolute style. The manner in which Paraguayans honor their "dictators" of the nineteenth century manifests their honest belief that these personalistic leaders were truly a product of the Paraguayan heritage. Citizens surprise themselves whenever they talk about installing a democratic, pluralistic, and competitive system. Their past has socialized them into supporting authoritarian rule. Competitive democracy remains a foreign concept that finds little application in the politics of Paraguay during the twentieth century. In light of the public's conviction about the desirability of authoritarian regimes, the leaders' ability to play up to time-honored symbols strengthens the foundation of authoritarianism and promotes its consolidation.

The tendency to accept paternalistic leaders with strong authoritarian traits was largely the consequence of Paraguay's experience during colonial times. With less wealth than most other peoples of Latin America, the native population of Paraguay enjoyed instead abundance from the soil and a salubrious climate. The Jesuit order, looking for a group of natives whom it could introduce to a "civilized" lifestyle, found in the Indian tribes a quiet, subdued, and gentle people. With the support and friendship of the Guaraní, the order labored extensively to create communities and promote the earthly and supernatural values that it endorsed.

Stroessner's ascendancy resulted from a series of complicated internal events that took place during the early part of the twentieth century. Whenever Paraguay departed from its authoritarian tradition, internal confrontations, instability, and chaos prevailed. Since the beginning of the century and until Stroessner took office in 1954, Paraguay had thirty-four presidents. Their average tenure was much less than the presidential terms of five years sanctioned by the Constitution. Rioting, personal clashes, and even a major war with Bolivia in the 1930s show that Paraguay's lack of political unity pushed the nation in a direction not congruent with its own traditions. The image of Paraguay in the hands of the nineteenth-century strongmen contrasted to the weak and unstable environment provided by the twentieth-century liberals forced many to hope for a return to the traditional authoritarian order, to what they believed were better times.

On the other hand, by no means all explanations concerning the consolidation of the Stroessner regime can be provided via a historical perspective. It is true that history to some extent determines the range of political options open to a society, but the entire experience of authoritarianism cannot be reduced merely to a successful connection with the past. Stroessner understood Paraguayan politics all too well. Although an army officer, he was aware of and learned from the personal confrontations between leaders of different political groups while he was still a battalion commander. He actively participated in coups and countercoups and mastered the operation of Paraguayan politics.

Furthermore, Stroessner devised an organizational network that permeated government and society. He utilized the Colorado party to penetrate neighborhoods and enlisted the support of different sectors of the population. The party offered him excellent communication channels to the people, and he had little trouble in using the party on his own behalf. During the early 1950s, the Colorados were no more internally united than any other party in Paraguay. The party's truce with Stroessner solved some of its internal discord and, along with the sanction of the armed forces, undergirded a long tenure for the regime.

The simple resolution of intraparty conflicts was not without tension. Other members entertained their own ambitions. The web of political support that brought Stroessner to power almost automatically crushed the chances that other serious contenders may have had for the presidential seat, but some did not understand the situation in such terms. Early in the life of the regime, Stroessner moved quickly to eliminate the challenges of Epifanio Méndez Fleitas and Edgar Ynsfrán by encouraging and exploiting their failures in their individual posts. Stroessner recognized that if the presidency was to be his for an undetermined duration, he needed to go beyond resolution of personal clashes and internal party strife.

Méndez Fleitas and Ynsfrán were much more than two men with presidential ambitions. They were leaders of Colorado party factions and received considerable support from local Colorado groups. By swiftly removing them from the political limelight, Stroessner reduced party matters to a single proposition: loyalty to him and his style of politics. After the removal of Méndez Fleitas and Ynsfrán, Stroessner's control of the party was unquestioned and he governed with his own brand of authoritarianism.

A uniform ideological base gathered support around the figure of the president himself. Indeed, it would be fair to say that his leadership did, in some sense, increase the role of "consensual" politics. Political positions were his own domain throughout the entire system, and identification with an ideology represented by a strong, personalistic figure consolidated the foundations of the regime. Stroessner created an ideological alternative both to the Colorado party and to the opposition. Of course, more negatively, he also drove into exile a large proportion of the Paraguayan population, that part unable to live under the norms, institutions, and elitism of the system that he nurtured for so long.

The combination of historical tendencies and strong personalism proved to be necessary conditions for the consolidation of authoritarianism in Paraguay. Stroessner's ideological orientations pervaded policy-making and produced reinforcing mechanisms by which the consolidation process gained strength. Among those orientations, control policies and economic co-optation were the foundation of Stroessner's administrative policy-making style.

Control policies rested on a combination of legal, constitutional, and ideological principles. The population was instructed as to how it could articulate political demands within the system. Dissent was silenced, the free press was persecuted, and bargaining institutions were crippled. Security institutions extended their role to civilian groups in an effort to undermine organized efforts to challenge the regime. The most important restrictions were those related to the functioning of the political system itself. In the past three decades, political parties were saddled with myriad new legal prerequisites to their gaining full rights. Congressional action became the seal of approval for the regime's policies and initiatives. The Stroessner administration's ability to function with impunity demonstrated that it could achieve its purposes through the normal channels of policy-making. Nevertheless, each institution reflected the limitations imposed on it through the extensive control apparatus of the regime.

The same message reached the population clearly and strongly. Open defiance and dissent were not tolerated and Paraguayans quickly adapted to that reality. They hedged their criticisms and resigned themselves to their contemporary fate. Repression, though not practiced on a grand scale, as in Chile or Argentina, was a constant reminder that the regime went beyond merely exercising power on a transitional or temporary basis. An environment of distrust, fear, and suspicion enveloped the nation. With a constant level of control articulated through key political institutions, the regime increased its ability to go on unchallenged.

Stroessner also understood that his most serious threat came not from outside elements but from within his own administration and support base. Paraguayan politics is rather special in this way: loyalty is given only so long as there exist some obvious gains. The regime could easily prevent challenges from outsiders but challenges from within proved less amenable to usual control practices. When members of the entourage mistakenly disapproved of the regime's policies, they were quietly ejected from the political system. A single mistake could easily end an entire political career.

Among those who presented the greatest risk of internal challenge were members of the armed forces. The Stroessner regime created a co-optation scheme by which military officers benefited as much from the regime as they did from staying out of politics. The combination proved a skillful move on the part of the president, and one that remained successful over the years. Stroessner "legalized" the right of military officers to engage in practices whose profits filled their pockets. Most of them became associated with a small sector of the government structure, and the government left it up to them to devise ways by which they could profit financially.

The most popular arrangement was in international trade. Paraguay's long border entailed many security problems, but its location made it a strategic transnational shipping hub. Paraguay was and is a player in the major leagues of international smuggling, and military officers skimmed off much of the cream. Although not all officers participated in "outside activities," the highest echelons of the armed forces were heavily involved in providing infrastructure and logistics to the smuggling network—at a price. Their example soon trickled down, so that other bureaucrats began to do the same. A bribe bought almost anything in Stroessner's Paraguay.

These economic benefits kept the military at bay, giving the regime virtual control of the country and allowing furtherance of the regime goals. Economic growth was impressive during the 1970s, once the new political system was consolidated, but the benefits were unevenly distributed. Many Paraguayans increased their ability to consume, and the regime gladly took credit for the new lifestyle. For the economy as a whole, however, there were no changes. Paraguay remains dependent on a few agricultural crops; it has developed little industry, partly because this would end the smuggling trade; it has not provided enough job opportunities; and migration to neighboring countries continues to drain human resources.

The consolidation of the regime was possible only because of the nature of Paraguay's political culture. The Stroessner experience redefined the political orientations of the population in a clear and particular authoritarian direction. Most of the population quietly accepted the autocratic form of government, whatever the cost, partially because of the political apathy that had developed. Paraguayans grew cynical about the political system. The younger generation was distancing itself from politics because it understood that politics was the province of a very select elite. Changes in individual attitudes toward politics help to explain why the transition from authoritarianism to democracy will be such a complex and difficult task in Paraguay. Unlike the transitional authoritarian governments of Brazil and Argentina in the early 1980s, the Stroessner regime was not a dictatorial administration helping the country grow toward a democratic future. The prospects for this sort of transition in Paraguay have increased under the administration of General Andrés Rodríguez, but much needs still to be done in order to prepare the nation for a more democratic style.

The level of support achieved by Stroessner promotes the interpretation that the regime had achieved a high degree of legitimacy. A closer inspection of the manner in which the support was gained necessitates a different conclusion. The legitimacy could have indicated Paraguayans' belief that the system worked well and therefore merited support, but—

given the defined roles of institutions, and the choices presented to the people—the support also reflected the constraints imposed on the population. The decision to support the regime may have been made because the system seemed to work well but also because it was impossible to uphold an alternative.

Paraguay under Stroessner achieved a high degree of consolidation, based, essentially, on successful policy-making and a correct reading of the historical and cultural traditions of the country. A foreign policy designed to keep the country isolated from the rest of the world, reinforced the nature of the regime. Even after the departure of the leader himself, the years of Stroessner's rule and the system that he created remain a laboratory of complexity and potential insights for those who wish to study the alternative processes of authoritarian consolidation. For the variables examined in this context to be better understood, the analysis must be extended to other authoritarian regimes. Similar cases in other geographical and socioeconomic contexts must be examined from this perspective. Only by the application of specific criteria to a number of comparative cases can we understand the consolidation of authoritarian regimes.

Selected Bibliography

Academia de Historia Militar del Paraguay. *Anuario de la Academia de Historia Militar del Paraguay.* Vol. 1, *Años 1984–1985.* Asunción: Estudio Gráfico, 1985.

Acevedo, Euclides, and Rodríguez, José Carlos. *Manifiesto Democrático: Una propuesta para el cambio.* Asunción: Editorial Araverá, 1986.

Adams, Nathan M. "The Hunt for André." *Reader's Digest,* March 1973, pp. 224–59.

Adorno, T. W.; Frenkel-Brunswik, Else; Levinson, Daniel J.; and Sanford, R. Nevitt. *The Authoritarian Personality.* New York: Norton, 1950.

Alegre, Heriberto. "La colonización en el Paraguay: El eje este." *Revista Paraguaya de Sociología* 14 (January-April 1977): 135–55.

Allardt, Erik, and Rokkan, Stein, eds. *Mass Politics: Studies in Political Sociology.* New York: Free Press, 1970.

Almond, Gabriel A. *Political Development: Essays in Heuristic Theory.* Boston: Little, Brown, 1970.

Almond, Gabriel A., and Coleman, James S., eds. *The Politics of the Developing Areas.* Princeton: Princeton University Press, 1960.

Almond, Gabriel A., and Powell, G. Bingham, Jr. *Comparative Politics: A Developmental Approach.* Boston: Little, Brown, 1966.

Almond, Gabriel, and Verba, Sidney. *The Civic Culture: Political Attitudes and Democracy in Five Nations.* Princeton: Princeton University Press, 1963.

———, eds. *The Civic Culture Revisited.* Boston: Little, Brown, 1980.

Alsina, Ezequiel González. *El Dr. Francia del pueblo y ensayos varios.* Asunción: Instituto Colorado de Cultura, 1978.

Amnesty International. *Prison Conditions in Paraguay: Conditions for Political Prisoners: A Factual Report.* London: Amnesty International, 1966.

———. *Report on Torture.* New York: Noonday, 1973.

Anderson, Bo, and Cockcroft, James. "Control and Co-Optation in Mexican Politics." *International Journal of Comparative Sociology* 7 (March 1966): 2–28.

Anderson, Charles W. *Politics and Economic Change in Latin America.* Princeton: Princeton University Press, 1967.

"Another Victim of Violence." *LADOC* 70 (September-October 1976): 14–15.

Apter, David A. *Choice and the Politics of Allocation.* New Haven: Yale University Press, 1971.

———. *Conceptual Approaches to the Study of Modernization.* Englewood Cliffs, N.J.: Prentice-Hall, 1964.

———. *Ghana in Transition.* New York: Atheneum, 1963.

———. *Political Change.* London: Cass, 1973.

———. *The Politics of Modernization.* Chicago: University of Chicago Press, 1965.

Argaña, Luis María. *Historia de las ideas políticas en el Paraguay.* Asunción: Biblioteca Colorados Contemporáneos, 1979.

Arendt, Hannah. *The Origins of Totalitarianism.* New York: World, 1958.

Arens, Richard, ed. *Genocide in Paraguay.* Philadelphia: Temple University Press, 1976.

Arnold, Adlai F. *Foundations of an Agricultural Policy in Paraguay.* New York: Praeger, 1971.

Asociación Nacional Republicana. *Acta de fundación del Partido Colorado y estatutos.* Asunción: Ed. Universo, n.d.

———. *Definiciones del coloradismo Paraguayo.* N.p., 1978.

———. *Homenaje de la Junta de Gobierno del Partido Colorado a la memoria del fundador Gral. de Div. Bernardino Caballero.* Asunción: Departamento de Prensa de la Junta de Gobierno de la ANR, 1976.

Asociación Nacional Republicana (Partido Colorado). *Declaración de principios y nuevo programa partidario.* Asunción: Casa América, Editorial Gráfica, 1984.

———. *El candidato del Partido Colorado a la presidencia de la república por el período 1973–1978, General de Ejército Alfredo Stroessner.* Asunción: Junta de Gobierno, 1972.

———. *El Coloradismo está para marcar rumbos, no para servir de furgón de cola de nadie.* N.p., 1980.

———. *El General Bernardino Caballero.* Asunción: Casa América, 1979.

———. *El trato a los disidentes en un régimen totalitario: El caso Melgarejo-Verón en el Paraguay.* N.p., 1981.

———. *El vice presidente 1o. de la honorable junta de gobierno del Partido Colorado, Dr. Sabino Augusto Montanaro.* Asunción: Casa América, Editorial Gráfica, 1972.

———. *Mensaje del coloradismo Paraguayo a toda la ciudadanía.* N.p., 1980.

Asociación Nacional Republicana (Partido Colorado) Junta de Gobierno del Exilio y la Resistencia. *Declaración de principios y programa mínimo.* N.p., 1973.

Baer, Werner. "The Paraguayan Economic Condition: Past and Current Obstacles to Economic Modernization." *Inter-American Economic Affairs* 29 (Winter 1975): 49–63.

Baer, Werner, and Birch, Melissa. "Expansion of the Economic Frontier: Paraguayan Growth in the 1970s." *World Development* 12 (August 1984): 783–98.

Báez Acosta, Pedro. *Trabajando también se construye una nación: Estudios económicos sobre el Paraguay.* Buenos Aires: Ediciones Patria Libre, 1956.

Bailey, Samuel L., ed. *Nationalism in Latin America.* New York: Knopf, 1971.

Barrett, William E. *Woman on Horseback.* New York: Frederick A. Stokes, 1938.

Bendix, Reinhard, ed. *State and Society: A Reader in Comparative Political Sociology.* Boston: Little, Brown, 1968.

Benítez, Justo Pastor. *Estigarribia: El soldado del Chaco.* 2d ed. Buenos Aires: Ediciones Nizza, 1958.

Bermejo, Idelfonso A. *Vida Paraguaya en tiempos del viejo López.* Buenos Aires: EUDEBA, 1973.

Blachman, Morris J., and Hellman, Ronald G., eds. *Terms of Conflict: Ideology in Latin American Politics.* Philadelphia: Institute for the Study of Human Issues, 1977.

Black, Cyril E., ed. *Comparative Modernization: A Reader.* New York: Free Press, 1976.

————. *The Dynamics of Modernization: A Study in Comparative History.* New York: Harper & Row, 1966.

Blomberg, Héctor P. *La Dama del Paraguay.* Buenos Aires: Editora Interamericana, 1942.

Bordón, F. Arturo. *Historia política del Paraguay: Era constitucional, 1869–1886*, vol. 1. Asunción: Orbis, 1976.

Bray, Arturo. *Hombres y épocas del Paraguay.* 3d ed. 2 vols. Buenos Aires: Ediciones Nizza, 1957.

Brodersohn, Mario S. "Sobre modernización y autoritarismo y el estancamiento inflacionario argentino." *Desarrollo Económico* 13 (October-December 1973): 591–605.

Brodsky, Alyn. *Madame Lynch and Friend.* New York: Harper & Row, 1975.

Bruneau, Thomas C. *Religiosity and Politicization in Brazil: The Church in an Authoritarian Regime.* Austin: University of Texas Press, 1981.

Bruneau, Thomas C., and Faucher, Philippe, eds. *Authoritarian Capitalism: Brazil's Contemporary Economic and Political Development.* Boulder, Colo.: Westview Press, 1981.

Cabrera, Gaspar N. *Carácter peculiar de la cultura Guaraní.* Asunción: Imprenta Zamphirópolos, 1965.

Campos, Hugo. *"Paz y progreso" en el Paraguay.* Buenos Aires: Ediciones Actualidad, 1977.

Canese, Ricardo. *Itaipú y la cuestión energética en el Paraguay.* Asunción: Universidad Católica, 1983.

————. *Transporte eléctrico en el Paraguay. Su conveniencia.* Asunción: Biblioteca de Estudios Paraguayos, Universidad Católica, 1981.

Canese, Ricardo, and Mauro, Luis Alberto. *Itaipú: Dependencia o Desarrollo.* Asunción: Editorial Araverá, 1985.

Caraman, Philip. *The Lost Paradise: The Jesuit Republic in South America.* New York: Seabury Press, 1976.

Cardoso, Fernando H. "On the Characterization of Authoritarian Regimes in Latin America." In *The New Authoritarianism in Latin America*, edited by David Collier, pp. 33–57. Princeton: Princeton University Press, 1979.

————. "Towards Another Development." In *From Dependency to Development*, edited by Heraldo Muñoz, pp. 295–313. Boulder, Colo.: Westview Press, 1981.

Cardoso, Fernando, and Faletto, Enzo. *Dependency and Development in Latin America.* English Translation. Berkeley: University of California Press, 1979.

Cardozo, Efraím. *Apuntes de historia cultural del Paraguay.* Asunción: Biblioteca de Estudios Paraguayos, 1985.

————. *Aspectos de la cuestión del Chaco.* Asunción: Imprenta Nacional, 1932.

————. *Breve historia del Paraguay.* Buenos Aires: EUDEBA, 1965.

Caroni, Carlos A. *Paraguay: Formación y supervivencia.* Asunción: N.p., 1975.

Carta Colectiva del Episcopado Paraguayo. *Año de reflexión eclesial.* Asunción: Secretariado General de la CEP, 1973.

Carta Pastoral de la Conferencia Episcopal Paraguaya. *El campesino Paraguayo y la tierra.* Asunción: Secretariado General de la CEP, 1983.

Céspedes, Roberto Luis; Herken, Pablo A.; and Simón, José Luis. *Paraguay: Sociedad, Economía y Política.* Asunción: El Lector, 1988.

Ceuppens, Henry D. *Paraguay: Año 2000.* Asunción: Editorial Zamphirópolos, 1971.

Chase-Sardi, Miguel. *La situación actual de los indígenas en el Paraguay.* Asunción: Centro de Estudios Antropológicos, Universidad Católica, 1972.

Chaves, Julio César. *El Presidente López: Vida y gobierno de Don Carlos.* Buenos Aires: Editorial Ayacucho, 1955.

————. *El supremo dictador.* 4th ed. Madrid: Ediciones Atlas, 1964.

Chaves, Osvaldo. *La formación del pueblo Paraguayo.* Buenos Aires: Ediciones Amerindia, 1976.

————. *El trabajo humano.* N.p., 1981.

Cheresky, Isidoro, and Choncol, Jacques, eds. *Crisis y transformación de los regímenes autoritarios.* Buenos Aires: Editorial Universitaria de Buenos Aires, 1985.

Chilcote, Ronald H. *Theories of Comparative Politics: The Search for a Paradigm.* Boulder, Colo.: Westview Press, 1981.

Claude, Richard Pierre. "The Case of Joelito Filartiga and the Clinic of Hope." *Human Rights Quarterly* 5 (1983): 275–301.

Cockcroft, James D.; Frank, André Gunder; and Johnson, Dale L. *Dependence and Underdevelopment: Latin America's Political Economy.* Garden City, N.Y.: Doubleday, 1972.

Collier, David. *Squatters and Oligarchs: Authoritarian Rule and Policy Change in Peru.* Baltimore: Johns Hopkins University Press, 1976.

————, ed. *The New Authoritarianism in Latin America.* Princeton: Princeton University Press, 1979.

Comblin, José. *The Church and the National Security State.* Maryknoll, N.Y.: Orbis Books, 1970.

Comisión Nacional Sobre la Desaparición de Personas. *Nunca Más.* Buenos Aires: EUDEBA, 1984.

Confederación Internacional de Organizaciones Sindicales Libres. *Paraguay: Historia de un dictadura.* N.p., 1982.

Confederación Paraguaya de Trabajadores en el Exilio. *Los trabajadores Paraguayos frente a la tiranía de Stroessner.* N.p., 1975.

————. *Los trabajadores Paraguayos frente a la tiranía de Stroessner.* N.p., 1983.

————. *27 de Agosto: 25o. aniversario de la gloriosa gesta obrera Paraguaya.* N.p., 1983.

Conferencia Episcopal Paraguaya. *Tierra y sociedad: Problemática de la tierra urbana, rural e indígena en el Paraguay.* Asunción: Equipo Nacional de Pastoral de la CEP, 1984.

Conferencia Episcopal Paraguaya, Equipo Nacional de Pastoral Social. *Fe cristiana y compromiso social.* Asunción: EDIPAR, 1984.

Corvalán, Grazziella. "Ideologías y origen social de los grupos políticos en el Paraguay." *Revista Paraguaya de Sociología* 9 (January-April 1972): 106–18.

Corvalán Vázquez, Oscar. "Recursos humanos y empleo en el Paraguay." In *Economía del Paraguay contemporáneo,* vol. 1, pp. 139–201. Asunción: Centro Paraguayo de Estudios Sociológicos, 1984.

D'Epinay, Christian Lalive, and Necker, Louis. "Paraguay (1811–1870): A Utopia of Self-Oriented Change." In *Self-Reliance: A Strategy for Development,* edited by Johan Galtung, Peter O'Brien, and Roy Preiswerk, pp. 249–68. London: Bogle-L'Ouverture Publications, 1980.

Dahl, Robert A. *Polyarchy: Participation and Opposition.* New Haven: Yale University Press, 1971.

————. *Regimes and Oppositions.* New Haven: Yale University Press, 1973.

Di Tella, Torcuato S. *Sociología de los procesos políticos: Una perspectiva latinoamericana.* Buenos Aires: Grupo Editor Latinoamericano, 1985.

Doldán, Enzo A. *Reflexiones sobre el liberalismo y los partidos políticos en el Paraguay.* N.p.: Orbis, 1980.

Domínguez, Jorge I. "Smuggling." *Foreign Policy* 20 (Fall 1975): 87–164.

Duarte, Silvio. *27 de Agosto: 23o. aniversario de la gloriosa gesta de la CPT, hoy en el exilio.* N.p., 1982.

Duarte Prado, Bacon. *Esquema de una doctrina y praxis para la juventud colorada.* Asunción: Editorial Alborada, 1977.

Easton, David. "An Approach to the Analysis of Political Systems." *World Politics* 9 (April 1957): 383–400.

Eckstein, Harry, and Apter, David E., eds. *Comparative Politics: A Reader.* New York: Free Press of Glencoe, 1963.

Eckstein, Susan. *The Poverty of Revolution: The State and the Urban Poor in Mexico.* Princeton: Princeton University Press, 1976.

Economía del Paraguay contemporáneo. 2 vols. Asunción: Centro Paraguayo de Estudios Sociológicos, 1984.

Eisenstadt, S. N. *Modernization: Protests and Change.* Englewood Cliffs, N.J.: Prentice-Hall, 1966.

Enríquez Gamón, Efraín. *Economía Paraguaya: Planteamientos.* Asunción: Instituto ·Paraguayo de Estudios Geopolíticos e Internacionales, 1985.

————. *Itaipú: Aguas que valen oro.* Buenos Aires: Editorial Guadalupe, 1975.

Estigarribia, José F. "Comments on the Constitution of Paraguay." In vol. 3 of *Constitutions of Nations,* 2d ed., 4 vols., compiled by Amos J. Peaslee, pp. 128–30. The Hague: Martinius Nijhof, 1956.

Estragó, Margarita Durán. "Los Domínicos en el Paraguay." *Estudios Paraguayos* 11 (1983): 171–253.

Evans, Peter. *Dependent Development: The Alliance of Multinational, State and Local Capital in Brazil.* Princeton: Princeton University Press, 1979.

"Father Caravias Tells of His Deportation." *LADOC* 2 (June 1972): 38a.

Fagen, Richard R., and Tuohy, William S. *Politics and Privilege in a Mexican City.* Stanford: Stanford University Press, 1972.

Federación de Entidades Democráticas de América Latina. *Estatuto.* Asunción: Editorial El Foro, 1983.

Fernández, Carlos J. *La Guerra del Chaco.* 5 vols. Buenos Aires: N.p., 1956.

Filartiga v. Peña-Irala, 630 F.2d 876 (2d Cir. 1980).

Fitzgibbon, Russell H., and Fernández, Julio A. *Latin America: Political Culture and Development.* Englewood Cliffs, N.J.: Prentice-Hall, 1981.

Flecha, Agustín Oscar. *Vía crucis del subdesarrollo.* Asunción: Centro de Publicaciones de la Universidad Católica de Asunción, 1978.

Fletschner, Carlos. *Cién capítulos de economía Paraguaya.* Asunción: Universidad Católica Nuestra Señora de la Asunción, 1983.

Fogel, Ramón. *Movimientos Campesinos en el Paraguay: Estudio de dos casos históricos.* Asunción: Centro Paraguayo de Estudios Sociológicos, 1986.

Frank, André Gunder. *Capitalism and Underdevelopment in Latin America.* New York: Monthly Review Press, 1969.

————. *Development and Underdevelopment in Latin America.* New York: Monthly Review Press, 1968.

Friedrich, Carl J., ed. *Totalitarianism.* New York: Grosset & Dunlop, 1954.

Friedrich, Carl J., and Brzezinski, Zbigniew K. *Totalitarian Dictatorship and Autocracy.* 2d ed. New York: Praeger, 1965.

Friedrich, Carl J.; Curtis, Michael; and Barber, Benjamin R. *Totalitarianism in Perspective: Three Views.* New York: Praeger, 1969.

Fromm, Erich, and Maccoby, Michael. *Social Character in a Mexican Village.* Englewood Cliffs, N.J.: Prentice-Hall, 1970.

Frutos, Juan Manuel. *Fundamentos históricos y políticos de la Federación de Entidades Democráticas Latinoamericanas.* N.p.: Editorial El Foro, 1984.

Galtung, Johan; O'Brien, Peter; and Preiswerk, Roy, eds. *Self-Reliance: A Strategy for Development.* London: Bogle-L'Ouverture Publications, 1980.

García Mellid, Atilio. *Proceso a los falsificadores de la historia del Paraguay,* vol. 2. Buenos Aires: Ediciones Theoría, 1964.

Gendzier, Irene. *Managing Political Change: Social Scientists and the Third World.* Boulder, Colo.: Westview Press, 1985.

Germani, Gino. *Authoritarianism, National Populism, and Fascism.* New Brunswick, N.J.: Transaction Books, 1977.

Gerschenkron, Alexander. *Economic Backwardness in Historical Perspective.* New York: Praeger, 1962.

Gómez Fleytas, José Gaspar. "Ubicación histórica de los partidos tradicionales en el Paraguay." *Revista Paraguaya de Sociología* 7 (September-December 1970): 144–64.

González, Antonio. *La rebelión de Concepción.* Buenos Aires: Editorial Guarania, 1947.

González, J. Natalicio. "Meditaciones Actuales." In *Cómo se construye una nación,* pp. 147–54. Asunción: Editorial Guarania, 1949.

González, Juan Natalicio. *Ideología Guaraní.* Ediciones Especiales, No. 37. Mexico: Instituto Indigenista Interamericano, 1958.

————. *Proceso y formación de la cultura Paraguaya.* Asunción: Editorial Guarania, 1948.

González, Natalicio. *Proceso y formación de la cultura Paraguaya.* Asunción: Instituto Colorado de Cultura, 1976.

González Delvalle, Alcibíades. *Mi voto por el pueblo y otros comentarios.* 2 vols. Buenos Aires: Ediciones Pigmalión, 1984–85.

González Delvalle, Alcibíades, and Brítez, Edwin. *Por qué clausuraron ABC Color.* Asunción: Editorial Histórica, 1987.

González Viera, Mauro. *Paraguay frente al futuro.* Asunción: N.p., 1972.

Graham, R. B. Cunninghame. *A Vanished Arcadia.* New York: Haskell House, 1968.

———. *Portrait of a Dictator: Francisco Solano López. Paraguay, 1865–1870.* London: William Heinemann, 1933.

Greenstein, Fred I., and Polsby, Nelson W., eds. *Macro-Political Theory.* Reading, Mass.: Addison-Wesley, 1975.

Griffin, Keith. *Underdevelopment in Spanish America.* Cambridge: M.I.T. Press, 1969.

Ground, Richard Lynn. " El auge y la recesión de la economía Paraguaya, 1972–1983. El papel de la política económica interna." In *Economía del Paraguay contemporáneo* 2:493–572. Asunción: Centro Paraguayos de Estudios Sociológicos, 1984.

Grow, Michael. *The Good Neighbor Policy and Authoritarianism in Paraguay.* Lawrence: Regents' Press of Kansas, 1981.

Guido y Spano, Carlos; Andrade, Olegario V.; Alberdi, Juan Bautista; Viola, Miguel Navarro; Gutiérrez, Juan María; and Seeber, Francisco. *Proceso a la guerra del Paraguay.* Prologue by León Pomer. Buenos Aires: Ediciones Caldén, 1968.

Gutiérrez, Ramón. "Estructura socio-política, sistema productivo y resultantes espacial en las misiones jesuíticas del Paraguay durante el siglo XVIII." *Estudios Paraguayos* 2 (December 1974): 83–140.

Harris, Louis K., and Alba, Victor. *The Political Culture and Behavior of Latin America.* Kent, Ohio: Kent State University Press, 1974.

Helfeld, David M., and Wipfler, William L. *Mbareté: The Higher Law of Paraguay.* New York: International League for Human Rights, 1980.

Herken, Juan Carlos. *Ferrocarriles, conspiraciones y negocios en el Paraguay: 1910–1914.* Asunción: Arte Nuevo Editores, 1984.

———. "El sector externo en la economía Paraguaya." *Estudios Paraguayos* 6 (September 1978): 87–114.

Herken Krauer, Juan Carlos. *El Paraguay rural entre 1869 y 1913: Contribuciones a la historia económica regional del Plata.* Asunción: Centro Paraguayo de Estudios Sociológicos, 1984.

———. "Proceso económico en el Paraguay de Carlos Antonio López: La visión del Cónsul Británico Henderson (1851–1860)." *Revista Paraguaya de Sociología* 19 (May-August 1982): 83–116.

Herken Krauer, Juan Carlos, and Giménez de Herken, María Isabel. *Gran Bretaña y la Guerra de la Triple Alianza.* Asunción: Editorial Arte Nuevo, 1982.

Herken Krauer, Pablo Alfredo. *Vía crucis económico, 1982–86.* Asunción: Editorial Arte Nuevo, 1986.

Hicks, Frederick. "Interpersonal Relationships and Caudillismo in Paraguay." *Journal of Interamerican Studies and World Affairs* 13 (January 1971): 89–111.

————. "Politics, Power and the Village Priest." *Journal of Inter-American Studies* 9 (April 1967): 273–82.

Hirschman, Albert. *A Bias for Hope: Essays on Development and Latin America.* New Haven: Yale University Press, 1971.

————. *Essays in Trespassing: Economics to Politics and Beyond.* New York: Cambridge University Press, 1981.

————. *Journeys toward Progress.* New York: Anchor Books, 1965.

————. *The Strategy of Economic Development.* New Haven: Yale University Press, 1958.

————, ed. *Toward a New Strategy for Development.* New York: Pergamon Press, 1979.

Huntington, Samuel P. *Political Order in Changing Societies.* New Haven: Yale University Press, 1968.

————. "Political Development and Political Decay." *World Politics* 17 (April 1965): 386–430.

————. "The Change to Change: Modernization, Development and Politics." *Comparative Politics* 3 (April 1971): 283–322.

Huntington, Samuel P., and Moore, Clement H., eds. *Authoritarian Politics in Modern Society: The Dynamics of Established One-Party Systems.* New York: Basic Books, 1970.

Huntington, Samuel P., and Nelson, Joan M. *No Easy Choice: Political Participation in Developing Countries.* Cambridge: Harvard University Press, 1976.

Instituto de Bienestar Rural. *Memoria 1982.* Asunción: Talleres Gráficos del Instituto, 1982.

"It is Calumny." *LADOC* 5 (August 1970): 1.

Jaguaribe, Helio. *Crisis y alternativas de América Latina.* Buenos Aires: Editorial Paidós, 1972.

————. *Economic and Political Development, A Theoretical Approach and a Brazilian Case Study.* Cambridge: Harvard University Press, 1968.

————. *Political Development: General Theory and a Latin American Case Study.* New York: Harper & Row, 1972.

Janowitz, Morris. *The Military in the Political Development of New Nations.* Chicago: University of Chicago Press, 1964.

Kabashima, Ikuo, and White, Lynn T., III, eds. *Political System and Change.* Princeton: Princeton University Press, 1986.

Kallsen, Osvaldo. *Historia del Paraguay contemporáneo, 1869–1983.* Asunción: Imprenta Modelo, 1983.

Kirscht, John P., and Dillehay, Robert C. *Dimensions of Authoritarianism: A Review of Research and Theory.* Lexington: University of Kentucky Press, 1967.

Kostianovsky, Pepa. *28 entrevistas para este tiempo.* 2d ed. Asunción: Universidad Católica de Asunción, 1985.

Laíno, Domingo. *Fronteras y penetración brasileña.* Asunción: Ediciones Cerro Corá, 1976.

———. *Paraguay: De la independencia a la dependencia.* Asunción: Ediciones Cerro Corá, 1976.

Lamounier, Bolivar. "Ideologia em regimes autoritários: Uma crítica a Juan J. Linz." *Estudos Cebrap* 7 (1974): 68–92.

Latin American Bureau. *Paraguay: Power Game.* London: Latin American Bureau, 1980.

Legislación Paraguaya: Recopilación de leyes, decretos leyes y decretos vigentes, vol. 1. Asunción: Universidad Católica, 1981.

Lerner, Daniel. *The Passing of Traditional Society: Modernizing the Middle East.* New York: Free Press, 1958.

Lernoux, Penny. *Cry of the People.* New York: Penguin Books, 1982.

Lescaze, Lee. "Paraguayan Police Figure Is Arrested in New York." *Washington Post,* April 5, 1979, p. A17.

Levine, Daniel H., ed. *Churches and Politics in Latin America.* Beverly Hills, Calif.: Sage Publications, 1980.

Lewis, Norman. "The Camp at Cecilio Baez." In *Genocide in Paraguay,* edited by Richard Arens, pp. 58–68. Philadelphia: Temple University Press, 1976.

Lewis, Paul H. *Paraguay Under Stroessner.* Chapel Hill: University of North Carolina Press, 1980.

———. *Socialism, Liberalism and Dictatorship in Paraguay.* New York: Praeger, 1982.

———. *The Politics of Exile: Paraguay's Febrerista Party.* Chapel Hill: University of North Carolina Press, 1965.

———. "Leadership and Conflict within the Febrerista Party of Paraguay." *Journal of Inter-American Studies* 9 (April 1967): 283–95.

Leys, Colin, ed. *Politics and Change in Developing Countries.* Cambridge: Cambridge University Press, 1969.

Liga Mundial Anticomunista. *Carta orgánica.* Asunción: Liga Mundial Anticomunista, 1979.

Lijphart, Arend. *Democracies: Patterns of Majoritarian and Consensus Government in Twenty-One Countries.* New Haven: Yale University Press, 1984.

Linz, Juan J. "An Authoritarian Regime: Spain." In *Mass Politics: Studies in Political Sociology,* edited by Erik Allardt and Stein Rokkan, pp. 251–83. New York: Free Press, 1970.

———. "Opposition to and under an Authoritarian Regime: The Case of Spain." In *Regimes and Oppositions,* edited by Robert A. Dahl, pp. 171–259. New Haven: Yale University Press, 1973.

———. "The Future of an Authoritarian Situation or the Institutionalization of an Authoritarian Regime: The Case of Brazil." In *Authoritarian Brazil: Origins, Policies and Future,* edited by Alfred Stepan, pp. 233–54. New Haven: Yale University Press, 1973.

———. "Totalitarian and Authoritarian Regimes." In *Macro-Political Theory,* edited by Fred I. Greenstein and Nelson W. Polsby, pp. 175–411. Reading, Mass.: Addison-Wesley, 1975.

Linz, Juan J., and Stepan, Alfred. *The Breakdown of Democratic Regimes: Latin America.* Baltimore: Johns Hopkins University Press, 1967.

Lipset, Seymour M. *Political Man: The Social Bases of Politics.* Expanded ed. Baltimore: Johns Hopkins University Press, 1981.

Los derechos de Bolivia sobre el Chaco Boreal y sus límites con el Paraguay. Buenos Aires: N.p., 1925.

Lott, Leo B. *Venezuela and Paraguay: Political Modernity and Tradition in Conflict.* New York: Holt, Rinehart & Winston, 1972.

Lugones, Leopoldo. *El imperio jesuítico.* Buenos Aires: Publicaciones de la Comisión Argentina de Fomento Interamericano, 1945.

Malloy, James M. *Authoritarianism and Corporatism in Latin America.* Pittsburgh: University of Pittsburgh Press, 1977.

Mannheim, Karl. *Ideology and Utopia.* Translated by Louis Wirth and Edward Shils. New York: Harcourt, Brace, 1936.

Marín, Reynaldo. "The Masses Will Decide the Outcome of the Battle." *World Marxist Review* 18 (December 1975): 21–35.

Martindale, Don. *The Nature and Types of Sociological Theory.* Boston: Houghton Mifflin, 1960.

Martz, John D. *The Dynamics of Change in Latin American Politics.* Englewood Cliffs, N.J.: Prentice-Hall, 1971.

Masi, Fernando. *Stroessner: La Extinción de un modelo político en Paraguay.* Asunción: Intercontinental Editora, 1989.

Mason, Paul T. *Totalitarianism: Temporary Madness or Permanent Danger?* Boston: Heath, 1967.

Meliá, Bartolomé, S.J. *Guaraníes y Jesuitas.* Asunción: Ediciones Loyola, 1969.

Meliá, Bartomeu. "Las reducciones jesuíticas del Paraguay: Un espacio para una utopía colonial." *Estudios Paraguayos* 6 (September 1978): 157–67.

Méndez, Epifanio. *Carta a un compañero.* Asunción: Editorial de las Catacumbas, 1980.

———. *Desatinos y calumnias al descubierto: Cartas polémicas.* Buenos Aires: N.p., 1957.

———. *El orden para la libertad.* Asunción: Editorial Cultura, 1951.

———. *El reencuentro partidario.* Montevideo: Ed. Firmeza, 1958.

———. *El valor social de la historia.* Asunción: La Colmena, 1951.

———. *Psicología del colonialismo: Imperialismo yanqui-brasilero en el Paraguay.* Buenos Aires: Instituto de Cultura Pane-Garay, 1971.

Méndez Fleitas, Epifanio. *Diagnosis Paraguaya.* Montevideo: Editorial Prometeo, 1965.

———. *Ideologías de dependencia y segunda emancipación.* Buenos Aires: Editorial Emancipación, 1973.

———. *Lo histórico y lo antihistórico en el Paraguay: Carta a los Colorados.* Buenos Aires: N.p., 1976.

Mendoza A., Raúl. "Desarrollo y evolución de la población Paraguaya." *Revista Paraguaya de Sociología* 5 (August 1968): 5–16.

Mendoza, Jaime. *La tragedia del Chaco.* Sucre, Bolivia: Imprenta y Litografía Salesiana, 1933.

Miranda, Aníbal. *Apuntes sobre el desarrollo Paraguayo.* Asunción: Universidad Católica, 1979.

————. *Desarrollo y pobreza en Paraguay.* Asunción: Comité de Iglesias e Inter-American Foundation, 1982.

————. *EE.UU. y el régimen militar paraguayo: 1954–1958: Documentos de fuentes norteamericanas.* Asunción: El Lector, 1987.

"Moral Healing of the Nation." *LADOC* 10 (November-December 1979): 1–14.

Mora Mérida, José Luis. *Historia social de Paraguay, 1600–1650.* Sevilla: Escuela de Estudios Hispano-americanos, 1973.

Moreira Alves, María Helena. *State and Opposition in Military Brazil.* Austin: University of Texas Press, 1985.

Moreno, Franciso José, and Mitrani, Barbara, eds. *Conflict and Violence in Latin American Politics: A Book of Readings.* New York: Crowell, 1971.

Morínigo A., José Nicolás. "El proceso de cambio en la estructura de la población económicamenta activa en el Paraguay." *Estudios Paraguayos* 6 (December 1978): 128–39.

————. "Hacia una cuantificación de la población pobre en Asunción." *Estudios Paraguayos* 9 (June 1981): 181–228.

Morínigo, José N., and Silvero, Ilde. *Opiniones y Actitudes Políticas en el Paraguay.* Asunción: Editorial Histórica, 1986.

Morínigo, Ubaldo Centurión. *Stroessner, defensor de las instituciones democráticas.* Asunción: Ediciones Epopeya del Chaco, 1983.

Muñoz, Heraldo. *From Dependency to Development: Strategies to Overcome Underdevelopment and Inequality.* Boulder, Colo.: Westview Press, 1981.

Münzel, Mark. "The Aché Indians: Genocide in Paraguay." IWGWIA Document No. 11. Copenhagen: N.p., 1973.

Nambeil, Ira. "Hydroelectric Projects Seen Key to Economic Growth in Paraguay." *Journal of Commerce,* January 16, 1973.

Nichols, Byron. "La cultura política del Paraguay." *Revista Paraguaya de Sociología* 8 (January-April 1971): 133–60.

————. "Las expectativas de los partidos políticos en Paraguay." *Revista Paraguaya de Sociología* 5 (December 1968): 22–61.

O'Donnell, Guillermo. *Modernization and Bureaucratic-Authoritarianism: Studies in South American Politics.* Berkeley: Institute of International Studies, University of California, 1973.

————. "Permanent Crisis and the Failure to Create a Democratic Regime: Argentina, 1955–66." In *The Breakdown of Democratic Regimes: Latin America,* edited by Juan J. Linz and Alfred Stepan, pp. 138–77. Baltimore: Johns Hopkins University Press, 1978.

————. "Reflections on the Patterns of Change in the Bureaucratic-Authoritarian State." *Latin American Research Review* 13 (1978): 3–38.

————. "Reply to Remmer and Merkx." *Latin American Research Review* 17 (1982): 41–50.

————. "Tensions in the Bureaucratic-Authoritarian State and the Question of Democracy." In *The New Authoritarianism in Latin America,* edited by David Collier, pp. 285–318. Princeton: Princeton University Press, 1979.

————. *Bureaucratic-Authoritarianism: Argentina, 1966–1973, in Comparative Perspective.* Berkeley: University of California Press, 1988.

O'Donnell, Guillermo, and Schmitter, Philippe C. *Transitions from Authoritarian Rule: Tentative Conclusions about Uncertain Democracies.* Baltimore: Johns Hopkins University Press, 1986.

O'Donnell, Guillermo; Schmitter, Philippe C.; and Whitehead, Laurence, eds. *Transitions from Authoritarian Rule: Comparative Perspectives.* Baltimore: Johns Hopkins University Press, 1986.

———. *Transitions from Authoritarian Rule: Latin America.* Baltimore: Johns Hopkins University Press, 1986.

Organization of American States. *Report of the Situation of Human Rights in Paraguay.* Washington, D.C.: Inter-American Commission on Human Rights, 1978.

Paciello, Oscar. *Código penal Paraguayo y leyes complementarias actualizadas.* Asunción: Ediciones Comuneros, 1981.

Pampliega, Amancio. *Misión cumplida.* 2d ed. Asunción: El Lector, 1984.

"Paraguay Obtains Washington Loans," *New York Times*, June 14, 1939, pp.1,12.

"Paraguayan Police Beat Exile," *New York Times*, June 25, 1986, p. A3.

Peaslee, Amos J. *Constitutions of Nations.* 4 vols. 2d ed. The Hague: Martinius Nijhof, 1956.

Pelleprat, P. Pierre, S. J. *Relato de las misiones de los padres de la Compañía de Jesús en las islas y en tierra firme de América meridional.* Caracas: Academia Nacional de la Historia, 1965.

Peña, Angel Florentín. *La democracia como régimen político.* Asunción: Ediciones NAPA, 1940.

Pendle, George. *Paraguay: A Riverside Nation.* London: Royal Institute of International Affairs, 1954.

Pereyra, Carlos. *Francisco Solano López y la guerra del Paraguay.* Madrid: Editorial-América, 1919.

———. *Solano López y su drama.* Buenos Aires: Ediciones de la Patria Grande, 1962.

Pérez Moreno, Sindulfo, and Meo, Carlos. *Stroessner.* Asunción: N.p., 1980.

Perlmutter, Amos. *Modern Authoritarianism.* New Haven: Yale University Press, 1981.

Phelps, Gilbert. *Tragedy of Paraguay.* New York: St. Martin's Press, 1975.

Pincus, Joseph. *The Economy of Paraguay.* New York: Praeger, 1968.

Plá, Josefina. "Elisa Alicia Lynch." *Estudios Paraguayos* 6 (December 1978): 28–32.

Plett, Rudolf. *Presencia menonita en el Paraguay: Origen, doctrina, estructura y funcionamiento.* Asunción: Instituto Bíblico Asunción, 1979.

Pomer, León. *Conflictos en la cuenca del Plata en el siglo XIX.* Buenos Aires: Riesa Editores, 1984.

———. *Proceso a la guerra del Paraguay.* Buenos Aires: Ediciones Calden, 1968.

Pozo Cano, Raúl del. *Paraguay-Bolivia: Nuevos documentos que prueban la jurisdicción del Paraguay en el Chaco.* Asunción: Imprenta Nacional, 1927.

Presidencia de la Nación. Secretaría Técnica de Planificación. *Diagnóstico demográfico del Paraguay, 1950–1977,* vol. 1. Asunción: Secretaría Técnica de Planificación, 1980.

_____ . *Plan nacional de desarrollo económico y social para el bienio 1965–1966*, vol. 2. Asunción: Secretaría Técnica de Planificación, 1965.

Presidencia de la República. Secretaría Técnica de Planificación. *Diagnóstico demográfico del Paraguay 1980*. Asunción: Secretaría Técnica de Planificación, 1980.

_____ . *Paraguay: Perfiles industriales*. Asunción: Secretaría Técnica de Planificación, 1977.

Presidencia de la República. Subsecretaría de Informaciones y Cultura. *Mensajes y discursos del excelentísmo Señor Presidente de la República del Paraguay, General de Ejército Don Alfredo Stroessner*. Asunción: Subsecretaría de Informaciones y Cultura, 1981.

Prieto, Justo J. *La Constitución Paraguaya concordada*. Asunción: Biblioteca de Estudios Paraguayos, 1981.

_____ . "El anteproyecto de constitución de Cecilio Báez." *Estudios Paraguayos* 9 (June 1981): 119–56.

_____ . "El estado de sitio en la constitución Paraguaya." *Estudios Paraguayos* 9 (December 1981): 353–68.

_____ . "El liberalismo como fuerza conductora para la democratización en el Paraguay." Paper presented at the 13th International Congress of the Latin American Studies Association, Boston, 23–25 October 1986.

Raab, Selwyn. "Paraguayan Alien Tied to Murders in Native Land." *New York Times*, May 15, 1979, p. B4.

Radin, Paul. *Indians of South America*. Garden City, N.Y.: Doubleday, Doran, 1942.

Remmer, Karen L., and Merkx, Gilbert W. "Bureaucratic-Authoritarianism Revisited." *Latin American Research Review* 17 (1982): 3–40.

República Argentina. Instituto Nacional de Estadísticas y Censos. *Anuario estadístico*. Buenos Aires: Instituto Nacional de Estadísticas y Censos, 1980.

República del Paraguay. Dirección General de Estadística y Censos. *Censo nacional de población y viviendas 1982* (Cifras provisionales). Asunción: Dirección General de Estadística y Censos, 1982.

Reyna, José L., and Weinert, Richard. *Authoritarianism in Mexico*. Philadelphia: Institute for the Study of Human Issues, 1977.

Richards, Donald G. "International Household Migration: The Case of Paraguay." Indiana State University, 1986.

Ríos, Angel F. *La defensa del Chaco*. Buenos Aires: Editorial Ayacucho, 1950.

Ríos, Francisco P. *La Obra Franciscana en América y Paraguay*. Asunción: Imprenta de las FF.AA. de la Nación, 1979.

Rivarola, Domingo. *Estado, campesinos y modernización agrícola*. Asunción: Centro Paraguayo de Estudios Sociólogicos, 1980.

_____ . "Universidad y estudiantes en una sociedad tradicional." *Aportes* 12 (April 1969): 47–84.

Rivarola Paoli, Juan Bautista. *Historia monetaria del Paraguay*. Asunción: Editorial El Gráfico, 1982.

Roa Bastos, Augusto, ed. *Las culturas condenadas*. Mexico City: Siglo XXI Editores, 1978.

Roett, Riordan. "Authoritarian Paraguay: The Personalist Tradition." In *Latin American Politics and Development*, edited by Howard Wiarda and Harvey Kline. Boston: Houghton Mifflin, 1979.

Ruffinelli, Roberto Céspedes. *El Febrerismo: Del movimiento al partido, 1936–1951*. Asunción: Editorial Luxe, 1983.

Salomoni, Víctor. *Fundamentos ideológicos del Partido Revolucionario Febrerista*. Asunción: EMASA, 1981.

Salum-Flecha, Antonio. *Historia diplomática del Paraguay de 1869 a 1938*. 3d ed. Asunción: Instituto Paraguayo de Estudios Geopolíticos e Internacionales, 1983.

Sánchez Quell, Hipólito. *Estructura y función del Paraguay colonial*. 6th ed. Asunción: Librería Comuneros, 1981.

———. *La diplomacia Paraguaya de Mayo a Cerro-Corá*. 6th ed. Asunción: Librería Comuneros, 1981.

———. *Stroessner, El desbrozador*. Asunción: Instituto Colorado de Cultura, 1977.

Schmitter, Philippe C. *Interest Conflict and Political Change in Brazil*. Stanford: Stanford University Press, 1971.

———, ed. *Military Rule in Latin America: Function, Consequences and Perspectives*. Beverly Hills, Calif.: Sage Publications, 1973.

———. "Still the Century of Corporatism?" *Review of Politics* 36 (January 1974): 85–131.

Seiferheld, Alfredo M. *Economía y petróleo durante la guerra del Chaco*. Asunción: El Lector, 1983.

———. *Nazismo y fascismo en el Paraguay: Los años de la guerra, 1939–1945*. Asunción: Editorial Histórica, 1986.

———. *Nazismo y fascismo en el Paraguay: Vísperas de la II Guerra Mundial, 1936–1939*. Asunción: Editorial Histórica, 1985.

Silvero, Ilde. "Opinión, interés y participación en la vida política Paraguaya." *Estudios Paraguayos* 11 (June 1983): 215–44.

Silvert, Kalman H., ed. *Essays in Understanding Latin America*. Philadelphia: Institute for the Study of Human Issues, 1977.

———. "Leadership Formation and Modernization in Latin America." In *Essays in Understanding Latin America*, edited by Kalman H. Silvert, pp. 17–30. Philadelphia: Institute for the Study of Human Issues, 1977.

Simón, José Luis. *Paraguay: Transición, Diálogo y Modernización Política*. Asunción: El Lector, 1987.

Smith, Brian H. *The Church and Politics in Chile: Challenges to Modern Catholicism*. Princeton: Princeton University Press, 1982.

Smith, Brian H., and Turner, Frederick C. "Survey Research in Authoritarian Regimes: Brazil and the Southern Cone of Latin America Since 1970." In *Statistical Abstract of Latin America*, vol. 23, edited by James W. Wilkie and Adam Perkal, pp. 796–814. Los Angeles: UCLA Latin American Center Publications, University of California, 1984.

Smith, Peter H. *Labyrinths of Power: Political Recruitment in Twentieth Century Mexico*. Princeton: Princeton University Press, 1979.

Sociedad de Análisis, Estudios, y Proyectos. *Ciudad y vivienda en el Paraguay.* Asunción: EDIPAR, 1984.

Souza, Paulo R., and Tokman, Victor E. "Características y funcionamiento del sector informal: El caso de Paraguay." *Revista Paraguaya de Sociología* 31 (September-December 1974): 51–63.

Speratti, Juan. *La Revolución del 17 de febrero de 1936: Gestación, desarrollo, ideología, obras.* Asunción: N.p., 1984.

_____ . *Los partidos políticos: Orientaciones, esfuerzos y realidades del adoctrinamiento Febrerista.* Asunción: EMASA, 1967.

Stefanich, Juan. *Paraguay nuevo.* Buenos Aires: Editorial Claridad, 1943.

Stein, Stanley J., and Stein, Barbara. *The Colonial Heritage of Latin America: Essays on Economic Dependence in Perspective.* New York: Oxford University Press, 1970.

Stepan, Alfred. *Authoritarian Brazil: Origins, Policies and Future.* New Haven: Yale University Press, 1973.

_____ . *The Military in Politics: Changing Patterns in Brazil.* Princeton: Princeton University Press, 1971.

_____ . *The State and Society: Peru in Comparative Perspective.* Princeton: Princeton University Press, 1978.

Sunkel, Osvaldo. *Capitalismo transnacional y desintegración nacional en América Latina.* Buenos Aires: Nueva Visión, 1972.

Susnik, Branislava. *El rol de los Indígenas en la formación y en la vivencia del Paraguay.* 2 vols. Asunción: Instituto Paraguayo de Estudios Nacionales, 1982.

"The World Needs Energy—And Little Paraguay's Got It." *Miami Herald,* December 29, 1977.

Tissera, Ramón. *De la civilización a la barbarie: La destrucción de las misiones guaraníes.* Buenos Aires: A. Peña Lillo, 1969.

Toro Ramallo, Luis. *Una síntesis del conflicto Boliviano-Paraguayo.* Santiago: Imprenta Universitaria, 1932.

Turner, Frederick C. *Catholicism and Political Development in Latin America.* Chapel Hill: University of North Carolina Press, 1971.

Ugarte Centurión, Delfín. *Evolución histórica de la economía Paraguaya.* Asunción: Editorial Graphis, 1983.

Un cuarto de siglo de paz y bienestar del pueblo Paraguayo. Asunción: Imprenta Nacional, 1979.

United Nations. *Economic Survey of Latin America, 1969.* New York: United Nations, 1970.

U.S. Congress. House. Committee on International Relations. Subcommittee on International Organizations. *Human Rights in Uruguay and Paraguay.* Washington, D.C.: Government Printing Office, 1976.

Velázquez, Rafael Eladio. *Breve historia de la cultura en el Paraguay.* 10th ed. Asunción: El Gráfico, 1985.

_____ . "La sociedad Paraguaya en la época de la independencia." *Revista Paraguaya de Sociología* 13 (January-April 1976): 157–69.

_____ . "Rebelión de los Indios de Arecayá en 1660." *Revista Paraguaya de Sociología* 2 (January-April 1965): 21–56.

Veritas. *Epifanio: El mago de la finanzas.* Asunción: N.p., 1970.

Vinocur, John. "A Republic of Fear." *New York Times Magazine,* September 23, 1984.

Viola, Alfredo. *Facetas de la política gubernativa del Dr. Francia.* 2d ed. Asunción: Ediciones Comuneros, 1976.

Volta Gaona, Enrique. *La Revolución del 47.* Asunción: By the author, 1982.

Warren, Harris G. *Paraguay: An Informal History.* Norman: University of Oklahoma Press, 1949.

———. *Paraguay and the Triple Alliance. The Postwar Decade, 1869–1878.* Austin: Institute of Latin American Studies, University of Texas, 1978.

———. *Rebirth of the Paraguayan Republic: The First Colorado Era, 1878– 1904.* Pittsburgh: University of Pittsburgh Press, 1985.

Washburn, Charles A. *The History of Paraguay.* 2 vols. Boston: Lee & Shepard, 1871.

White, Richard. *Paraguay's Autonomous Revolution, 1810–1940.* Albuquerque: University of New Mexico Press, 1978.

White, Richard Alan. "In New York a Key Paraguayan Murder Suspect Faces U.S. Justice." *Los Angeles Times,* April 15, 1979, sec. 5, p. 3.

Wiarda, Howard. "Towards a Framework for the Study of Political Change in the Iberic-Latin Tradition : The Corporate Model." In *Political System and Change,* edited by Ikuo Kabashima and Lynn T. White III, pp. 249–78. Princeton: Princeton University Press, 1986.

Wiarda, Howard, and Kline, Harvey, eds. *Latin American Politics and Development.* Boston: Houghton Mifflin, 1979.

Wilkie, James W., and Perkal, Adam, eds. *Statistical Abstract of Latin America,* vol. 23. Los Angeles: UCLA Latin American Center Publications, University of California, 1984.

Williams, John Hoyt. *The Rise and Fall of the Paraguayan Republic, 1800– 1870.* Austin: Institute of Latin American Studies, University of Texas, 1979.

———. "Dictatorship and the Church: Doctor Francia in Paraguay." *Journal of Church and State* 15 (Autumn 1973): 419–36.

———. "From the Barrel of a Gun: Some Notes on Dr. Francia and Paraguayan Militarism." *Proceedings of the American Philosophical Society* 119 (February 1975): 73–86.

———. "Paraguayan Isolation under Dr. Francia—A Reevaluation." *Hispanic American Historial Review* 52 (February 1972): 102–22.

———. "Paraguay's Nineteenth Century Estancias de la República." *Agricultural History* 47 (July 1973): 206–15.

———. "The Conspiracy of 1820 and the Destruction of Paraguayan Aristocracy." *Revista de Historia de América* 75–76 (January–December 1973): 141–55.

———. "Paraguay's Stroessner: Losing Control." *Current History* (January 1987): 25–35.

World Bank. *Paraguay: Regional Development in Eastern Paraguay.* Washington, D.C.: World Bank, 1978.

Ynsfrán, Edgar L. *La irrupción moscovita en la Marina Paraguaya.* Asunción: By the author, 1947.

———. *Tríptico republicano: Democracia, agrarismo, paraguayidad.* Asunción: Editorial América-Sapucai, 1956.

Ynsfrán, Pablo Max. *La epopeya del Chaco: Memorias de la guerra del Chaco del Mariscal José Felix Estigarribia.* Asunción: Imprenta Nacional, 1972.

———, ed. *The Epic of the Chaco: Marshal Estigarribia's Memoirs of the Chaco War, 1932–1935.* Austin: University of Texas Press, 1950.

Young, Henry Lyon. *Eliza Lynch, Regent of Paraguay.* London: Anthony Blond, 1966.

Zook, David H. *The Conduct of the Chaco War.* New Haven: Bookman Associates, 1960.

Index